PUBLIC SEX

PUBLIC SEX

The Culture of Radical Sex

Pat Califia

CLEIS
PRESS

Published in the United States by Cleis Press Inc., P.O. Box 8933, Pittsburgh, Pennsylvania 15221, and P.O. Box 14684, San Francisco, California 94114.

Book design and production: Pete Ivey
Cover photo: Phyllis Christopher
Cleis logo art: Juana Alicia

Printed in the United States.
First Edition.
10 9 8 7 6 5 4 3 2 1

Library of Congress Cataloging-in-Publication Data

Califia, Pat
    Public sex: the culture of radical sex / by Pat Califia — 1st ed.
        p.   cm.
    Includes bibliographic references.
    ISBN 0-939416-88-3 : $29.95. —
    ISBN 0-939416-89-1 (pbk.) : $12.95
        1. Homosexuality—United States. 2. Sex customs—
    United States. 3. Pornography—United States.   I. Title.
    HQ76.3.U5C354   1994
    306.7'0973—dc20   94-21652
                                                        CIP

Copyright information continues on page 261.

This book is for
S. Bryn Austin
(Amazon Copy Editor, Bluestocking, and Killer Cartoonist)
because she waded through a very tall pile
of Xeroxed articles and got excited

and

Gayle S. Rubin
because it's time
because of what she went through
because she's still standing

with my deepest love and gratitude

Contents

Acknowledgments

I want to thank several people (despite the fact that some of them are no longer living) for their invaluable help and inspiration. Some of them assisted me with research, some engaged in lively debate with me, others were willing to share intimate parts of their experience which hopefully infused my politics with some compassion, some are my heroes because of their choice to live as sexual outlaws despite the penalties for being out on the erotic frontier, others gave me work that allowed me to keep on writing, and some of them simply loved me (albeit for varying amounts of time). If I have left anyone out, it is because of poor memory, not a lack of gratitude. All conclusions, opinions, and errors in the book remain my own responsibility.

Their names are: Skip Aiken, Dorothy Allison, Sasha Alyson, Jo Arnone, Noreen Barnes, Kate Bornstein, Tala Brandeis, Beth Carr, the Bad Boys with Big Hearts and Bigger Buttholes of the Catacombs, Wendy Chapkis, Mark Chester, J. C. Collins, John P. De Cecco, Ph.D., Jack Fertig, Peter Fiske, Janine Fuller, Jack Fritscher, Fred Goss, Chris Gutierrez, William Henkin, Ph.D., Mike Hernandez, Amber Hollibaugh, Jim Kane, Richard Kasak, Stuart Kellogg, the founders, volunteers and staff of the Lesbian Herstory Archives, Teddy Matthews, V. K. "Mamselle" McCarty, Robert McQueen, Steve McEachern, Laura Miller, John Mitzel, Fakir Musafar, Joan Nestle, Scott O'Hara, Jim Olander, Ph.D., Marcia Pally, Pam Parker, N. Drew Parkin, Ph.D., John Preston, Mark Pritchard, Carol Queen, Tom Reeves, Sky Renfro, Wendell Ricketts, John Rowberry, Gayle Rubin, Joanna Russ, Terry Sapp, Marjan Sax, Amy Scholder, Mikal Shively, Cynthia Slater, Bob Smolin, Annie Sprinkle, Wickie Stamps, Lawrence Stanley, David Stein, Sam Steward, Thor Stockman, Kat Sunlove, Robin Scott Sweeney, Abby Tallmer, Morgan Tharan, Zoriah Tharan, Mark Thompson, David Thorstad, Daniel Tsang, Carole S. Vance, Ph.D., Lamar Van Dyke, Anne Williams, Stormy Williams, Layne Winklebeck, Marcus Wonacott, Carla Wood, Tim Woodward, and Sid Zweibel.

Introduction:
Or It Is Always Right to Rebel

Public Sex represents the bulk of my nonfiction work from 1979 to the present. That's a decade and a half of fuming and fussing about sexual repression and censorship, bragging about my search for an ever more forbidden way to have an orgasm, struggling (with many others) to form and preserve the modern leather community, making alliances with other sexual minorities, and incurring the wrath of Big Brother, Big Sister, and a lot of other people who have too much power and no sense of humor. I've been pretty busy.

The subtitle of this book, *The Culture of Radical Sex*, raises a definitional question. By "radical sex," I do not simply mean sex which differs from the "norm" of heterosexual, vanilla, male-dominant intercourse. People whose erotic practices are deviant do tend to acquire an outsider's critical perspective on marriage, the family, heterosexuality, gender roles, and vanilla sex. But being a sex radical means being defiant as well as deviant. It means being aware that there is something unsatisfying and dishonest about the way sex is talked about (or hidden) in daily life. It also means questioning the way our society assigns privilege based on adherence to its moral codes, and in fact makes every sexual choice a matter of morality. If you believe that these inequities can be addressed only through extreme social change, then you qualify as a sex radical, even if you prefer to get off in the missionary position and still believe there are only two genders.

It seems appropriate to trace the history of my own personal and professional development as a sex radical to give you, the reader, some background to these pieces and some idea of where they fit in an overall scheme of radical sexual politics.

The oldest article in the book, "A Secret Side of Lesbian Sexuality," was published in *The Advocate* in 1979. The process of writing this single article and dealing with public reaction to it had a great impact on all the work I did after that. It created an ecological niche for me as a journalist whose work was simultaneously pornographic, political, and educational.

This was one of the first pieces to appear in the gay press about women who do S/M with other women. I was terrified when I wrote it. I kept getting up in the middle of typing to lie down until my nausea subsided and my hands stopped shaking. When that issue of *The Advocate* hit the newsstands, it was days before I could actually look at my words in print. Why write and publish something that felt so dangerous? Because I was pissed off. I was tired of reading lies about my sexuality, tired of being told I didn't exist—and if I did, it was only as a distant cousin to a rapist or a chainsaw killer. I was tired of being alone, and I knew there would never be a leatherdyke community if somebody didn't announce that one already existed. I figured if I was public enough about being into leathersex, either I would get squashed and my misery would be over, or other perverse girls would find me, and then I wouldn't be so lonely.

There was another reason to come out. After watching the destructive impact the "feminist" antiporn movement had on the lesbian community here in San Francisco, I was dying to write a critique of its inflammatory tactics and circular reasoning. But members of that movement fought really dirty. They attacked anybody who argued with them as an advocate of violence against women, a child molester, or (gasp) a sadomasochist. They weren't above calling employers, publishers, or dissertation committees to inform them of the "perverts" in their midst. These storm-trooper tactics had intimidated most mainstream feminists from fighting head-on the Bay Area's Women Against Violence in Pornography and the Media (WAVPM).

Mainstream feminists were also reluctant to get down in the muck and wrestle with WAVPM's more successful New York City heirs, Women Against Pornography (WAP). They were embarrassed by WAP's frank focus on sexually explicit material and uncomfortable with the idea of championing pornography. The divisive issue of lesbianism had done so much damage to the women's movement in this country that there was very little chance feminist leaders would risk an even dirtier debate about S/M, which could result from their taking a strong stand against WAP. So in the beginning, only leatherwomen were willing and able to take on WAP and its satellite organizations. We did it because we didn't have much choice. We either had to find vehicles for public criticism of these people or resign ourselves to being drummed out of the women's movement and stand helplessly by while it was turned into a single-issue campaign for moral purity.

It wasn't until members of WAP, Women Against Violence Against Women, and New York Radical Feminists organized a picket of the Scholar and the Feminist IX conference "Towards a Politics of Sexuality" in 1982—known now simply as the Barnard conference—that more respectable feminists began to realize they had to mount some opposition to the "feminist" antiporn movement. The picketers handed out leaflets that denounced invited speakers as immoral, antifeminist, and beyond the pale of academic discourse or progressive activism. Anonymous informants contacted Barnard College, who was hosting the conference, and the college administration seized the conference program as suspected pornography. The brouhaha caused the Helena Rubinstein Foundation to withdraw funding for the conference series. Coverage of the conference in *off our backs* (*oob*) and other feminist newspapers basically took the side of the protesters. As part of their smear of "Towards A Politics of Sexuality," *oob* featured detailed coverage of a totally unrelated event, a women's S/M play party, and published the names of attendees. The collected papers of the conference appeared in Carole S. Vance's anthology, *Pleasure and Danger* (Boston: Routledge & Kegan Paul, 1984), only because she is a very brave and stubborn woman who could not be turned aside by slander.

But in 1979 none of that had happened yet. No one had said publicly, "I don't think pornography causes violence against women. I don't think feminists should be trying to ban pornography. This is a right-wing, homophobic, misogynist ideology. I think the only problem with pornography is that there's not enough of it, and the porn that does exist reflects the sexual fantasies of aging Catholic gangsters. I do some of the things that you find so scary when they are depicted in pornography, and I refuse to be tarred and feathered and ridden out of the lesbian ghetto on a rail." This was pretty much my position, and I knew I was not the only lesbian feminist in the world who felt this way.

The history of the '50s and McCarthyism made it clear that you cannot save yourself by keeping your head down and hoping the people who made you a member of a proscribed class will not ferret you out. If I was going to be called all those bad names anyway, I might as well be the first one to spread the good news. When you come out, you make yourself vulnerable to disapproval, criticism, and discrimination. But you also get to define your own terms. You get to go first and be the one to say who you are and what that means. And after you've already admitted in public that you're a hopelessly twisted slut, what are your detractors going to do? A whisper campaign of slurs and innuendoes doesn't have much power if the object of the campaign has already given the general public abundant details about her sexual practices.

The immediate consequences of publishing "A Secret Side of Lesbian Sexuality" could hardly have been more dire. I got a call at two o'clock in the morning from Barbara Grier of Naiad Press, threatening to cancel the publication of my first book, *Sapphistry*, a lesbian sex-education manual. It was hard to tell which upset her more: the fact that I had publicly revealed my identity as a leather person ("You might as well tell people you are a murderer!") or my statement that S/M was so important to me I would rather be marooned on desert island with a male masochist than a vanilla dyke ("We do not publish books by bisexual women!").

Sapphistry did hit print, and it went on to garner wheelbarrows full of vicious reviews. ("*Sapphistry*: Striking Out At Feminism 'Til It Hurts," read the headline in *Big Mama Rag*.) The feminist press was incensed because I focused on lesbianism as a way that two women could give pleasure to one another rather than as the paradigm for a feminist relationship. Not only did the book defend S/M, it also talked about butch/femme as a viable language of lesbian passion instead of as an embarrassing anachronism eschewed by enlightened modern lesbians. And casual sex! And dildos! And...well, there was also all that stuff about disabled women...and how to prevent sexually transmitted diseases...and it was pretty hard to bitch about that. Nevertheless, *Sapphistry* got maybe two positive reviews.

But real dykes, both feminist and nonfeminist, didn't care what their self-appointed leaders thought. They bought *Sapphistry*. If their local women's bookstores wouldn't carry it, they mail-ordered it. In 1992 this book was still one of Naiad Press's top thirty sellers.

These early publishing experiences taught me several things. First of all, I found out that the dyke on the street wanted to talk about sex. She might have a lot of questions, she might want to argue about whether or not it was okay for women to use pornography or tie each other up or strap it on. But she was willing to talk about it. And she most definitely did not want feminist newspaper editors or bookstore owners telling her what she could and could not read, think about, talk about, or perform as a sexual experiment. Women did not want to be protected from controversy or from new ideas. Most lesbians were really clear that sex was an important part of their lives, and they were happy to hear anything that would make sex easier, more fun, more available, and less terrifying.

While coming out as an S/M dyke and looking for kindred souls, I found out that lesbian life was a lot more diverse than the stock portrayals of our community in the lesbian-feminist fiction of the '80s. There was no such thing as a typical or average lesbian. There were bar butches, femmes who came out in the '50s, lesbian sex workers, couples who had been monogamous for forty years, bikers and their babes, girls whose sex partners outnumbered the population of Alaska, transgendered lesbians, lesbians in cross-generational relationships, and a hundred more "types." We came in all colors, classes, ages, and physical (dis)abilities. This rich, complex body of interlocking social networks never got portrayed in print because, I believe, our writers were ashamed of us.

Even in the '80s, many lesbian authors, in bids for literary legitimacy, chose to remain closeted and write about things other than their own lives. Even novelists, journalists, and academics who were ostensibly out of the closet could only bear to write about lesbian reality in sanitized, strained, and compartmentalized ways. It was almost as if on some level they were still hoping to have Mom or the parish priest pat them on their heads and say, "There, there, I understand now. Being a lesbian is a good thing. You're not a sexual misfit. You're a freedom fighter."

Many of the women whom this assimilationist literature rendered invisible were the most visibly lesbian members of our community. Most of them had never had to come out because people had started telling them they were queers when they were just little kids. They could not and would not hide their dyke identities. They were committed to living in the company of and for the good of other women. They had kept a lesbian community alive through very hard times. They defended the bars where women's-studies majors who despised them went cruising. Their physical and emotional scars from those battles frightened middle-class white girls who formed their lesbian identities over books by Ti-Grace Atkinson, Kate Millett, and Shulamith Firestone. But Amazons always have scars. It drove me crazy that these women, who were my ancestors and heroes, were being written off and ignored. Not only did they get beaten up, ridiculed, and pathologized by straight society, but their own elite, their own intelligentsia, wanted to deny them a place in our history. This was just plain wrong.

Adrienne Rich's essay, "Compulsory Heterosexuality and Lesbian Existence," which originally appeared in a special sexuality issue of *Signs* in 1980, is a perfect example of this approach to lesbian history.[1]

Rich outlined a "lesbian continuum" which included "a range...of woman-identified experience, not simply the fact that a woman has had or consciously desired genital sexual experience with another woman."[2] This concept was necessary, Rich believed, because "Any theory...that treats lesbian existence as a marginal or less 'natural' phenomenon, as mere 'sexual preference'...is profoundly weakened...whatever its other contributions."[3] Rich says, "As we delineate a lesbian continuum, we begin to discover the erotic in female terms: as that which is unconfined to any single part of the body or solely to the body itself; as an energy not only diffuse but, as Audre Lorde has described it, omnipresent in 'the sharing of joy, whether physical, emotional, psychic,' and in the sharing of work; as the empowering joy which 'makes us less willing to accept powerlessness.' "[4]

Thus Rich found it possible to include in the lesbian continuum many women who she believes opposed the institution of heterosexuality without necessarily being dykes (Chinese marriage-resistance societies, female trading societies and secret sororities in Africa, the Beguines' lay religious movement in Europe, and just about any form of "female friendship and comradeship"[5]). However, she excluded lesbians whose sexual practices she believed were antifeminist: butch/femme lesbians and sadomasochists. She also excluded lesbians who allied themselves with gay men. (Rich cautioned us not to view lesbianism as merely the female version of homosexuality. She objected to "the patterns of anonymous sex among male homosexuals, and the pronounced ageism in male homosexual standards of sexual attractiveness."[6]) A footnote says, "The issue of 'lesbian sadomasochism' needs to be examined in terms of dominant cultures' teachings about the relation of sex and violence [nota bene: in the original published version of this essay, in Signs, Rich added, "and also of the acceptance by some lesbians of male homosexual mores"]. I believe this to be another example of the 'double life' of women."[7] (In Rich's theories, the double life of women is "apparent acquiescence to an institution founded on male interest and prerogative"[8]). And in another footnote she writes, "I would suggest that lesbian existence has been most recognized and tolerated where it has resembled a 'deviant' version of heterosexuality—e.g., where lesbians have, like Stein and Toklas, played heterosexual roles (or seemed to in public) and have been chiefly identified with male culture."[9] The same footnote assigns female Berdaches (crossdressing Native American women warriors and shamans) and by implication all passing women, to the same ash heap.

Rich's essay is a brilliant explication of the way our society denies, punishes, and ruthlessly eliminates lesbianism. But she seems every bit as afraid of lesbian lust as the people and institutions who hunt us down. Why can sexual preference be dismissed with the adjective "mere"? Is it such a little thing to know in every fiber of your being that only a woman's touch will ignite your body and heart and make your life whole? Why can't sex be honored for its own sake, instead of being prettified by the euphemism "the erotic" and blurred with human experiences that are necessary and worthwhile, but not orgasmic? Do we really need to look so far afield from the lesbian community to justify the value of our lives? Women can resist male domination and even the institution of heterosexuality without being lesbians. We should honor them for that costly and difficult effort. But don't we lose more than we gain when we elevate them to the status of role models and excommunicate huge segments of our own community? Why is it that butch/femme and S/M dykes are dismissed as the products of sexism and misogyny while, for example, a religious order of celibate, Christian women is not? Rich even has room within her roster of feminist heroes for women who bound their daughters' feet or excised their clitorises. She refers to them as "token torturers" who were forced to carry out the wishes of their husbands, fathers, and religious leaders.[10] She swallows this, but strains at a spanking or a crewcut?

The work of Caroll Smith-Rosenberg ("The Female World of Love and Ritual: Relations between Women in Nineteenth-Century America," *Signs*, Autumn 1975) and Lillian Faderman (*Surpassing the Love of Men: Romance between Women from the Renaissance to the Present*, New York: William Morrow & Co., 1981) also shifted the attention of lesbian-feminist academics toward female relationships that were not necessarily sexual. If we lived in a world where heterosexuality was not, in fact, compulsory, I would be more willing to rejoice at the existence of scholarship which extended the boundaries of lesbianism to nonsexual female bonding. Since women have been killed, mutilated, imprisoned, and suffered a hundred other dire penalties for seeking erotic gratification with one another and rejecting men, it seems cruel and incomprehensible for feminist scholars to dismiss *any* form of lesbianism as a tool of the patriarchy.

And so I decided that my own work would take a different tack. It would be about disenfranchised people and topics, even if that meant I would stay poor and be widely hated. Even if that meant nobody would take my work seriously. Even if that meant I'd have trouble getting published or never make it to graduate school and never teach at a university. Like a '50s stone butch or a male-to-female transsexual in the '60s, I didn't have any place to hide. I decided if I could simply clear some ground for myself and other women like me, where we could live with less fear and more freedom, that would be enough. I didn't have to accomplish anything else in this lifetime.

My experience with the volcanic beginnings of the lesbian S/M community made me curious about how other communities (including the early gay community) had come into being, had grown, and had changed. The works of Jonathan Katz and Jeffrey Weeks were especially helpful and informative. By including crossdressing women and many others whose lesbian identities were been questioned by 1980s feminists, Katz showed me who my dyke ancestors were. His first book, *Gay American History* (New York: Thomas Y. Crowell, 1976) tracked the progress that gay men and lesbians had made from being isolated freaks and psychiatric case histories to members of an above-ground, powerful subculture that lobbied for increased protection and civil rights. The message of this book was that pride, self-esteem, and self-disclosure were the building blocks of that progress. Nobody ever built a community by going into therapy, tackling somebody else's causes, or pretending to be something they were not.

Weeks authored several books on gay history and sexual politics: *Coming Out* (London: Quartet Books Limited, 1977), *Sex, Politics and Society* (Essex: Longman Group Ltd., 1981), and *Sexuality and Its Discontents* (Boston: Routledge & Kegan Paul, 1985). This body of work is too large to summarize here. But common themes emerged from all three books. Weeks made it clear that there was more than sex going on in the sexual fringe. He put struggles for sexual freedom within the context of class differences. He was always suspicious of the state even when it ostensibly liberalized sex law, and he saw gay sexual minorities as being important for challenging the status quo. This was a big improvement over simplistic theories that explained butch/femme sex, S/M, public sex, or cross-generational relationships as oppressive recastings of abusive heterosexual institutions or the result of internalized homophobia. Weeks was also critical of socially progressive movements for being willing to back down on their radical agendas, and he was scathing about the notion of "natural" sexuality. He justly pointed out that if any sexual identity (even heterosexuality) was natural, it would not need to be supported by such a powerful system of reinforcement for those who could produce the desired behavior, and punishment for those who could not. Weeks also described the ways that sexual identity and the meanings assigned to certain specific sex acts had changed from Victorian times to the present. He observed that the meaning assigned to an act by the dominant culture is not necessarily the same meaning assigned by those who perform the act; from this insight came the possibility that the dominant culture is not entitled to say which sexuality is healthy or unhealthy, loving or vicious. Power, Weeks reiterated, comes from insisting on the right to say what your sex means. (And wisdom, I might add, comes from asking other people what their sex means before you jump to any conclusions.)

18

Battles over freedom of expression thus have implications far beyond the mere ability of print to circulate without being hampered by agents of the state. The line between word and deed is a thin one. A desire that cannot be named or described is a desire that cannot be valued, acted upon, or used as the basis for an identity.

The process of coming out as a kinky dyke forced me to question many of my own assumptions about gender, sexuality, identity, and oppression. It was woefully obvious that simply coming out as a lesbian had not eliminated my sexual prejudices or given me any special insight into the way other marginalized people dealt with their stigmatized status. Hence my curiosity about virtually every sexual variation, whether gay or not, and my willingness to support transgendered people, boy-lovers, sex workers, bisexuals, tearoom cruisers, straight swingers, and just about anybody else who gets treated badly because most people are afraid of sex and politicians can get elected by sponsoring moral panics. This position has been as controversial within the S/M community as it is outside of it. Unfortunately, most people's sexual tolerance ends at their own bedroom (or dungeon) door.

"A Secret Side of Lesbian Sexuality" was followed by a series of articles about the antiporn movement, public sex, prostitution, the age of consent, fetishism, and crossing the boundaries of gender and sexual orientation. During this period, most of my work appeared in *The Advocate* because the paper was willing to pay me for it, and the editors did not subject me to the endless rounds of wrangling that more politically correct and impoverished publications expected from their authors. I was fortunate indeed to have the support of editor-in-chief Robert McQueen, a former Mormon who shared my missionary zeal for speaking one's mind. Perhaps because of his fundamentalist upbringing, McQueen was outraged by any suggestion of prudery. He belonged to an earlier generation of gay activists who had spent their whole lives battling the cops to keep gay bars and bathhouses open and gay publications on the newsstands. He had first-hand knowledge of the repressive power of the state. And he was perfectly comfortable with editing a biweekly magazine that was widely perceived outside the gay community as a piece of homo porn.

It's tempting to take the soothing view that progress is inevitable, and things are better now than they were ten years ago. But as far as the gay press is concerned, I don't think that's true. One of the major consequences of the AIDS epidemic has been a retreat from sexual politics. The gay movement has been transformed from a broad-based attempt to address several issues (sodomy laws, antigay discrimination, homophobia in religious institutions, military witch-hunts, porn laws, police crackdowns on public sex, registration of so-called "sex offenders," the age of consent, child custody, etc.) to a crusade for a cure. Our agenda has pretty much shrunk to one item.

True, the gay press is almost completely above-ground these days. You can buy a copy of *Out* or *The Advocate* or *10 Percent* at almost any big-city magazine rack, and you don't have to look over your shoulder or hide it in your bag. The local cops will rarely confiscate gay news magazines, and the post office won't detain them and charge them with obscenity. But it seems to me that the gay press has traded censorship by the chief of police or the postmaster general for a more subtle form of social control by Absolut Vodka. We are like a white-trash family who doesn't mention the uncles and cousins who are in jail, pretends that car up on blocks is going to be fixed any day now, and scrimps and saves to have one nice suit of clothes to wear to church so the neighbors (who are also impoverished) won't be able to run us down. We are pretending we have already arrived, achieved legitimacy, and taken our place at the Thanksgiving table.

What pathetic crap. What we do in bed is illegal in about half of the states. There are only a few tiny parts of the country where we are legally protected from discrimination. Young, working-class gay people who try to escape their families and get a college education by enlisting in the military still have a good chance of being caught in a witch-hunt and dishonorably discharged. In small cities and towns and even in big cities, there are still many, many gay men and lesbians who don't know how to find our community. Most of us can't get a date, much less a domestic partner.

Most of the pieces in this book would never appear in today's version of *The Advocate*. The advice column I've written for ten years can't even appear in the main book. It has to be relegated to the *Advocate Classifieds*, a separate publication that features sex ads (as opposed to ads seeking long-term, committed partners), nude photos, and erotic fiction. During the '80s, the owners and editors of *The Advocate* made a political decision to keep the classified ads in the main book because they thought part of their job as publishers of a gay paper was to create a gay community. They succeeded in part by helping men find each other for sex, friendship, and love. Now the owners of the magazine have chosen to distance themselves from the sex ads (while still taking the advertisers' money) so they can devote advertising space in the magazine to things that are much less dangerous than casual sex, i.e., booze. Personally, I'd rather be funded by buggery than delirium tremens.

I was told that my column couldn't remain in the main book because letters about foreskins did not belong in a serious news magazine. I'm not sure why foreskins were singled out for Jeff Yarbrough's opprobrium, and since I have no absolute knowledge on this point, I will refrain from speculation. Of course, *The Advocate* proper still runs advice columns—about AIDS. It seems that the only way we can legitimately talk about our sexuality is under the rubric of death and disease. We can't celebrate, defend, or describe queer pleasure even though it was the quest for pleasure that made so many of us HIV-positive. This hypocrisy and prissiness robs the gay press of much of its old feistiness, earthiness, and power to rock the world.

More than ten years into the epidemic, I no longer believe a cure or a vaccine or even a treatment for AIDS will be found, no matter how much money the government throws at this problem. For a decade now, we've been beating ourselves up because we can't seem to force the government and pharmaceutical companies to take AIDS seriously and to save our precious lives. Sadly, the resources it takes for medical research on this scale is beyond the scope of individuals. We're like ants trying to turn over a car. The state is not going to save us, and we should stop wringing our hands and hoping it will come to our rescue.

We have the means at hand right now to save our own lives. Prevention will be the key to ending this epidemic. If every one of us used latex barriers every time we had any kind of sex and did not share needles, within ten years there would be no plague. Implementing this strategy would require us to talk a whole lot more about sex and drugs. We need more information about what it is that people really do. We need to know what kind of risks they take, and why. Each of us needs to become a peer sex educator and defend our loved ones' health. We need to stop indulging in the ridiculous fantasy that if we could just get legally married like heterosexuals, we could all be monogamous, and then we would be safe.

The gay movement also needs to throw its weight behind needle-exchange programs. Drug abuse *is* a gay issue because drugs work even better than orgasms to ease the pain of being different. Activists have ignored the politics of drug trafficking and narcotics laws in this country at their own peril. Needle cleaning is not an effective way to prevent transmission of HIV and other blood-borne diseases. The right to a clean syringe should be as inalienable as the First Amendment or the right to an abortion. But have you ever read about a gay civil-rights organization taking on the defense of a needle-exchange volunteer?

We don't want to take responsibility for our pleasures. It's not just the barriers and the way it feels to use them that make safe sex cumbersome and unattractive. It's the fact that you have to talk about it and think past your inflamed genitalia to the consequences of letting it run free like wild mustangs. There's something even sadder than that: we won't do it because some of us still hate ourselves. We're guilty about being queer. We can't get rid of all that programming that says we are inferior, filthy, disgusting, godless, and pathological. We need the euphoria of orgasm the way a junkie needs a fix, to kill some of the pain of being outcasts. And so we keep on dying and killing each other before we die. Because we believe we deserve it.

If we cannot be our brothers' and our sisters' keepers, then we do not deserve to live in the sunlight. Until we can pass this enormous test, we won't be a free and loving people because we will not have earned the right to live with pride. We did not create this heritage of shame and hate. But shifting it from our shoulders will take the most enormous outpouring of sex-positive propaganda that this world has ever seen. We are going to have to fall in love with lust and defend it, claim it, and make it a source of affirmation. I don't know anybody in the gay press or in our national organizations who is qualified to champion this drive, but the cool part is that we don't need anybody to lead us. This is something each one of us can do on her or his own recognizance.

So I continue to write my advice column: For the sake of those who are so freaked out about being gay that it doesn't occur to them to just buy a gay guide and find out where the nearest gay bar or community center is. For the sake of teenagers who are suicidal because they think they might be gay and believe that means they are just going to die of AIDS anyway. Because there are still grown men out there who need to be told to go to public-health clinics to ask the doctors about those nasty-looking things on their peters. And well-meaning guys who are confused about what safe sex is, exactly. And people who think masturbation will damage their genitals or make them sick. And couples who are in danger of splitting up because one of them cheated, or one of them has just revealed that she or he has some unconventional sexual tastes. Promoting fag lust is a weird career for a dyke. Perhaps it's just my bad karma for being a biphobic, transsexual-hating separatist for so many years.

Ironically, much of my work has found a new haven in the straight press. Without magazines like *The Spectator*, *Skin Two*, and *Gauntlet*, the table would be pretty bare. So I continue to write think pieces about sex and the law, the antiporn movement, and sexual variation from a lesbian-feminist perspective—for a heterosexual audience. I guess it isn't any more strange than giving gay men advice about fellatio and crabs.

It's sad that the majority of the feminist press remains under the control of women who think a dyke in a leather jacket is a bigger threat to their movement than a fundamentalist Christian legislator who's just dying to pass the Pornography Victims Compensation Act or some other hare-brained blue law a là Catharine MacKinnon.

I would not want you to think that being a sex radical has ruined my life. I've gotten a lot more out of my chosen path than an opportunity to become a workaholic or the demon goddess of profligacy. Thanks to my many readers and a handful of enlightened editors, I've been able to make a living at my keyboard. There are probably about ten gay writers who can make this claim. Okay, maybe by now there are a dozen of us. This has given me more freedom to think, read, and play than most people ever experience. When my partner became ill with chronic fatigue syndrome, I was able to schedule my work around taking care of her. I am convinced that the five-day work week is truly evil. If we can't have a world without bosses, we should at least have a world with flex time, day care, six-week vacations, six-hour work days, and three-day weekends.

My insides and my outsides match. I do not have to hide my identity or my feelings. The stress that I experience around my sexual difference is manageable because it comes from other people's prejudices, not from self-hate or self-doubt. Without this consistency, I would never be able to live more freely in the world or have an intimate relationship. You can't love or let yourself be loved if you're busy juggling lies and papering over your libido. Because my life is so weird, I have no shortage of things to think or write about. I have been blessed with the friendship of some exceptional men and women who compose a family that is more loving and more supportive than any of those dreadful people I was saddled with at birth. I even made it into graduate school.

And I have seen progress. There is a nascent industry that promotes lesbian passion. Dykes who come out today are much more likely to read On Our Backs than they are to read off our backs. Despite all the campaigns to close the baths, irrepressible fans of public nudity and sex (including dykes) continue to organize sex parties or open clubs where responsible casual sex is encouraged. The women's bookstores that refuse to censor dissident voices have flourished for the most part, because they meet their customers' needs. Today there is a National Leather Association that sponsors an annual conference. There are support groups for S/M people all over the country. We are beginning to acquire enough critical mass to make some serious changes. And that's a good thing, because the next decade is going to see major legal battles over images and descriptions of S/M sexuality and even the freedom to practice S/M without police interference. The quality of life for almost every sort of pervert everywhere is much better than it was ten years ago. Transpeople are organizing a protest for this year's Michigan Womyn's Music Festival. Bisexuals are forcing both gay and straight people to listen to their issues. Heterosexuality is getting more recreational, less procreational. The only sex radicals who are worse off now than in the late '70s are boy-lovers and sexually active youth.

The new frontier of the fight for freedom of expression is in the realm of virtual reality. Computerized information services are often guilty of imposing censorship upon their customers, which hampers the potential of telecommunications to form international networks of people, including gay men and lesbians, with many different common interests. The U.S. government has used the pretext of looking for kiddy porn to institute a wide-ranging campaign of on-line surveillance and entrapment. Recently, the Canadian government tried to ban all Usenet groups from the state-funded university system. And Great Britain may try to prevent all Internet newsgroups from the "alt" hierarchy from being transmitted into that country. These groups include discussion of kinky sex, but they also include medical information, rock 'n' roll fandom, sci-fi readers, political rebels, and a bunch of other interesting conversation. If this effort succeeds, an antiporn rationale will have been used to cut off British citizens from a rich culture capable of generating many kinds of social change.

■ ■ ■

There are some holes in this book which I regret. An entire book should be written just about the issue of who controls cyberspeech. There's also no comprehensive article on sex work, transgenderism, or narcotics laws.

Nor does *Public Sex* reflect many of the changes that have happened in my life since I got clean and sober three years ago. Sobriety has made it necessary for me to develop the spiritual basis of my life and publicly acknowledge it. If the Goddess does not exist, we must certainly invent Her. The current fascination with goddess imagery and mythology is important not to locate objective archeological proof that there were once matriarchal societies, but to create that possibility for the future. By picking over the ambiguous relics of the past, we dream ourselves into a world where women wield power and create peace and justice. We need the sage counsel of the female archetypes who speak from the collective unconscious because our own mothers did not teach us how to be warriors. These new, fierce voices are on our side; they want us to win. All those legends about Amazons may simply be tales about men's fear of the unleashed rage of women. If so, it is inevitable that those fears will take on flesh and women will learn to polish their weapons, keep them sharp, and wield them as a disciplined unit. The force of women united to defend one another and shape a society closer to our hearts' desire is a world-shaking power, and if that does not qualify as a sort of divine energy, nothing can.

In a roundabout way, I have come back to some of the separatist principles that I espoused when I was coming out as a lesbian in 1971. I don't intend to give up any of my male friends or stop learning from the gay men's community. But it is necessary for women to have some space where we can spend time only with each other and create a culture that is as free as possible from the influence of male domination. While I support full civil rights for everyone, I also think that lesbians have a right to participate in events and institutions that are for lesbians only. It seems strange to me that every other group in society is automatically accorded the right and privilege of self-definition and association, but dykes who want to hook up with other dykes are inevitably trashed.

This modified separatism has been fueled by my concern over the huge appropriation of women's time and energy that has occurred as a response to the AIDS pandemic. While the health crisis is a dire emergency that every thinking, caring person must address, it alarms me to see gay men blindly absorb women's caretaking without making much of an effort to reciprocate. The majority of gay men remain woefully ignorant about feminism, and too many are contemptuous of women's bodies and hostile toward lesbians. When I see a mass movement among gay men to raise money for breast-cancer research, or a volunteer army of gay men who are taking care of women with chronic and life-threatening illnesses, this resentment will be appeased.

Despite the fact that I had to quit consuming drugs and alcohol, I still believe that laws that turn intoxicating substances into contraband are self-defeating. When being an addict means committing illegal acts, people become more reluctant to seek treatment. The price of drugs is inflated, the quality of the product is compromised, and the result is increased street crime and mortality. The U.S. prison population has tripled since 1980. In California the increase has been more than five-fold. We lock up a larger portion of our own citizens than any other nation: 455 out of 100,000. The old South African government came in second to us, at 311 per 100,000. The Bureau of Justice Statistics attributes half of this growth to increases in the number of drug criminals entering prison. In 1992 drug offenders made up 30 percent of the prison population, compared with 7 percent in 1980. There is no evidence that imprisonment is a workable strategy to eliminate drug abuse or the crimes that people commit to purchase drugs. This prison system is funded by your tax money. It would be cheaper to send every incarcerated drug addict to treatment and then to college than it is to keep all of them in jail. The cost is not merely economic. A disproportionate number of those incarcerated are people of color. The damage done to their lives and communities corrodes the soul of America. The invisible men and women in prison have made each of us into a jailer and a prisoner of fear.

But this and other topics will have to wait for another book. I can't imagine that there won't be another book, just as I once couldn't imagine living past thirty. Today, at the amazing age of forty, I am trying to cause just as much trouble as I did when I was twenty-five. Fifty should be awesome, and sixty incendiary.

Notes

1. This essay originally appeared in *Signs* (vol. 5, no. 4, 1980) and was reprinted in Rich's book, *Blood, Bread, and Poetry* (New York: W. W. Norton, 1986). Since the newer version is the one most accessible today, all page citations refer to the reprint.
2. Rich, Adrienne. "Compulsory Heterosexuality and Lesbian Existence." *Blood, Roses, and Poetry* (New York: W. W. Norton, 1986), 51.
3. *Ibid.*, 27.
4. *Ibid.*, 53.
5. *Ibid.*
6. *Ibid.*
7. *Ibid.*, 40.
8. *Ibid.*, 60.
9. *Ibid.*, 50.
10. *Ibid.*, 37.

I.
Sexual Outlaws v. The Sex Police

I.

Sexual Outlaws v. The Sex Police

"Sexual Outlaws v. The Sex Police" deals with age-of-consent laws, the state's attempt to control solicitation and public sex, the results of then-President Ronald Reagan's Meese Commission on pornography, and the implications of narcotics laws and public policy for IV drug users and the AIDS pandemic. From time to time, our government declares war on nearly every aspect of libidinal expression, so of course it would have been possible to address the issue of the social control of sexuality and other pleasures by looking at a dozen other topics. But these four battlegrounds are keys to understanding how and why cops and politicians go after vice.

■ ■ ■

Few issues generate more anger than the dreadful specter of child abuse and sexual molestation. "The Age of Consent: The Great Kiddy-Porn Panic of '77" and "The Aftermath of the Great Kiddy-Porn Panic of '77" were very scary to write. After they appeared in print, I had a bad bout of paranoia that was exacerbated by all the funny clicks on my telephone and by mail that arrived at my house already opened. To those of you who feel that the only solution to the problem of child abuse is to raise the age of consent and increase penalties for the manufacture and distribution of child pornography, let me just say this: The penalties for having sex with a minor or having anything to do with creating erotic images of minors could hardly be more drastic. Are children and teenagers safe yet? Have we managed to stem the tide of violence against young people? Is it any easier to come out as a sixteen-year-old gay man or a fifteen-year-old lesbian than it was seventeen years ago, before many of these laws got passed?

I find that many people undergo a weird process of internal splitting when this issue is discussed. Very few of us waited until we were eighteen to have sex. And some of us who waited would rather have been active earlier. How many of us remember having a crush on an older person whom we admired? Were these feelings evil? If they had been reciprocated, would the sexual experiences or relationships that followed necessarily have been any more painful or awkward than our first clumsy sexual experiences with peers who were just as dumb about sex as we were? Wouldn't it have been easier to have a warm and caring escort through some of the pitfalls of becoming an adult gay man or woman? And why doesn't this information color the discourse on the sexual rights of young people?

I believe that we are afraid to give children and teenagers the support, information, and power they need to be safe and to control their own bodies. The family as we know it simply could not survive such a challenge. I urge everyone to take a look at the actual letter of the law that controls young people's sexuality and outlaws child pornography. Look at how age-of-consent and antipornography laws are implemented and what their effects have been on society. Don't simply take them at face value. The kiddy-porn panic is one of the biggest con games ever run on a gullible public.

The federal child-pornography law is both broad and vague, ostensibly because protecting children is so important that law enforcement must be given great latitude in going after the monsters who prey on young people. The kiddy-porn panic it fuels has had some truly alarming results. Just this year, Wayne State University photography professor Marilyn Zimmer found herself being investigated when she threw away a roll of film that contained nude photos of her three-year-old daughter. A janitor discovered the film and turned it over to the university's Department of Public Safety (DPS). The DPS tried to have Zimmerman charged with criminal child sexual abuse. The Wayne County Prosecutor's Office eventually refused to press charges against her. But before that, they searched her home and office, seizing eight boxes of her family photos and some other personal belongings. No other photos of nude children were found. Wayne County prosecutor Nancy Diehl sought testimony from art experts about the nature of such photos. More than fifty photographers and artists from around the country contacted Diehl's office on Zimmerman's behalf. This response, plus the fact that the contact sheet was never developed, persuaded Diehl to drop all charges. Zimmerman is now suing the university for invasion of her privacy. This is not an isolated case. Photographer Robyn Stoutenberg was embroiled in a similar controversy in Pima County, Arizona, over a nude photo of her son that was displayed in an art gallery. While Stoutenberg was never prosecuted, her home was searched, her name was damaged by sensationalistic press coverage, and the prosecutors decided to keep the controversial photo of her four-year-old son!

This law is so poorly written that the Supreme Court recently agreed to decide whether or not the government must prove that those who distribute or receive sexually explicit films or photographs of minors are aware that the performers are not adults. This issue arises because federal law-enforcement agencies have been conducting huge kiddy-porn entrapment schemes. People's names are taken from confiscated mailing lists of adult bookstores and video companies, U.S. customs lists of seizures of allegedly obscene material, and the personal address books of people arrested earlier. These people are sent flyers, brochures, or letters urging them to order erotic material. The notices often don't specify that the material will depict minors. Euphemisms may be used, such as "students" or "youthful-appearing" models. If anyone is careless or stupid enough to take the bait, the government ships a package of child pornography (of which it seems to have an ample supply). Postal officials have been known to correspond with some people for years before persuading them to violate the law in this fashion. When the package arrives, the luckless individual is arrested, and her or his home and business is searched.

A federal appeals court ruled in 1992 that because the child-pornography law does not require knowledge that the material depicts minors, it violates the First Amendment. The Justice Department is seeking to have that ruling overturned. Federal prosecutors are also seeking a new trial in the child-pornography case of Stephen A. Knox. Last fall the Supreme Court asked the Third U.S. Circuit Court of Appeals in Philadelphia to review his case after the Justice Department admitted that Knox had been convicted on a faulty legal premise. This "faulty premise" was the fact that the so-called "pornography" in his case consisted of videos of girls dressed in leotards, bathing suits, or underwear. There was no sexual activity in the material; there wasn't even any nudity. President Clinton reprimanded Attorney General Janet Reno for making such an admission and directed the Justice Department to draft legislation to tighten laws against child pornography! The Senate unanimously passed a resolution calling for the same thing. In this social climate, it does not seem very likely that the Supreme Court will substantially alter the wording or interpretation of this law.

The fact that many of the founders of the gay-liberation movement were (and are) boy-lovers has well-nigh disappeared from the official history of our rebellion. The very term "boy-lover" is rarely heard in gay discourse. True, there have always been political disagreements within our community about the age of consent and cross-generational relationships. But the decade of FBI harassment suffered by the North American Man/Boy Love Association (NAMBLA) probably has more to do with the mainstream gay movement's drawing away from this issue. It is a serious and terrifying thing to confront such a powerful institution. So perhaps it was inevitable that the Stonewall 25 organizing committee would vote to exclude all organizations advocating the repeal of age-of-consent laws from its June 26, 1994, march. A group called the Spirit of Stonewall (SOS) formed to protest this ban, and has invited NAMBLA to march with them. I was proud to be among the people who signed SOS's petition for inclusion of all gay organizations in the Stonewall anniversary celebration. Perhaps Father Bruce Ritter, one of the original Meese Commission members, will be marching with SOS. (Ritter resigned from his position as president of Covenant House, a New York City shelter for runaways, after private investigators found "extensive evidence" confirming sexual misconduct with shelter residents.)

■ ■ ■

Today the issue of public sex is, if anything, even more hotly debated in the gay community than it was in 1982. Two years after the article "Public Sex" was written, the bathhouses in San Francisco were shut down. Then-Mayor of San Francisco Dianne Feinstein, under the prodding of openly gay journalist Randy Shilts, ordered Public Health Director Mervyn Silverman to close them in 1984. The city of New York closed its bathhouses in 1985, beginning with the notorious S/M club, the Mineshaft. Perhaps to head off any perception that they were discriminating against gay people, the same authorities also closed down Plato's Retreat, a straight swing club. About a dozen gay men's public-sex establishments were also closed. This action was taken against the recommendation of the New York City Health commissioner Dr. David Sencer, who said in a letter to Mayor Koch that "closure of the bathhouses will contribute little if anything to the control of AIDS." Around the same time, many bathhouses were closed in other major American cities.

Gay people who advocate closing the baths feel that their existence is indefensible in the age of AIDS. The baths have come to represent an age of sexual license and irresponsibility which many gay men resent both because it is over and because it was supposedly responsible for creating or spreading a lethal sexually transmitted disease. Those who believe the baths should remain open claim that they provide good central locations for conducting safer-sex education. They point out that closing the baths doesn't really stop unsafe sex; it simply moves it to more dangerous locations where it's more difficult to enforce safer-sex guidelines, such as highway rest areas and adult bookstores. Many anti-baths activists seem to have forgotten that it was mass arrests in places like these which led to the creation of the baths.

Local newspapers routinely print the names and addresses of men arrested in sweeps of public cruising areas. This recently prompted a New Hampshire man named Arthur Richardson to fight the charge of public lewdness. When cops arrested him, he says he was only taking a leak, but he planned to keep quiet about the charges and plead guilty until he learned that one of his fellow defendants, Paul Eastman, had shot himself to death with a rifle before going to trial. Richardson went public. He told reporters this was "a needless tragedy" and found an attorney who would defend him. He said, "Whether Mr. Eastman was guilty of anything more than having to relieve himself...will never be known with certainty, but the fact remains that his arrest and the reaction which followed made his life unbearable." Richardson, an apparently straight man who had lived with a woman for fourteen years, labeled the rest-area crackdown "homophobic." It's interesting that so many of us have trouble seeing it in the same clear light.

In most cities, the baths have acquired twilight status similar to that of gay bars in the '60s. They are allowed to remain open as long as they are not too large or public (and as long as the appropriate palms are greased). But in an election year or at the whim of a newspaper editor who decides to boost circulation by running an exposé about "AIDS dens," they can be closed. This marginal status makes the baths harder to find. Since the profits that owners can rake in from these clubs is limited, they usually have little motivation to make them attractive or safe or keep them clean or well-lit. Fire codes and other safety regulations are routinely ignored. This fosters a stereotype that public sex is inherently furtive, dangerous, and dirty.

Was sexual license the only thing that the baths promoted? I don't think so. As the most visible gay institutions, they made it possible for many men to experiment sexually with other men. They facilitated coming out (as well as made it easier for some men to remain in the closet and still have lots of gay sex). The baths generated large profits, some of which funded early gay-rights organizations. By offering employment to out-of-the-closet gay men, these businesses created an economy that could support activism and assumption of a full-time, totally open gay identity. By allowing large groups of men to come together and bond with one another, the baths became the heart and soul of '80s gay activism. They taught gay men to see themselves as members of a common tribe with similar interests and needs. The same men who prowled those steamy hallways in their little white towels also turned over police cars and set them on fire during the May 21, 1979, White Night riots in San Francisco, which followed Dan White's trial for the murders of Mayor George R. Moscone and city supervisor Harvey Milk.

Throughout the '70s and '80s, the "gay family" consisted of the entire community. There was a strong sense that an injury to one was an injury to all. Gay baths and backroom bars were part of a system of territorial marking that delineated the boundaries of our neighborhoods. This was important because it made the community palpable. We had territory that we could defend. And people did police these neighborhoods to eliminate gay bashing and police harassment.

The gay family of the '90s is an isolated couple committed to its own financial success and perhaps a desire to raise a child. The emphasis on monogamy and long-term couples has created a less radical style of activism. I do not wish to deride the dedication it takes to hold such a relationship together. Same-sex partnerships ought to be accorded the same respect and benefits that heterosexual couples receive. However, I am uncomfortable with claims that we are "just like everybody else" or "want the same things straight people do." Do people have value only if they go about in pairs? It's wonderful when health insurance, for example, is extended to a domestic partner. But people should not have to be in a relationship to qualify for health care. This raises the issue of what will happen to those of us who are obviously not just like sedate, married heterosexuals. Does privatization and the retreat to a ranch house in the suburbs really make us safer, happier, or more free?

The baths are often condemned for enforcing a narrow, racist standard of masculine attractiveness. It is certainly true that many establishments did (and still do) exclude men who are overweight, nonwhite, effeminate, middle-aged or elderly, or men who simply piss off whoever is minding the door. These egregious acts of discrimination frequently provoked boycotts and protests, as well they might. However, the baths (along with gay literature, pornography, disco culture, and radical politics) created a new sort of homosexual man—one who was not necessarily a sissy. For the first time, it was possible for a gay man to be butch without trying to pass as straight. The concept of masculinity was changed forever by the specter of body-builders and other macho types who were hot to go home and fuck each other.

Not every gay man was capable of synthesizing an identity that incorporated both nelly and butch components, but a lot of them did. This emphasis on reclaiming masculinity made it imperative for gay men to demonstrate physical courage. They began to fight back against gay bashers, the police, right-wing politicians and religious authorities, and the rest of their enemies.

■ ■ ■

Liberals and civil libertarians snickered when the Meese Commission turned in its final report. Nobody took this bunch of political-cartoon types seriously. The panel had been selected with such a heavy hand that its bias was pathetically obvious. Its hearings had been kangaroo courts in which porn was tried and found guilty of causing everything from premarital sex to homosexuality to serial murder. Although it generated some opposition, everyone basically heaved a sigh of relief and went away after the commission issued its report.

That was a tactical blunder. The fact is that the Meese Commission has gotten practically everything asked for in its report. The Justice Department promptly formed the Child Exploitation and Obscenity Section (CEOS), a title which guaranteed the unit's activities would not be subject to much scrutiny, and proceeded to use it to crack down on the adult-entertainment industry. In its heyday, CEOS had at least ten litigators working in its national headquarters and trained U.S. attorneys all over the country in new techniques and strategies for obscenity prosecutions. In cooperation with the FBI, the IRS, the postal service, U.S. customs, and state and local police, CEOS has chalked up hundreds of porn busts. Whenever possible, it mounted multiple prosecutions of the same company in different states, thus making the cost of defense astronomically high. Many people in this predicament chose to just plead guilty, pay big fines, and sign pledges to never again do business in the sex industry.

Federal Court of Appeals Judge Joyce Hens Green recently issued an injunction that forced the Justice Department to drop multiple prosecutions against Phil Harvey, the owner of Adam and Eve, but it is not clear if they have abandoned the tactic completely. They still have the Racketeer-Influenced and Corrupt Organizations Act (RICO) to fall back on. RICO was originally passed by lawmakers who believed it was necessary to give the police sweeping powers to wipe out organized crime. But RICO's definitions are extremely broad. If you commit an illegal act in concert with another person, you could qualify for a RICO prosecution. In at least one case, a drug dealer has been busted under RICO for conspiring to commit a crime with the police informant who bought his merchandise and then placed him under arrest. In a RICO case, police are allowed to seize anything that might have been used to commit criminal acts—personal and business records, computers, vehicles, business property and homes, inventory, etc. This obviously makes it very difficult to muster a defense or even make a living until the case is settled, and that can take years.

Sexually explicit material has not only become less available in this country; the content is also restricted. Since the law is not clear about exactly what constitutes obscenity, most porn producers overreact and delete anything that might be controversial (such as interracial sex, anal sex, fisting, or any hint of domination) from their magazines and videos. If there's any chance that a particular image might catch the eye of an ambitious attorney general or district attorney, a digitized patch is placed over the action. While the quality of the merchandise has steadily declined, the cost of pornography has increased. Small companies that were trying to make higher-quality films or videos that would appeal to women are finding it difficult to stay in business under these conditions. Many straight companies that used to have gay product lines have shut them down.

Civil libertarians were unsuccessful in preventing these developments because most people still find it difficult to defend the freedom to rent or buy pornography. A lot of the people who turned up to testify before the commission on behalf of the First Amendment did not focus their testimony on the issue of pornography. They chose instead to speak about the dangerous impact that censorship could have on the arts, theater, and literature. Although the chilling effects of the Justice Department's antiporn campaign have spread beyond the adult entertainment industry, the commission was always very clear about its intention to simply wipe out smut, beginning with the most explicit and stigmatized images, then proceeding to images of mainstream sexual practices. So the folks who could not stand up at the Meese Commission and say, "I want to be able to see somebody get spanked, tied up, and soundly fucked in a full-color film with a gorgeous soundtrack," the folks who could only muster an embarrassed reference to the innocence of *Playboy*, now find themselves in the quandary of not being able to enjoy much vanilla porn.

This is the price that we pay for driving sexuality underground. Most people seem to want to visit sex as if it were a brothel or a shooting gallery, get their fixes, and then go home without getting busted and publicly labeled as perverts or sex fiends. They don't want to try to integrate whatever they find in pornography that is so rewarding with the rest of their lives. We routinely trade sexual frustration for respectability. The fact that porn, prostitution, and other illicit pleasures can be found only in sleazy neighborhoods where they are meted out by disreputable characters allows us to lie and tell ourselves that these experiences are not very important. But they are. They must be. Otherwise the sex industry could not continue to thrive in these harsh circumstances. Erotic entertainment is the only thing that gets a lot of people through bad and boring marriages, hateful jobs, health problems, divorce, aging, or tedious relationships with their friends and families. But it seems that consumers won't wise up about this until the secret source of juice and joy dries up completely.

■ ■ ■

This section of *Public Sex* includes a piece about IV drug users and AIDS. Its age can be seen by the references to HTLV-III (this was before "the virus" was known as HIV). Government policies toward this vector of AIDS transmission have not changed significantly. But one important recommendation in the article needs to be updated—the suggestion that people clean needles and cookers with a 10 percent bleach solution.

Recent studies have found that cleaning needles with diluted bleach does not kill HIV in the injection equipment. In fact, a Baltimore study found no difference in seroconversion rates between injection-drug users who cleaned their works regularly and folks who never bothered. A 10 percent bleach solution apparently causes blood to clot, which makes the virus inaccessible to the disinfectant. Now the Centers for Disease Control (CDC) is recommending that people rinse their needles three times with clean water, completely fill the needle and syringe at least three times with full-strength bleach (leaving it in for at least thirty seconds each time), shake the rig to loosen any debris, then rinse it three times with new, clean water.

These guidelines were apparently formulated by people who have never hurt for their next shots. I'd like to see some white-coated M.D. from the CDC try to remember how to count to three while his upper lip is beaded with sweat, his hands are shaking, and his stomach is turning over. It is unreasonable to expect that an addict will go through this tedious and time-consuming process. Not only are people usually in a hurry to get high, they are often injecting in situations where the environment won't allow them to set out all this paraphernalia and wait for the bleach to work.

It is more important than ever for injection drug users to have access to clean needles. Lawmakers keep arguing that such access will encourage drug use. But many researchers, including Dr. Peter Lurie and Dr. John Watters at the University of California, have found that needle-exchange programs reduce HIV infection without increasing the numbers of drug users. Dead junkies don't go into treatment. If we want people to get help (instead of just writing them off as subhumans who deserve to die because they are addicts), we have to adopt a more compassionate and reasonable public policy. Before they die, HIV-positive drug users often infect their sexual partners, and their children also become infected. The numbers of new HIV infections among women could be cut dramatically if only people could walk into pharmacies and buy clean needles as easily as they can buy condoms.

Nevertheless, many district attorneys continue to prosecute needle-exchange volunteers, charging them under the laws against possession of drug paraphernalia. The defense that these people are forced to break the law because a health emergency exists has often been successful. Alameda District Attorney John Meeham recently lost a case in Berkeley against health worker Scott Halem. A jury unanimously acquitted him of illegal possession of syringes. This case cost taxpayers an estimated $50,000 to $150,000 to prosecute. But Meeham turned right around and busted volunteers at Alameda County Exchange (ACE). It took four squad cars to give one volunteer a citation and to seize five hundred needles. The minute the cops left, ACE volunteers resumed their life-saving work.

The next time officials in your area complain about not having adequate funds to feed, clothe, house, and treat people with AIDS, they should be reminded that we can't afford to waste public money on wild goose chases like Meeham's vendetta. Any police crackdown on "immoral" behavior is very expensive and does little if anything to eliminate the targeted behavior. In this era of hard times, it's difficult to understand why the public continues to allow its elected officials and public employees to engage in these spendthrift public-relations boondoggles.

The Age of Consent:
The Great Kiddy-Porn Panic of '77
1980

At what age did you realize you were a sexual being? Most people (if they're honest) can recall having tingly feelings and nasty thoughts when they were little cherubs with lamentable table manners. I have a much clearer memory of naughty experiments performed with my prepubescent companions (oh, those golden days of carefree crossdressing, lighthearted medical malpractice, and simulated white slavery) than I do of more pragmatic experiments with shoelaces and buttons, the telephone, and prayer. I was more worried about finding enough privacy to masturbate than I was about almost anything else except perhaps getting rid of my lima beans before my mother got back to the dinner table. I don't remember learning my alphabet or singing nursery rhymes, but I do remember prying sex secrets out of my mother while she gave me my bath.

Culturally induced schizophrenia allows parents to make sentimental speeches about the fleeting innocence of childhood and the happiness of years unburdened by carnal lust—and then exhaust themselves policing the sex lives of their children. Children are celibate because their parents prevent them from playing with other little kids or adults. They are shy because they are not allowed to go naked any longer than is absolutely necessary to take a bath. They are not innocent; they are ignorant, and that ignorance is deliberately created and maintained by parents who won't answer questions about sex and often punish their children for being bold enough to ask. This does not make sex disappear. The erotic becomes a vast, unmapped wilderness whose boundaries are clearly delineated by averted eyes. Sex becomes the thing not seen, the word not spoken, the forbidden impulse, the action that must be denied.

Even though many prominent sex researchers have documented the existence of sexual capacity in children (for instance, Kinsey verified the occurrence of orgasm in girls and boys at less than six months of age),[1] our society is fanatically determined to deny it. Legally, young people are assumed to be incapable of agreeing to engage in a sexual act until they reach the age of consent, which in many states is still eighteen. Sex between an adult and a minor is called statutory rape, and someone convicted of this dubious crime can receive a heavier sentence than someone convicted of manslaughter. Contrary to what you would expect from a system ostensibly committed to protecting and nurturing its children, the minor partner is often subjected to blackmail, humiliating and punitive police interrogations, and public exposure (which can lead to painful conflicts with parents and peers). She or he may be coerced into testifying against her or his adult partner or lover in court. Age-of-consent laws don't make sense even if you believe that the desire and ability to have sex don't develop fully until puberty. These laws are completely arbitrary and do not take into account the varying degrees of physical and emotional maturity possessed by young people or the fact that puberty is occurring at earlier and earlier ages. Unfortunately, new laws that make this bad situation truly nightmarish were railroaded through state and federal legislatures in 1977 and 1978.

■ ■ ■

There are few adult lesbians and gay men who have not suffered under the campaign to extirpate any sign of eroticism in young people. Even heterosexuality, the choice approved by church and state, is hedged about with ominous warnings and tainted with guilt. Young women and men who would like to have sex with each other are impeded by lack of privacy and free time and by very limited access to birth control, abortion, sex counseling, and medical treatment for sexually transmitted diseases. Parents are so panicked by the possibility that their children might grow up to be gay that they sometimes try to prevent their children from even hearing the words "homosexual" or "lesbian." I don't know what's worse—having a persistent, vague, uneasy feeling that you just won't grow up to be like Mommy and Daddy or hearing your secret self described with mockery, pity, and opprobrium. Many kids who should be gay because they would be happier that way probably give up and conform and never find their way into our community. The young women and men who refuse to recant have an ugly fight on their hands. At the very least, they must learn to do without approval and love from their families and friends. They may have to cope with the loss of economic support and defend themselves against physical violence at home or at school. If they are religious, they will be threatened by the loss of salvation and God's love. They may be forced to submit to homophobic "counseling." As a last resort, parents may turn an "incorrigible" youth over to the juvenile justice system and wash their hands of her or him.

These young people are our next generation. Whatever we suffered in the process of coming out is still being inflicted on them. Why is there no systematic attempt to reach out to them, bring them into our movement and our community, and help them to reach healthy gay adulthood?

The squeamish attitude of today's lesbian and gay movement toward youth liberation can be traced directly to the Great Kiddy-Porn Panic of 1977. We all know that 1977, the year of Hurricane Anita and Dade County, was a very bad year for gay liberation. But most of us don't realize just how serious it was. In 1977 our march toward civil rights was met by a tidal wave of hysteria over the issue of gay sex and kids. The mainstream lesbian and gay movement was frightened into a hasty and ill-conceived retreat from this issue, which allowed the police to mount a terrorist campaign against gay youth and their adult lovers. In 1980 we are in the middle of a homophobic backlash that can only be compared to McCarthyism. Boy-lovers (and girl-lovers, though they are less visible) are the new communists, the new niggers, the new witches.

The flurry of panic over child prostitution, kiddy porn, and gay youth was engineered on a national level by a group of right-wing politicians, would-be celebrities, fundamentalist Christians, and vice cops. These people took advantage of the public's ignorance, fear of sex, and hatred of homosexuality to pass repressive laws that are probably unconstitutional; obtain state and federal grants; build powerful careers; and make themselves famous. Unfortunately, they succeeded in doing even more than that: They split our movement. Other gay men are turning against boy-lovers, and lesbians are turning against all gay men. No matter what your position on the issue of young people and sex, it is clear that this split makes it much more difficult for us to organize action on any gay issue. The April 12, 1980, "March on Albany for Lesbian and Gay Rights" is a perfect example. Because David Thorstad of the North American Man/Boy Love Association (NAMBLA) was asked to speak, the Coalition for Lesbian and Gay Rights and New York NOW withdrew their endorsement of the march. Participation was drastically reduced to only a couple of hundred people.

This controversy could destroy the modern gay movement, which is why we must understand how and why the Great Kiddy-Porn Panic of 1977 developed. In February 1977, Dr. Judianne Densen-Gerber, director of New York's Odyssey House, a drug-addiction treatment facility, toured the country, making inflammatory speeches about the "huge" child pornography industry and warning Americans that homosexuals were seducing their children into prostitution. Robert Leonard, president of the National District Attorneys' Association, set up a special Task Force on Sexual Exploitation of Children at the Association's spring meeting. CBS, that great friend of gay people, broadcast a "60 Minutes" special on kiddy porn on May 15.[2] After a brief mention of adult males with sexual interests in young girls, the program focused on magazines full of erotic pictures of young boys and footage of teenage male hustlers working the streets. Also in May 1977, the *Chicago Tribune* ran a series of articles linking rape, prostitution, pornography, and child molestation with gay liberation. Shortly thereafter, three Chicago men were arrested and accused in the press of constituting a child pornography ring. One of the men was eighteen years old. It turned out that they could hardly have formed a "ring" of any kind since they didn't know each other. Anita Bryant surfaced in the news with her crusade to Save Our Children from the lavender menace, and Los Angeles cop Lloyd Martin traveled to many cities, making speeches similar to Dr. Densen-Gerber's and helping local police track down pedophiles. Martin's Sexually Exploited Child Unit received funding from the city of Los Angeles in 1977, which supposedly made him a national expert on the subject.

All this furor culminated in a call for federal legislation against the sexual abuse of children. On May 23, 1977, the Kildee-Murphy hearings began. Congressmen Dale E. Kildee and John W. Murphy proposed federal legislation that would make it a felony to photograph or film a "child" (anyone under sixteen years of age) in the nude, engaged in sexual activity with another person, or masturbating. The penalty would be a fine not to exceed $50,000 or up to twenty years in prison or both. The Kildee-Murphy Bill would impose a similar penalty on depictions of simulated acts, clerks who knowingly sold child pornography, or anyone who knowingly permitted a child to engage in prohibited sex acts. The existence of a "feminist" antipornography movement made it possible for some politically active women to sympathize with the campaign against kiddy porn and cross-generational sex, which *Ms.* magazine exploited in a special issue in August 1977 ("Is Child Pornography... About Sex?"). *Ms.* included an article, "America Discovers Child Pornography" by Helen Dudar, which featured uncritical interviews with Densen-Gerber and Martin.

As the media blitz continued, so did arrests. Peter LeGrow, the owner of a Seattle disco for gay youth, was busted on August 30 and charged with promoting the prostitution of two teenage boys. The local newspapers covered his arrest in a distorted way; columnist Hilda Bryant's series on boy hustlers debuted the next day. LeGrow was clearly the victim of entrapment. His alleged crime was assisting an undercover cop to find two young men for a date. He took no money for making this introduction, and one of the boys was also employed by the police as an informer. But the most outrageous bust of the year occurred on December 8, 1977. Twenty-four men were arrested in the Boston area and indicted in what the newspapers called a child-pornography and prostitution ring. The police established a hotline to take anonymous tips that would lead to further arrests, and lesbian legislator Elaine Noble actually urged the gay community to cooperate. Luckily, her point of view did not prevail, and the Boston/Boise Committee organized to publicize the arrests, challenge the media's sensationalistic coverage, and help the defendants.[3] As a matter of fact, none of the indictments were for pornography, none of the men arrested knew each other, and of the sixty-three boys involved, most were fourteen years of age or older.

This pattern of homophobic mass-media exposés, arrests, and public pressure for harsher penalties for cross-generational sex was not limited to the United States. In December of 1977, *The Body Politic*, a Toronto gay monthly, was busted for obscenity after publishing an article on boy-love. The article included no erotic illustrations or descriptions, and *The Body Politic* is still in court defending itself against these charges in 1980.[4] Similar campaigns against kiddy porn, child prostitution, and boy-lovers have been conducted in Australia, England, Turkey, Sweden, Denmark, and other countries. Kiddy porn was outlawed or penalties dramatically increased in England, Australia, Sweden, and Denmark.

The language used by Densen-Gerber, *et al*, makes it difficult to figure out what is wrong with their position. The term "child abuse" conjures up images of babies scalded with boiling water or children beaten with blunt instruments. "Sexual exploitation of children" makes us think of teenagers being fed drugs and forced onto the street by unscrupulous pimps. "Kiddy porn" evokes a picture of little bodies torn and damaged from copulation with adults. Who wouldn't oppose such dreadful things? Who doesn't feel heart-rending sympathy for the children who are helpless to resist the violence of their parents, teachers, or other adults? Three-minute "interviews" on television or one-page articles in *Time* magazine don't give detailed enough pictures of what Densen-Gerber, Martin, Leonard, etc., think of human sexuality. Happily, all of the stars of the kiddy-porn crusade turned up to testify at the Kildee-Murphy hearings, and their testimony has been published by the U.S. Government Printing Office. This book, *Sexual Exploitation of Children*, should be required reading for membership in the gay liberation movement. It should certainly have received closer attention from the editors of *Ms.*, who should be embarrassed for not digging a little deeper into the political beliefs of Lloyd Martin and Judianne Densen-Gerber.

The hearings (portions of which were televised) provided an amusing yet distressing glimpse into American sexual mores. Everyone on the committee and every speaker assumed that it is a terrible thing for children to have sex—any kind of sex. It was stated as fact that sexually active children grow up to be prostitutes, drug addicts, incestuous parents, impotent, frigid, homosexual, or some combination of the above. Yet no research was cited to prove this. Numbers were tossed around: there were 1 million children being used in pornography; no, 2 million; 30,000 boys in Los Angeles were working as prostitutes and 120,000 in New York; the child pornography industry was grossing $1 million a year; no, $1 billion. None of these statistics was substantiated. The testimony revealed the unexamined beliefs that fondling a child's genitals is just as abusive as punching her or him in the mouth; that the term "child prostitution" just as accurately describes a man who picks up a teenage runaway and gives him a ride, $5, and a blow job as it describes a pimp with his stable of addicts; and that "kiddy porn" includes snapshots taken by boy-lovers of their young friends as well as the commercial material sold in adult bookstores. The committee was not concerned with preventing rape or violence against children. It was concerned with keeping them asexual. Information indicating that children may seek sexual contact or enjoy it was manipulated as additional evidence that society has become hopelessly corrupt. Descriptions of affectionate, cross-generational relationships were presented as the ultimate perversion—as if people who would engage in such relationships were too sick and depraved to feel the appropriate guilt and remorse. The term "child" was used indiscriminately to refer to infants, grade-schoolers, and teenagers. The only witness to offer a dissenting opinion was Heather Grant Florence of the American Civil Liberties Union. She said:

> The ACLU's basic position is that while it is perfectly proper to prosecute those who engage in illegal action, constitutionally protected speech cannot be the vehicle. Accordingly, the ACLU submits that those who directly cause and induce a minor to engage in a sexual act, or engage in it with a minor, are those who violate the laws; those who recruit and offer children for sexual acts clearly should be prosecuted...In contrast, those who have not participated in causing or engaging in the sexual activity but who may profit as a result of it, such as a publisher, editor, distributor, or retailer, are not violating the law.[5]

Florence's only objection to the Kildee-Murphy bill was the threat it posed to the First Amendment. She did not object to the committee's position that sex is bad for children, and she even suggested that it would be appropriate for them to increase the legal penalties for adults who have sex with minors. The committee greeted this comparatively mild speech with derision and outrage.

■ ■ ■

Who are the stars of the Great Kiddy-Porn Panic, and how have they fared since their moment in the limelight? Ironically, after making it easier for police to entrap pedophiles, Congressman John Murphy was himself the victim of entrapment, caught in the Abscam scandal. Anita Bryant (who did not testify at the Kildee-Murphy hearings) is getting a divorce, and her Ministries for Counseling Homosexuals have been charged with financial mismanagement; 1978 tax returns show that the Ministries raised $1 million; $450,000 was spent on "direct fees for raising contributions," including the antiporn and anti-child abuse activities of the illegal subsidiary Protect America's Children. Only $150 was spent on counseling.[6]

The National District Attorneys' Association's Robert Leonard's primary contribution to the hearings was a diagram drawn for him by an incarcerated boy-lover which was supposed to outline a "national network" of pedophiles. This ridiculous document consists of a page of boxes, circles, and triangles connected by a tangled network of arrows and dotted lines. The "network" is apparently made up of such entities as the Internal Revenue Service, *The Advocate*, porno shops, mail-o-matic operations, children's nudist camps in Vermont, a geologist, the Church of the New Revelation, Walnut Creek, legal assistance, Frank's second car, Big Brothers of Ann Arbor, Wayne State University, and the European network. After condemning those who would corrupt the morals of youth by buying their sexual favors, Leonard was convicted of embezzling $100,000 in federal money to build himself a house on the California coast.

Detective Lloyd Martin is still going strong, so he bears closer examination. Martin began working on the sexual exploitation of children in 1971, when Sam Yorty was mayor of Los Angeles and Ed Davis was chief of police. He was assigned to the pornography squad in 1973 and founded the Sexually Exploited Child (SEC) unit in 1976. His main contribution to the hearings was to provide estimates of the number of children involved in prostitution and pornography and to reaffirm the paranoid fantasy of a national porn/boy hustler ring by claiming that a book called *Where the Young Ones Are* had sold seventy thousand copies. This book, supposedly a directory of playgrounds and bus stations where loose kiddies convene, was never presented for the committee's examination.

Martin wants every police department in the country to set up an SEC unit. To this end, he frequently gives interviews and helps organize entrapment schemes. He readily admits that children can initiate sexual activity with adults. In his testimony at the Kildee-Murphy hearings, he said, "The most difficult concept for most people to understand and accept is that very often, these children are consenting partners in the sexual activity. In some cases they initiate the sexual activity with direct propositions or with seductive behavior."[7] Martin has also said that the relationship between a man and boy is often very warm and affectionate, and that "only 1 case in 200 involves a child who is the victim of force."[8] He complains that the affection children feel for their adult "molesters" is so intense that they rarely can be forced to testify against them. He defines a pedophile as "somebody paying more attention to the child than the parent would,"[9] an odd definition that would place all kinds of people under suspicion and hardly seems to imply sinister or damaging behavior. Nevertheless, Detective Martin has made a career of hunting down boy-lovers because he believes that having sex with minors is worse than murdering them:

> To me a crime against a child has no equal. It's worse than a homicide. A homicide is terrible, but it is over with very shortly. The victim of sexual exploitation has to live the rest of his or her life with those memories of what pornography and sexual deviation brings upon them.[10]

The "sexual deviation" Martin refers to is homosexuality. He believes that boys who have sex with men grow up to be gay, and it is obvious to him that they would be better off dead. Martin is so obsessed with homosexuality that he hardly mentions heterosexual pedophilia when discussing the sexual exploitation of children. He tries to hide his homophobia by publicly stating that he is not after homosexuals, just boy-lovers, but he urges other gay men to turn in pedophiles to the police. He believes that pedophiles cannot be cured, so they should receive lifetime prison sentences.

Martin advocates raising the age of consent in California to eighteen. He teaches a course on child sexuality and the exploitation of children at the University of Southern California and announces that he has never read the Kinsey reports.[11]

Some of the most colorful testimony for the Kildee-Murphy bill was given by Dr. Judianne Densen-Gerber. She turned up at the hearings with a trunk full of child pornography which she told the committee had been purchased by her seventeen-year-old daughter and a friend. To the consternation of the committee, she flashed covers and read titles while the TV cameras rolled. When Congressman Ertel chided her for displaying this material on television where his children might see it, she snapped, "So why don't you clean it up so I don't have any magazines to show?"[12] Densen-Gerber has a lot of spunk.

She also has a lot of ambition. Her career began in 1966 when she established Odyssey House, a drug-addiction treatment program in New York City. What is the connection between drug addiction, kiddy porn, and child prostitution? Densen-Gerber believes that sexual activity in childhood is one of the primary causes of drug addiction and prostitution, and that drug addicts and prostitutes (she makes little or no distinction between these two groups) sexually abuse their own children.

By making powerful friends, capturing the attention of the mass media, and putting pressure on government agencies, Densen-Gerber expanded Odyssey House into a little empire, including programs in seven other American cities and in Australia. At its high point, Odyssey was receiving about $3 million annually in state and federal funding. Odyssey's spin-offs included a briefly funded program for teenage prostitutes and a house for addicted mothers. Densen-Gerber did not restrict her activities to the United States. She instigated another kiddy-porn panic in Australia and traveled to England to help Mary Whitehouse and Cyril Townsend pass the Protection of Childhood Act, a measure that resembles the Kildee-Murphy bill.[13]

In 1979 Attorney General Robert Abrams announced that he was launching an investigation of alleged financial mismanagement at Odyssey. Former staff members and patients have claimed that private donations and government funds were used to maintain Densen-Gerber's expensive lifestyle; that the census of patients was tampered with to inflate reimbursements from state and local agencies; that patients were kept in filthy conditions and sent to beg for food at supermarkets; that residents were forced to wear paper donkey ears and tails or made to scrub the floor with toothbrushes to learn humility; that Densen-Gerber used patients as personal servants; that staff were asked to light candles to her to pledge their loyalty; that residents were punished for such things as holding hands; that the treatment program was not clearly understood by staff; that patients were allowed to write their own evaluations; and that there was no follow-up to determine whether or not Odyssey successfully treated drug addiction.[14] These accusations are still under investigation.

In January 1979, Odyssey received a federal grant of $90,000 for the Midtown Adolescent Resource Center (MARC), a program for teenage prostitutes. This grant proposal was funded after being turned down by the three reviewers, which is very unusual. After about nine months of controversy, which included the resignation of two directors and apparent difficulty keeping kids in the program, the federal government sent out a review team and cut off funding for MARC. Had they not done so, the original grant could have been renewed for three years. The first director of MARC claims he quit because Densen-Gerber was exploiting two teenage prostitutes in national-television appearances instead of treating them. The review team found that these two young women were housed with, treated like, and counted as addicts to boost state funds. They were subjected to strip searches, including rectal examinations, when they entered and left the building. Their personal belongings were confiscated, and they were forced to wear punishment signs—cards with humiliating messages written on them, such as "I lie" or "I steal"—when they misbehaved. One member of the review team said these women had been "misused" and quoted Densen-Gerber as stating, "There are times when as in war children must be sacrificed for other long range ends." This evaluator believed that some Odyssey practices "might have constituted child abuse."[15]

Odyssey's Mabon program on Ward's Island, the project to assist addicted mothers, has encountered similar embarrassing charges. The Mabon project sometimes included women who were not addicts but needed temporary shelter for themselves and their children. On at least three occasions, when such women tried to leave, Odyssey officials reportedly tried to keep them in the program by refusing to release their children. Mobilization for Youth had to get a writ of habeas corpus to get two children returned to their mother and filed a $100,000 suit for false imprisonment that is still pending.[16]

In her Kildee-Murphy testimony, interviews with the press, and her own writings, Densen-Gerber shows herself to be a flamboyant source of misinformation. She repeatedly refers to child pornography as "mutilation" and agrees with Detective Lloyd Martin that parents who batter their children cause less psychological damage than parents who have sex with them.[17] Among her bloopers are such curious statements as "The fact that the children for sexual snuff films are...purchased from Mexico is well known,"[18] and "The prepubescent child having intercourse does not have a vaginal pH which protects against infection...

children who have prepubescent intercourse have the highest incidence of cervical carcinoma of all women."[19] While she concedes that good sex education is needed, she believes that "anatomy and warnings about masturbation are not a substitute for dealing with the very real concerns and frustrations of adolescence."[20] The fact that such distortions were never questioned by the committee is a gauge of its total lack of objectivity. Most child pornography consists of nude pictures of kids and teenagers. There are no commercially available snuff films, despite rabid references to them in feminist antipornography literature and the Kildee-Murphy hearings. Pedophiles report that they rarely engage in intercourse with their young partners. Oral and manual techniques are most commonly used, and if anyone gets fucked, it is usually the older partner.[21] Densen-Gerber's claim that sex with a parent is more damaging than being beaten and her apparent belief that sex education should include warnings about masturbation are ludicrous.

It was easy to classify Anita Bryant as politically regressive since she enthusiastically identified herself with the right wing. Densen-Gerber, on the other hand, has won a lot of liberal support. After all, she was involved in treating drug addiction and ending child abuse. But her sexual politics don't really seem to be that different from Anita Bryant's. Densen-Gerber believes that "something has to be done to help the American family be able to rear its children in less oppressive permissiveness"[22] and warned the Kildee-Murphy committee that "present child rearing is not working. We can't leave it all in the present *laissez-faire* state."[23] She blames politically liberal and permissive parents for child abuse (which includes allowing a child to be sexually active), drug addiction, prostitution, pornography, and homosexuality.

At least one researcher, Dr. James W. Prescott, would dispute Densen-Gerber's beliefs about the causes of child abuse. His cross-cultural studies and other investigations have led him to conclude that child abuse is caused by our society's acceptance of violence and hatred of sexual pleasure. He points to corporal punishment by parents and schools, unwanted births, lack of physical affection between parent and child, and repression of premarital and extramarital sexuality as factors that lead to brutal treatment or the murder of children. Dr. Prescott theorizes that people who espouse traditional values (e.g., that pain and suffering build character, that sex is dirty, that war is necessary, that adultery should be punished by law and abortion made unavailable) are more likely to batter or murder their children than people with more positive attitudes toward sex, who do not believe violence is an effective way for individuals or nations to resolve conflicts.[24]

Densen-Gerber believes that the fringe or minority elements of our society are not entitled to rear children. Referring to Harlow and Prescott's work on infant monkeys who were separated from their mothers, she says:

> Their work showed that when there is no family socialization these monkeys compensated by precocious and promiscuous sexualization. That is what we are seeing. We have 2.4 million children in the care of substance-abusing mothers. Prostitutes average 2.8 children and they are selling their kids.[25] [Author's note: This study actually showed that infant monkeys deprived of physical contact with their mothers were unable to engage in sexual activity.]

Densen-Gerber also told the committee that foster parents are led to abuse children in their care when the state gives them financial aid. Monetary assistance supposedly encourages foster parents to view these children as potential sources of profit, and from there it's one short step to the porno studio.[26] She also told the committee that "researchers working with deviant women report that 50 to 70 percent have been sexually traumatized as children,"[27] and went on to repeat her theory that depraved parents prey on their children, who then grow up equally depraved and ready to prey on *their* children. Her list of unfit parents thus includes "deviant" women as well as prostitutes, drug addicts, poor people, and those whose politics are not conservative. Frankly, this reminds me of a Nazi eugenics program.

People who are nonconformists, disenfranchised, or underprivileged can raise children with love and care. But Densen-Gerber and her compatriots in the Great Kiddy Porn Panic are concerned with maintaining the nuclear family and everything it stands for—middle-class values, homophobia, uniformity, and puritanism—at all costs. The Kildee-Murphy committee bewailed the existence of one million runaways, acknowledged that most of them were mistreated at home, and did nothing to address this problem but outlaw child pornography and prostitution. A minor in America is, with rare exceptions, unemployable. A young woman or man who wants to exist independent of the family has few options other than the sex industry. Closing down this industry without providing alternative employment is equivalent to sentencing young people to frustration, abuse, or suicide in cozy little suburban ranch-style prisons. The fact that Densen-Gerber hinted at ending financial aid to foster parents, thus closing off another escape route from a bad family situation, is an outrage.

The Great Kiddy-Porn Panic of 1977 was a huge success. The Kildee-Murphy Bill is now Public Law No. 95-225, and many states have enacted similar legislation. Police have closed down many boy-love publications in this country and are using confiscated mailing lists and entrapment to bust shocking numbers of gay men. Sentences of twenty to forty years are common. The campaign against kiddy porn succeeded because it confused the issue of violence against children with the issue of children and sexuality. Everyone, gay and straight, is appalled at the idea of children or teenagers being raped, forced into performing sex acts in front of a camera, or exploited by a pimp. But many gay people are not appalled at the idea that young people want to break away from their families and sometimes grow up to be gay.

The members of the Kildee-Murphy committee were much more upset by a teenage hustler who leaves home to get away from his alcoholic father than they were by parents who starve their kids or beat them. The law that they passed is being used to punish gay men who cross the barrier of age and establish sexual intimacy with consenting young men. It has done nothing to prevent violent child abuse. Kids need better sex education, so they can understand the implications of sexual proposals and make informed choices. They need economic independence so that their parents can no longer use money to coerce them into stultifying lifestyles. They need protection from adults who use or threaten assault to intimidate them. Instead the Great Kiddy-Porn Panic has locked minors even more firmly into the status of property and has increased the risk that parents who do not raise their children according to traditional values will lose them.

Notes

1. Wolman, B.B., and J. Money, eds. *Handbook of Human Sexuality*, Englewood Cliffs, New Jersey: Prentice-Hall, Inc., 1980, 20.
2. On April 26, 1980, CBS aired "Gay Power, Gay Politics," a schlockumentary anchored by Harry Reasoner which made San Francisco look as if it were run from behind the scenes by leathermen and drag queens. The report focused on the 1979 mayoral election and was especially derogatory in its treatment of Dianne Feinstein. Randy Shilts eventually managed to get the producer of the show, George Crile, and his associate, Grace Diekhaus, censured by the National News Council. My sarcastic remark about CBS in this essay was an attempt to remind readers that we could not trust CBS to tell the truth about child pornography any more than we could trust the netwrok to honestly depict the grassroots struggle to gain civil rights for gay men and women in San Francisco.

3. The Boston/Boise Committee was named in reference to a McCarthy-era roundup of gay men in Boise, Idaho. Dozens of lives were ruined by this witch-hunt. For more information, see the comprehensive book by former *Time* and *Newsweek* editor John Gerassi, *The Boys of Boise: Furor, Vice and Folly in an American City*, New York: MacMillan, 1955.

4. *The Body Politic* was busted in 1979 for obscenity after publishing Gerald Hannon's article, "Men Loving Boys Loving Men" and found not guilty. But because Canada has no law against double jeopardy, the Crown filed for a new trial. This trial was still pending in 1980 when the entire collective was arrested again, this time for publishing "Lust with a Very Proper Stranger," an article about fisting by Angus MacKenzie. Eventually *The Body Politic* stopped publishing.

5. U.S. House Committee on the Judiciary, *Sexual Exploitation of Children*. Hearings before the Subcommittee on Crime, 95th Cong., 1st sess., May 23, 25, June 10, and September 20, 1977, Serial #12, 118-119.

6. *Pan: A Magazine about Boy-Love*, Vol. 1, No. 5, May 1980, 8.

7. House Committee, *Sexual Exploitation of Children*, 57.

8. "The Men Behind the Kidporn Industry." *San Francisco Examiner*, February 17, 1980, 13.

9. *ibid.*, 12.

10. Mitzel, John. "The Great Kiddie Porn Panic of 1977." *NAMBLA Journal #3*, 6-8.

11. *Gay Community News*, February 9, 1980, 3-8.

12. House Committee, *Sexual Exploitation of Children*, 49.

13. *Pan: A Magazine About Boy-Love*, Vol. 1, No. 2, August 1979, 24.

14. Komisar, Lucy. "The Mysterious Mistress of Odyssey House." *New York*, November 19, 1979, 43-50.

15. *ibid.*, 46.

16. *ibid.*, 47.

17. "The Battle-Line: Dr. Judianne Densen-Gerber as Witch of the Week." *Pan: A Magazine about Boy-Love*, Vol. 1, No. 3, November 1979, 28.

18. House Committee, *Sexual Exploitation of Children*, 43.

19. *ibid.*, 47.

20. "The Battle-Line: Dr. Judianne Densen-Gerber as Witch of the Week," 28.

21. Thorstad, David. Interview by Guy Hocquengheim in *Semiotext(e) Special Large Type Series: Loving Boys*, Summer 1980, 21.

22. House Committee, *Sexual Exploitation of Children*, 47

23. *ibid.*, 51.

24. Prescott, James W., Ph.D. "Child Abuse in America: Slaughter of the Innocents." *Hustler*, no date available.

25. House Committee, *Sexual Exploitation of Children*, 45.

26. *ibid.*, 51.

27. *ibid.*, 40.

The Aftermath of the
Great Kiddy-Porn Panic of '77
1980

How would you feel if you could be sentenced to spend twenty years in prison for owning a nude photograph of your lover and another twenty years for actually having sex with her or him? If your partner is a minor, you could easily receive such a sentence under new kiddy-porn laws and old age-of-consent legislation. It is a federal offense to produce, own, or distribute sexually explicit material if the subject is sixteen or younger. Thirty-five states enacted similar legislation in 1977 and 1978. The penalties for "statutory rape" (sex between a legal adult and a minor) are grim. Convicted pedophiles may do more time for having sex with minors than they would for manslaughter. Once incarcerated, they have a difficult time securing probation or parole, and other prisoners harass, beat, and even kill inmates who are known to be "child molesters."

The kiddy-porn laws were passed during a flurry of public outrage over violent child abuse and the sexual exploitation of children, but they have done nothing to diminish the brutal treatment of young people. Children and teenagers are still being sexually abused, beaten, and sometimes put to death by their adult custodians. Young people are still the property of their parents (or, if the parents are not appropriately conservative, the state). They are the poorest group in our society. A minor who attempts to become self-supporting faces discrimination in jobs, housing, and every other area of her or his life. Minors have no control over their educations, their places of residence, or their religious beliefs. They are routinely denied the full protection of the Bill of Rights and thus are subject to searches, curfews, and other indignities that would be illegal if applied to any other group. The laws that make it illegal for minors to work in the sex industry or have adult lovers also make it unlikely that a young woman or man will be able to escape from an abusive family. So, under the guise of protecting children, the great kiddy-porn panic has intensified their oppression.

These laws are being used against segments of our society which are far more vulnerable than the porn business. For instance, artists often do not have the resources or the experience to successfully defend themselves against vice charges, and they may have suspect politics or unconventional lifestyles, making them ideal targets for censorship and harassment. Photographer Jacqueline Livingston's 1980 *Village Voice* interview was illustrated with erotic photographs she had taken of her son, Sam. These illustrations prompted the American Society for the Prevention of Cruelty to Children to insist on a meeting with staff members of the *Voice* to discuss "kiddy porn" in their newspaper. Livingston was accused of child abuse, investigated by the Tompkins County Department of Social Services, and only narrowly missed losing custody of her son.[1]

Gay men who have sexual relationships with boys (and the boys themselves) are the *real* victims of the kiddy-porn crusade. This result could have been predicted by anyone familiar with Dr. Judianne Densen-Gerber, Anita Bryant, Detective Lloyd Martin, and their compatriots. These people repeatedly condemn youthful sexual activity of any kind because they believe it turns kids queer. This absurdity is being touted as the new theory of the etiology of homosexuality.

In fact, since 1977 the media has latched onto this theory, conducting and publishing numerous exposés on the subject of child sexuality and its relationship to adult homosexuality. In a *New York Post* three-part series published in 1979, Stephen F. Hutchinson, vice president and general counsel for Odyssey Institute, is quoted as saying that most pedophiles were seduced themselves at early ages. The article also makes the dubious claims that pedophiles operate a national underground network through which they exchange "millions of dollars worth of filth"; that federal, state, and local laws dealing with pedophilia are weak; and that "There is a marked tendency toward leniency toward pedophiles." Typical of the "statistical" evidence quoted are these two contradictory estimates: Lloyd Martin's claim that there are thirty thousand kids up for sale in New York alone and an estimate that there are twenty thousand pedophiles in this country. The article also states, "The venereal disease rate among children under fourteen has doubled in the last decade and has been termed epidemic."[2]

In a 1980 *San Franciso Examiner* article, the experience of Berkeley police officer Seth Goldstein (Northern California's version of Lloyd Martin) is reported as follows: "ten pedophiles have confessed to him. Each one had sexual experience as a child. As adults, their desire for children is overpowering." Paul Burkhardt, director of the Sexual Orientation Program at Atascadero State Hospital, states that most of the two hundred male pedophiles confined there "had sexual activities with other children as youngsters."[3] Since most kids experiment sexually with other children, this reminds me of Krafft-Ebing's contention that masturbation must cause criminal behavior and insanity since most of the inmates of prisons and asylums he interviewed confessed to practicing self-abuse.

Also in 1980, the *San Francisco Chronicle* published a piece which implied that young female prostitutes can be transformed into lesbians by the nature of their work: " 'I'm thinking about women who like to trick with women,' said Brown Sugar, a small boned girl with several gold chains around her neck. 'I'd go for it because men treat me like trash. Seems like women treat a lady the way they are supposed to.' " Although the article repeatedly refers to the young female and male prostitutes in the article as "children," the youngest one interviewed was a fifteen-year-old boy. Brown Sugar, the "child" quoted above, has one child of her own and has served a year in a Los Angeles prison for the attempted murder of a trick.[4]

■ ■ ■

Erotic pictures of boys play an important role in a subculture where actual contact between youths and adults is difficult to arrange. Some pedophiles express their sexuality primarily through the use of erotic materials as aids to masturbation. So the federal government's making kiddy porn illegal was a brilliant stroke because it is now actually possible to enforce age-of-consent laws.[5] Boy-lovers often take pictures of their youthful partners (doesn't everybody take pictures of loved ones?) and help each other get these pictures developed. They may share photographs with friends. This is a far cry from the myth of the Hydra-headed kiddy-porn industry that is trotted out to horrify and agitate the public, but such photographs do fall under the legal definition of child pornography. So, if police can find such material in the possession of a boy-lover, they usually can locate the boy and try to pressure him into testifying against his adult partner.

Armed with these draconian laws, the police are already making a frightening number of arrests.[6] Even more frightening, however, is evidence that the police may be preparing for mass arrests on an unprecedented scale. Three major busts have given the police literally thousands of names and addresses of gay men who might possess prosecutable material.

On October 30, 1979, New York City police broke up a call-boy ring and seized the mailing list of clients, some three thousand names. A few of the call boys were minors. On November 30, 1979, Lloyd Martin raided the Athletic Models Guild (AMG) and seized its photographic equipment and mailing list. AMG produced a wide range of erotic gay male material; however, they are not a source of kiddy porn. The justification for this raid was an alleged complaint from a fourteen-year-old whom police say was photographed at the studio. Police do not have the name or address of this complainant.

George Jacobs, a commercial photographer, was arrested in Woods Hole, Massachusetts, on September 13, 1979. His photographic equipment and mailing list were also seized. The police claimed Jacobs was the center of an international child-porn ring. Jacobs says he helped a group of eight to ten men get their pictures of boys developed, and kept some copies for himself.

The police went to a lot of trouble to get Jacobs. Lloyd Martin apparently got his hooks into a boy-lover named Ralph Bonnell and pressured him into becoming an informer. Bonnell was flown all the way from California to Massachusetts, where he set up a meeting with his old friend Jacobs. After spending a few hours at Jacobs's home, Bonnell was picked up by Irving M. Peterson, team leader of the Mail Fraud and Prohibitive Mailings Investigation Unit for the Northeast. After grilling Bonnell, Peterson got enough information to obtain a search warrant. This elaborate effort resulted in Jacobs's being arrested, tried, and sentenced to thirty-nine years in prison. After the verdict, Judge Wagner told Jacobs, "You are a despicable, vile creature, a disgrace to the human race. This conduct is worse than murder." All but fourteen months of Jacobs's sentence was waived, possibly because he threatened to challenge the constitutionality of the Massachusetts kiddy-porn law. But his troubles are far from over. He could be diagnosed a sexually dangerous person, which means he would stay in prison until that diagnosis is reversed.[7] Also, Peterson is urging the feds to try Jacobs under the federal kiddy-porn law.[8]

In addition to the mailing lists, address books, and correspondence they have obtained via arrests, the police are assisted by photo labs which turn in customers who send in film of young people. There is some evidence that they may have acquired names from the Gay and Lesbian Community Services Center VD Clinic in Los Angeles.[9] Martin Locker, New York's "prohibited mail specialist," inspects foreign mail specifically to intercept incoming kiddy porn. He has also resorted to placing sex ads soliciting boy-lovers whom he asks to exchange porn with him, and to answering ads. Locker has counterparts in other cities. For example, in Washington, D.C., Postal Inspector Obie Daniels has been involved in actions against child pornography.[10]

What are the police going to do with all this information? United

States vice cops may share their lists with agents in other countries and solicit similar material from them.[11] Irving Peterson has been quoted as saying that the U.S. Attorney General has informed him that actions against pedophiles and child pornography are a priority for 1980. It looks like a full-scale offensive is being planned. The gay civil-rights movement ought to be worried.

Boy-lovers are of course frightened already, and they have reacted the way oppressed groups traditionally do: they have organized. In December 1978, a group of concerned individuals sponsored a Boston conference, "Man/Boy Love and the Age of Consent." After the conference, thirty legal adults and minors formed the North American Man/Boy Love Association (NAMBLA).

Members of NAMBLA risk penalties which a garden-variety lesbian or gay man currently doesn't have to sweat about. It obviously takes considerable courage for them to go public, but the mainstream gay movement has not been supportive. Many gay papers refuse to carry ads for pedophile individuals, publications, or groups. Three exceptions are *Pan: A Magazine About Boy-Love* (published in the Netherlands), *Gay Community News*, and *Gay Insurgent*. The ban on open debate of boy-love is so pervasive that at least one gay journalist, Sidney Smith, lost his job for not observing it. Smith worked for a gay radio show in New York City. He aired an interview with Dutch Senator Edward Brongersma, a regular contributor to *Pan*. Smith was fired on the grounds that the material did not represent and might hurt the interests of the gay community.[12] Ironically, Smith was also employed by the station's art and literature department, which retained him despite its being a "straight" department.

At least three major gay events have been disrupted by conflicts over how much support should be given to boy-lovers and sexually active youth. In addition to drastically reduced participation in the April 12, 1980, March on Albany that resulted from a dispute over NAMBLA spokesperson David Thorstad's participation, the October 14, 1979, March on Washington dropped its demand for the abolition of age-of-consent laws because conservative lesbian and gay groups threatened to withdraw their support, and New York City's gay-pride march was torn in half this year because members of the Lesbian and Gay Pride March Committee were "vociferous in their opposition to the abolition of age-of-consent laws and the participation of NAMBLA...as well as transpeople, in the gay rights movement."[13]

This hostility is sad, but it isn't surprising. Despite all our hard work, the economic and political situation in this country is getting worse, not better. Our standard of living is dropping. Jobs are getting harder to find, and working conditions are worse than ever. Financial hardship results in more violence in the streets (much of it directed against visible lesbians and gay men) and makes it more likely that our nation will go to war. This atmosphere of scarcity and patriotism encourages the use of gays as scapegoats. Our civil liberties are being eroded by a Supreme Court that steadfastly refuses to extend equal protection under the law to homosexuals. We can't even get the ERA passed! The right wing has got us on the run.

In this climate, the cost of dissent has risen sharply. Gays comprise one of the most well-behaved minorities, perhaps because we are always trying to get back into our parents' good graces. We also have the illusion of the option to go back into the closet if things get too tough. Nobody wants to come under surveillance by the secret police. Nobody wants to go to prison. We can't seem to do anything to halt inflation, curb jingoism, or silence the well-financed voices of bigotry. And yet we can succeed at purging our own movement, jettisoning the controversial planks of our platform, and doing some of the vice squad's dirty work. But in so doing, we postpone open warfare—and our own liberty—for a few more decades, perhaps indefinitely.

Many well-intentioned people in our movement are working overtime to do just that. Steve Endean, our first gay lobbyist in Washington, D.C., and a speaker at a NAMBLA-sponsored forum, expressed this fear: "What NAMBLA is doing is tearing apart the movement. If you attach it [the man/boy love issue] to gay rights, gay rights will never happen."[14]

Endean's view of boy-lovers corresponds to Edmund White's:

> That's the politics of self-indulgence. Our movement cannot survive the man-boy issue. It's not a question of who's right, it's a matter of political naïveté.[15]

Who's being naïve is debatable. First of all, nobody is fooled when we proclaim that the gay movement has nothing to do with kids and their sexuality. Lesbians and gay men don't magically spring into existence at some arbitrary age of consent. Many of us know from the time that we are small children that we are attracted to members of our own sex. Many of us—both women and men—had our first homosexual experiences with partners who were older than ourselves. Parents start looking for signs of homosexuality in their kids at about age two. Sexual repression isn't one hundred percent effective, but it does keep some young women and men from forming gay identities. To leave that repression unchallenged is to leave a major bastion of gay oppression untouched. It's absurd to say that sex between a man and a boy or a woman and a girl is not a gay issue. It certainly isn't a heterosexual issue.

Second of all, the police do whatever we let them get away with. They don't bust the biggest gay-lib organization or the most popular bar in town. They close down the hustlers' bars, the drag bars, and the leather bars. Right now they can get away with collecting the names and addresses of gay men who might be pedophiles, entrapping boy-lovers, and putting them in prison. They can get away with intimidating and persecuting lesbian and gay minors. Does anybody seriously think they will stop there unless we force them to? There are enough archaic sex laws on the books—laws relating to pornography, sodomy, public sex, and prostitution—to put many of us in prison if the police are allowed to use entrapment and surveillance. Even states that have decriminalized sodomy could easily alter their statutes so that they applied only to *heterosexual* activity, making homosexual oral and anal sex special, prosecutable offenses. It would take only an uproar of public outrage similar to the Great Kiddy-Porn Panic of 1977. Are you sure the police don't have your name and address?

Endean and others who argue for a politics of expedience are dead wrong. Gay rights *is* a question of right and wrong. Our strength comes from the conviction that we are combating injustice. Our enemies espouse simple-minded obedience to outmoded, inhumane superstitions. They are not moral; they are moralistic. But our movement *is* profoundly moral. It stands for the ethics of self-determination, for human happiness, and against the tyranny of conformity. By abandoning boy-lovers to the police and gay kids to their homophobic families, we may hasten the day when adult lesbians and gay men have full civil rights, but will we ever be able to forgive ourselves? Can we honestly say we have freedom if gay minors do not? Our movement cannot survive the loss of its conscience.

Of course, there are those who claim that we must disassociate ourselves from pedophiles as a matter of principle. They agree with the stars of the great kiddy-porn panic that it is wrong for adults and young people to have sex with each other. It is sometimes hard to tell the right-wing position on this issue from the position that many prominent lesbian-feminists have promulgated. For instance, there's Elaine Noble's response to the 1977 Boston/Boise arrests:

> Gross personal abuse and effrontery of innocent children is a
> sacrilege of the highest order. Adults involved in the corruption
> of unprotected, impressionable children by drugs, alcohol and

sex must be immediately halted and reprimanded. We will not tolerate nor in any way condone through lack of aggressive action the perpetuation of such deviant, defiant behavior.[16]

When the police set up a hotline to take anonymous tips that would lead to further arrests, this lesbian legislator actually urged the gay community of Boston to cooperate.

As a sacrilegious, defiant deviant bent on corrupting anyone who's susceptible, I am angered by the sight of another lesbian's vehemently waving the American flag and spouting apple-pie slogans. Noble blindly accepts the Judeo-Christian belief that sex is dangerous and bad and the ridiculous notion that children are asexual. Young lesbians and gay men don't need to be protected from "corruption"—they need protection from their repressive families; nonjudgmental information about human sexuality and gay lifestyles; and the economic freedom to make their own choices. The "gross personal abuse and effrontery" they suffer usually does not occur in their relationships with older lesbian and gay male friends and lovers. It takes place on the school playground, where they are hounded for being "bulldaggers" or "fags." It takes place in the school counselor's office, the rabbi's or the minister's office, and over the supper table, where they are bullied and harangued about being freaks and about disappointing their parents. Robin Morgan has congratulated Noble for having the courage to express this "unpopular" opinion. I do not see how it could have taken great courage for Noble to urge the gay community to inform on itself and turn its back on its younger generation. In the middle of a police crackdown, a right-wing backlash, and inflammatory attacks in the press, Noble chose to side with the police, the right wing, and journalists eager to discredit the gay movement. This choice represented a simple loss of nerve. It is no cause for congratulation.

Robin Morgan gave to Jill Clark her own views on cross-generational sex. They are less simplistic than Noble's, but have the same law-and-order flavor.

> I think boy-love is a euphemism for rape, regardless of whether the victim seems to invite it. That is what has been said of the woman rape victim. When somebody relatively powerless is getting fucked, literally and figuratively, by somebody powerful, that is a rape situation. Let's not blame the victim.[17]

Morgan acknowledges that children are sexual, but states, "the only way that sexuality has a chance of flowering in any non-damaging,

60

power-free relationship is with another child." If there is a difference of more than three or four years between the children or if one partner is bigger and stronger than the other, Morgan questions the consensuality of their relationship. She believes that young people are not attracted to adults because they are sexually appealing or have likable personalities, but because "power is attractive and interesting, especially to the powerless." She perceives a female/male split over the issue of boy-love (and pornography, sadomasochism, and promiscuity) which she attributes to "the bonding of women, straight or gay," which opposes "the bonding of men." She goes so far as to state that "the issue of child-love is almost zilch among lesbians." Her theory is that women don't eroticize children because they raise them. Specifically, she mentions the process of changing a diaper and dealing with baby shit as an experience that prevents women from being sexually turned on to children's asses. She suggests that if more men performed child care, fewer of them would find children sexy. This interview includes an interesting statement: "There comes a point when you realize that sexuality and emotions are involved with one another, and to break the one off from the other is to do something horribly divisive to your own psyche and spirit, let alone to the other person."[18]

The core of Morgan's argument is her characterization of boy-love as "a euphemism for rape." Feminist antirape activists have worked long and hard to educate the public about the difference between consensual intercourse and rape. Many people, if not most, blur these two categories and believe that every sexual act involves a degree of force which a woman invites and enjoys. Thus there is no such thing as rape, just a more or less forceful attitude on the part of the male partner. This view of sex is based on the assumption that women don't enjoy sex, don't initiate it, and never give clear consent to engage in it. Thus, women must be taught to initiate sex and explicitly indicate their interest or lack of interest in it.

The onus of guessing when "no" means "maybe" must be taken from men's shoulders. People also need the kind of sex education that makes mutually pleasurable sex possible. Morgan's specious redefinition of rape could undo years of laborious public education. There is a clear difference between a consensual sex act which takes place between two people of different social status and a sexual assault (which can easily take place between people of equal social status). Her concept of rape implies that all kinds of relationships are inherently nonconsensual—sex between men and women, between people of different racial or ethnic backgrounds, between people of different socioeconomic levels, between able-bodied and physically challenged people, and even between partners who differ greatly in size and strength. It harks back to the days when everyone believed that homosexuals forcibly seduced impressionable victims into lives of vice and misery. It seemed obvious then that nobody would freely choose a lesbian or male homosexual lover.

Our society is made up of class systems and runs on arbitrarily assigned privilege. Loving relationships provide ways to cross barriers, forge alliances, and redistribute power. Granted, they cannot substitute for full-scale social change. But we cannot forgo all intimacy until these inequities are finally abolished. There is nothing wrong with a more privileged adult offering a young person money, privacy, freedom of movement, new ideas, and sexual pleasure.

Morgan's assumption that adults have more power than young people is not an adequate description of the social conditions that surround cross-generational relationships. Any minor has the potential power to send an adult partner to jail for half of her or his life. It is condescending to assume that young people are so dazzled by the power of adults that they cannot tell the difference between being molested and being in love or being horny. Any child old enough to decide whether or not she or he wants to eat spinach, play with trucks, or wear shoes is old enough to decide whether or not she or he wants to run around naked in the sun, masturbate, sit in somebody's lap, or engage in sexual activity. We should be working to end the artificial state of sexual ignorance in which children are kept—not perpetuating or defending it.

Morgan's contention that there is a natural female/male split on this issue is questionable. It seems to be based on an acceptance of traditional sex roles. To begin with, all women are not mothers. Some of us find the notion of pregnancy and child rearing repugnant. It is possible that sexual activity occurs more often between mothers and children or other women than between men and children. Women have more access to kids, and there are fewer taboos surrounding women's handling young people's bodies. Granted, given feminine conditioning the women who have erotic contact with young people probably don't think of it as sex, but this is hypocrisy, not liberation.

The assumption that only men engage in cross-generational sex with girls and boys permeates nearly every feminist argument against it. Lesbian Feminist Liberation of New York (LFL) is against *any* lowering of the age of consent because "the repeal of the age of consent laws presents greater dangers to young women as 97–99 percent of molested children and teenagers are girls who are raped or taken advantage of by heterosexual men." This dubious statistic comes from Florence Rush, who is achieving some prominence in the lesbian-feminist press as an expert on child molestation. LFL's position is based in part on Rush's research, which supposedly "shows vast differences between young women's and men's feelings about their sexual experiences with adults." Rush reports that most of the young women in her sample felt coerced into sex and carried fear, guilt, and shame about the experience. The boys tended to have mixed reactions. "Those who were approached 'man-to-man' tended to feel natural about the experience while those who were coerced like the young women felt ashamed or guilty." LFL rather smugly denies that age-of-consent laws are a children's liberation issue.[19] This position is heterosexist, homophobic, and ageist.

Why is there no discussion of the frustrating and tragic situation of young girls who know they are lesbians in grade school, junior high, or high school? As Beth Kelly has pointed out in her autobiographical article, "Speaking Out: Woman/Girl Love,"[20] relationships between young girls and women do exist. Kelly's article contains a moving and beautiful description of her relationship with her great-aunt, which began when she was about eight years old. She says, "I think I can safely say, some 20 years later, that I was never exploited physically, emotionally, or intellectually...I can only empathize with all of the young women and men out there now, who are being and will be sold short by adults who will not or cannot face these issues...We seem to be so hung up on trying to protect ourselves and our hard-won gains that we are willing—and quick—to deny powerless others the right to be and affirm themselves sexually...I must reiterate that lesbians have no room for righteous indignation."

Why are lesbians willing to cooperate with the patriarchal conspiracy to silence the truth about the intensity and diversity of female sexuality? This attempt to define pedophilia as a male issue simply alienates and estranges women whose lesbian experiences include cross-generational contact. It is one more brick in the Great Wall of Feminist Propriety that separates the ladylike lesbians from the female sex perverts. This new category of sexual deviant, created by real feminists, includes women who do S/M, women who crossdress, butches and femmes, women who are promiscuous, women who use pornography, transsexual women, women who work in the sex industry, women who have fetishes, girl-lovers, bisexual women, and just about anybody who has a clearly defined sexual preference and spends time trying to fulfill it.

Rush's research clearly demonstrates that it is consent, not gender, that makes the difference in young people's reactions to sex with adults. It also seems to indicate that the sexual orientation of the adult is an important factor. Boy-lovers seem to have more concern that the desire for sex be mutual than heterosexual men do. The study might justify a condemnation of heterosexual child rape (not pedophilia, since the sample included no consenting sexual activity between young girls and men), but it is being used to trash gay men.

LFL has no right to speak for children's liberation. That is the right of young people. It is odd that LFL's definition of liberation does not include a young person's right to control her or his own body. This implies that sex isn't so important for young people as for adults. Try telling that to a fourteen-year-old who's in love with her gym teacher.

The antiporn movement's position on boy-love doesn't differ that much from the other arguments cited above. It's just more extreme. Women Against Violence in Pornography and the Media (WAVPM) sees erotic activity between adults and young people as a part of the back-lash against feminism. According to their analysis, as women become more powerful men become so intimidated that they turn to helpless little girls and pictures of helpless little girls. Thus, by definition, every pedophile is antifeminist. A 1977 issue of WAVPM's newsletter stated the following argument:

> We see this proliferation of pornography, particularly violent pornography and child pornography, as part of the male back-lash to the women's liberation movement. Enough women have been rejecting the traditional role of subordination to men to cause a crisis in the collective male ego...As women have become stronger and more assertive, some men find it easier to feel powerful with young girls, including children. Hence the enormous increase in child pornography in recent years.[21]

This argument is tautological: Boy-love is bad because it is antifeminist. How do we know David Thorstad is antifeminist? Because he is a boy-lover. Never mind that Thorstad has worked for many years to support the goals of the women's movement (and made himself unpopular with many gay men in the process). His political identity is being defined by his sexual identity—which is like saying that all homosexuals are godless communists or that all sadomasochists are secret fascists. There is no one-to-one correlation between an individual's sex life and her or his political views.

WAVPM's theory does not explain why an adult man would prefer boys (who have more social and physical power than girls) if he is moti-vated simply by a fear of powerful partners. It also does not explain why women have sexual relationships with girls. Yet this theory, which might explain *heterosexual* pedophilia, is being used to attack gay men.

What is missing from all this sanctimonious cant is the fact that some adults and young people care so deeply about each other that they are willing to risk long prison sentences, social stigma, and violence to make contact with each other. Morgan is right: sexuality and emotions cannot be separated from each other without doing something horrible to the human spirit. But what makes her think that tenderness is not present in cross-generational relationships? The shrink establishment used to say that about lesbian relationships—that they were hopelessly neurotic because two women couldn't really love each other.

I think it is interesting that so much of the new, ostensibly feminist morality dovetails with the old, Judeo-Christian morality. But while the American left is used to dealing with its own sectarian elements, the women's movement is not. We do have a conservative wing trying to turn feminism into a campaign against pornography, boy-lovers, sado-masochists, drag queens, transsexuals, and prostitutes. It cannot be mere coincidence that so many groups of people who already have been outlawed, depersonalized, and termed sick are being turned into symbols of women's oppression. The feminist jargon that justifies this process is becoming the new language of sexual repression, the new justification for punishing or eradicating dissenting sexualities. It may replace the language of the New Testament and psychiatric rhetoric.

Fortunately, not every feminist falls back on conventional sexual mores when the issue of sexual variation comes up. Jane Rule has written a very sensible article, "Teaching Sexuality," in which she argues that adults should take more responsibility for educating children about sex. She says, "When the relatively simple task of teaching table manners takes so many years, why do we assume that sexual manners need not be taught at all?" She argues:

> Children are at our mercy. They are at each other's mercy as well. It makes about as much sense to leave children's sexual nourishment to their peers as it would to assume that the mud pies they make for each other are an adequate lunch...If we accepted sexual behavior between children and adults, we would be far more able to protect our children from abuse and exploitation than we are now. They would be free to tell us, as they can about all kinds of other experiences, what is happening to them and to have our sympathy and support instead of our mute and mistrustful terror.[22]

Kate Millett has also made a statement supporting youth sexuality, including children's right to express themselves sexually with adults if they choose to do so. Of course she believes that increased sexual freedom for young people must be part of a complete program for their liberation.[23]

It is disheartening that some boy-lovers have not taken note of the diversity of feminist thinking on this issue and assume that all women oppose cross-generational sex. This assumption has been the excuse for some boy-lovers' misogynist statements, which do nothing to further their cause with lesbians and feminists.

Perhaps the most disappointing aspect of the whole debate over youth sexuality is that the opinions of young people and youth liberation groups are rarely solicited. Back in 1978, when this controversy was heating up, *FPS: A Magazine of Young People's Liberation* put out a special editorial statement on children and sex. It's a pity that more adult lesbians and gay men have not used *FPS's* position to inform their own. The editors of *FPS* believe that children (even very young children) are capable of making their needs and wishes known if adults will pay attention to them and that there is nothing intrinsically wrong with young people's having sex with each other or with adults. They say, "current morality more often inhibits people who would be good with children rather than the abusers." They believe that in a sexually liberated, economically just society, prostitution would not exist. However, until that time they support the right of young people to have access to all jobs, including prostitution. They call for better working conditions, decriminalization, and an end to stigmatization of prostitution. They oppose any attempt to ban child pornography because such a ban would weaken the Bill of Rights, and they remind their readers that "taking nude photographs of children doesn't necessarily involve force or evil." Instead of censorship, they support working to end the sexual repression they believe makes such material profitable. *FPS's* editors acknowledge that many other issues are crucial to the liberation of young people and regret having to defend youth liberation on the grounds of prostitution and pornography. However, they point out that these areas of young people's liberation are currently under attack, and that we have no choice but to meet that attack head on.[24]

Mark Moffett, a fifteen-year-old boy who has had relationships with men, was interviewed for *FPS* by Sylvere Lotringer. This interview provides rare insight into cross-generational sex from the point of view of the minor partner. Moffett believes that it is easier for gay boys to find adult gay men than it is for men to find boys, and he documents the fact that boys often must locate, proposition, and persuade their older partners. This is his position on age-of-consent laws:

> I think the age of consent should be lowered and probably abolished. But only after coercion laws have been strengthened and there has been an adequate education of prepubescent children. As it stands now, a lot of kids would be in danger since they don't know that much about sex and sexual relationships...It all comes back to education. After that children can be expected and given the freedom to have sex with whomever they want to have sex with...I don't think rape is being stopped now with the age of consent laws.

The lesbian and gay movement must stand firm against attempts to isolate us from gay youth and their adult partners. We must make it costly for the state to attack any segment of our community. The police must be taught that they cannot go after drag queens, leathermen, boy-lovers, visible lesbians, or hustlers without having to deal with all of us. There is no other way to keep the witch-hunt from spreading. We are, after all, a *minority*. We must present a unified front. There are not enough of us to make any other strategy practical.

We also must avoid replicating oppression within our own movement. Straight society would like to deny us the right to choose our lovers, our sexuality, and our lifestyles. Gay freedom means freedom to choose, freedom to be different, freedom to live openly without fear. The outside world does not make the same fine distinction between political theory and sexual practice that we do. Conservative gays may object to drag, leather, sex with youth, hustlers, or other fringe aspects of gay culture because they aren't erotically appealing, seem shocking, or don't appear to be politically correct. But straight society recognizes only two categories—heterosexuals and queers. America does not reward conservative gays for being emotionally stable, working hard at their jobs, or having long-term relationships. It rewards them for being invisible. And America does not hesitate to use whatever vicious tactic is necessary to destroy homosexuals who get too rebellious. The irony is that fringe gays are often the most active, committed, and vocal workers in the lesbian and gay liberation movement. There is nothing more embittering than being sold out by other lesbians and gay men to a society that holds all of us in contempt.

Feminists must realize that we have little to gain by perpetuating outmoded concepts of childhood and repressive methods of child rearing. The subservience of women is built on the idea that every adult human female ought to spend most of her life caring for helpless children. We ought to be creating child-rearing methods that produce self-managing girls and boys. We also ought to be prepared to have them talk back to us. Truly autonomous girls and boys are entitled to accurate information about sex, and lots of support—but they will make their own choices.

Kids should not have to become prostitutes or porn models in order to escape their families. But if we support a campaign to do away with youth prostitution, ban kiddy porn, and stop at that, we leave the nuclear family intact and mandatory heterosexuality unchallenged. We should probably be doing just the opposite—demanding that workers in the sex industry receive the same decent, safe working conditions, wages, respect, and benefits that other workers feel entitled to. We need openly lesbian and gay teachers in the schools. We need to get good information about homosexuality into sex education programs. Foster homes should be available for lesbian and gay kids who cannot live with their parents. We have to make our movement more accessible to young people—let them know where to find it, hold our events in places and at times that will allow them to attend, listen to them, and help them instead of ignoring them and discounting them. Gay money should be allocated to provide employment for young lesbians and gay men, and our social-service agencies should be educated and pressured into giving them full assistance.

Boy-lovers and lesbians who have young lovers are the only people offering a hand to help young women and men cross the difficult terrain between straight society and the gay community. They are not child molesters. The child abusers are teachers, therapists, cops, and parents who force their stale morality onto the young people in their custody. Instead of condemning pedophiles for their involvement with lesbian and gay youth, we should be supporting them. They need us badly. Forty years in prison is a long, long time. Only a very sad society with some very sick attitudes toward sex could think such a sentence is just. Forty years for *what?* For experiencing sexual pleasure? When the capacity to have orgasms is present at six months of age and possibly even earlier? God help us, it's a wonder any of us manage to feel love or make love with training like that.

We were capable of smashing windows at City Hall and torching police cars when somebody we loved was taken away from us—and it was already too late. It is not too late to stop the police from seizing vulnerable members of our community and sentencing them to a living death. We should not allow one more boy-lover to go to prison. If we do, his misery is on our heads.

Notes

1. Stambolian, George. "Creating the New Man: A Conversation with Jacqueline Livingston." *Christopher Street*, Vol. 4, No. 9, May 1980, 8-17.
2. Ruffini, Gene. "Those 'Solid Citizens' Who Lust for Children." *New York Post*, November 6, 1979.
3. "The Men Behind the Kidporn Industry." *San Francisco Examiner*, February 17, 1980.
4. Sward, Susan. "A Sordid Story of Life on the Street." *San Francisco Chronicle*, August 18, 1980, 6.
5. Thorstad, David. Interview by Guy Hocquenghem in *Semiotext(e) Special Large Type Series: Loving Boys*, Summer 1980, 30.
6. Mitzel, John. "Clown Nabbed in NY on Kid Porn Charge." *Gay Sunshine News*, July 5, 1980. Martin Locker, New York's prohibited mail specialist, arrested a priest who is also a boy-lover by entrapping him through *Fetish Times* and other sex ads. The priest led Locker to Ronald Drew, a teacher. Since his arrest, the education commissioner has tried to take away Drew's pension. Locker also entrapped Marvin Matthow, who did children's television programs as "Baldy the Clown." Undercover police entrapped Matthow by offering him money to procure models for a film.

   Pan: A Magazine About Boy-Love. Vol. 1, No. 3, November 1979, 6. Officers of the Pedophile Information Exchange (PIE) were arrested in London and charged with a conspiracy to corrupt the public morals. The PIE newsletter is not pornographic and repeatedly warned readers against committing any illegal act. Nevertheless, police apparently went after PIE simply because its newsletter put boy-lovers in touch with one another. The charge carries a potential life sentence, and the "conspiracy" need not even be for an illegal purpose.

   Pan, Vol. 1, No. 4, February 1980, 9. It's hard to sympathize with some of the people who get caught by these laws. Pennsylvania Republican State Representative David S. Hayes protested when Governor Dick Thornburgh proclaimed a Gay Pride Week. On December 17, 1979, he was arrested and charged with anal and oral intercourse with a seventeen-year-old boy.

   Pan, Vol. 1, No. 3, November 1979, 4. Anti-boy-love sentiment does more than get people arrested. It can get them killed. In July of 1979, Edgar Quann was reportedly beaten to death by members of a small New York Muslim sect for having sex with the son of a church member.
7. Richard Peluso, one of the Boston/Boise defendants, is still in prison because he was diagnosed as a sexually dangerous person. Most of the other defendants are either out on probation or had their charges dropped.
8. Mitzel, John. "Man Sentenced to Total of 39 Years on Charges of Child Pornography, Rape." *Gay Community News*, February 9, 1980, 3, 8-9.

9. Homosexual Information Center News Release, November 20, 1976.

10. Penn, Stanley. "Martin Locker is a 'Prohibited Mail Specialist.'" *Wall Street Journal*, January 23, 1980, 48. Locker is fortunately prohibited from opening first-class mail within the United States.

11. "The Battle-Line: Los Angeles Cop Lloyd Martin." *Pan: A Magazine About Boy-Love*, Vol. 1, No. 5, May 1980, 28. A *Pan* correspondent in Sydney, Australia, reported that the police there had received a list of names and addresses of gay men from the FBI and had been asked if they had received any complaints about unsolicited child pornography. The FBI also stated that they were willing to fly such a person to the U.S. to testify, according to this article. *Pan* states that Sydney newspapers reported that it was Lloyd Martin who gave George Jacobs's list to Australian police.

12. *Pan*, Vol. 1, No. 5, May 1980, 8-9.

13. *Gay Community News*, Vol. 7, No. 49, July 5, 1980, 1.

14. Shehadi, Philip. "Adult/Youth Relationships Discussed at NYC Forum." *Gay Community News*, July 5, 1980, 7.

15. White, Edmund. *States of Desire*. New York: E.P.Dutton, 1980, 320.

16. Hudson, John Paul. "The Gay Almanac: The Boston Boise Affair and the Censorship of Sexual Minorities." *Gaysweek*, March 6, 1978.

17. Clark, Jill. "Interview With Robin Morgan." *Gay Community News*, January 20, 1979, 11-12.

18. *ibid.*

19. Shapiro, Lynne. "Women Loving Women Denounce Men 'Loving' Boys." *Lesbian Tide*, September/October 1979, Vol. 9, No. 2, 14.

20. Kelly, Beth. "Speaking Out on 'Women/Girl Love'—or, Lesbians *Do* 'Do It'." *Gay Community News*, March 3, 1979, p 5.

21. Lederer, Laura, and Diana Russell. "Questions We Get Asked Most Often." WAVPM *Newspage*, November 1977, 3.

22. Rule, Jane. "Teaching Sexuality." *The Body Politic*, June 1979, 29.

23. Millett, Kate. *Semiotext(e) Special Large Type Series: Loving Boys*, Summer 1980, 44.

24. "A View from the Staff: Children and Sex." *FPS: A Magazine of Young People's Liberation*, No. 60, April-June 1978, 13-16.

Public Sex
1982

Since its inception, the American gay liberation movement has demanded that all sex acts performed in private between consenting adults be decriminalized. This is no surprise given the well-documented determination of the state to invade our bedrooms and regulate what goes on there. In fact, for some this single demand is the total content of gay liberation, and if that demand were met they would dismantle the movement and trot home to do you-know-what behind locked doors.

Such a reform of sex law would be a definite improvement over what we have now. But we have to be wary of making unwise concessions or being forced into too narrow an interpretation of our demands. If we restrict ourselves to protecting the rights of consenting adults, we leave young gay men and lesbians and their adult friends and lovers vulnerable to persecution. While pressing for social change, we could easily be trapped into becoming guardians of the "morals" of our nation's youth in exchange for protection of consenting adults. Similarly, we need to be careful how the term "sex in private" gets defined. Too narrow a definition of privacy could leave us with little or no right to be visibly gay, meet each other in public places, or participate in sex outside of monogamous, closeted relationships.

The law is the context within which the issue of public sex is defined and debated. The Supreme Court has used the nebulous "right to privacy" to give people the right to use contraceptives, get abortions, read pornography, and talk on pay telephones without sharing their conversations with Uncle Sam. But our highest court has refused to use the right to privacy to strike down state sodomy laws that regulate private sexual behavior (although it will allow a lower court's liberal ruling to stand). This means that your right to read about oral or anal sex in your own bedroom is protected but not your right to actually do these things.

The Supreme Court's passivity leaves sexual minorities vulnerable to state and local sex codes, where the bulk of control over sex in America rests. Clark Norton, author of "Sex in America: An Outlaw's Guide," describes this situation with accuracy and anger.

In state after state across the country, a variety of archaic sex laws ranging from the repressive to the absurd remain in force...Many sex laws are blatantly discriminatory against various minorities—gays, young people, the handicapped—but they are often so vague and generalized that they could apply to virtually anyone. Most are only selectively enforced...And they vary so widely from state to state that a moment's innocent pleasure in one state could lead to life in prison in the state next door.[1]

Despite the fact that the vice squads and the courts limit or protect our privacy, some gay men and lesbians seem to feel that the men who engage in public sex are actually responsible for attacks on the civil liberties of homosexuals. Tearoom cruisers are frequently described as enemies of the gay movement, and public sex is portrayed as a major obstacle to winning some modicum of protection for gay people.

This position is aptly summarized in an enraged commentary by Eric Jay which appeared in the *Washington Blade* shortly after the Hinson scandal broke on Capitol Hill. According to Jay, public sex is responsible for "the tension between us and our Gay sisters." He denies that public sex has any validity because "we are not living any longer in the 1950s" when police raids on gay bars and the impossibility of coming out made "furtive encounters in public places" excusable. He chastises gay activists who protest police harassment of men in cruising areas and "bemoan the plight of Gays who get brutalized by redneck thugs" for "squandering their limited resources on those who refuse to accept responsibility for themselves and whose behavior threatens to deflect public attention from the basic...goals and principles of the Gay human rights movement."

Instead, Jay claims, "Campaigns should be conducted within the gay community both to warn against and to condemn behavior that, in short, is indefensible." Such campaigns would apparently include seeking "cooperation with the police in confronting issues of vital importance to the Gay community rather than mindlessly decrying 'police brutality.' " Jay believes that "the overwhelming majority of Gay people do indeed reflect the general moral code of our society"; besides, he says, we all "know the location of a Gay bath house." He asks "our responsible spokespersons" to "totally disavow the practice of public sex by Gay men and definitely disassociate the Gay rights movement from such behavior."[2]

I believe that this very common position is based on false stereotypes

I. SEXUAL OUTLAWS V. THE SEX POLICE

about the nature of public sex; misinformation about how this offense is handled by police and the courts; embarrassment about our own sexuality; premature optimism about our safety from police harassment in bars, bathhouses, and our own homes; and a short-sighted view of gay liberation's potential to alter the place of sex in our society.

We don't need to rely on speculation to discover what our lives would be like if private gay sex between consenting adults were legalized. England passed legislation to this effect in 1967 at the recommendation of the Wolfenden Committee. British gay historian Jeffrey Weeks explains why this recommendation was made:

> The paradox at the heart of the Wolfenden Committee's work...can be partly grasped if we see its roots in [a] search for a more effective regulation of sexual deviance...The problem the Committee was established to consider was not how to liberalize the law...but whether the law was the most effective means of control...What they proposed therefore was a partial retreat of the law from the regulation of individual behavior...so male homosexuality in private should be decriminalized...But the logic of the distinction between private and public behavior was that the legal penalties for *public* displays of sexuality could be strengthened at the same time as private behavior was decriminalized...The key point is that privatization did not necessarily involve a diminution of control.[3]

In fact, this so-called law reform actually made it easier for the state to penalize male homosexuality. (Lesbian sex has never been illegal in England.) According to Weeks:

> The Sexual Offenses Act of 1967 decriminalized male homosexual activities in private for adults over the age of 21. But its restrictions were harsh from the start...It tightened up the law with regard to offenses with "minors" and to male importuning. And it absurdly restricted the meaning of "private": for the sake of the Act, "public" was defined as meaning not only a public lavatory but anywhere where a third person was likely to be present...And in the next few years [after decriminalization] *the number of prosecutions actually increased.* [Emphasis added].[4]

We have yet another good example of what happens when the state decriminalizes private sex between consenting adults. Canada's sex laws closely resemble England's, and Toronto's gay community can give bitter testimony to the great freedom they enjoy under this "liberal" law.

Toronto police have relentlessly raided bathhouses, which are not considered to be private places because people theoretically can witness each other having sex in them. The presence of a third party makes sex an indecent rather than a protected, private act. The police have even charged gay men with operating "bawdy houses" in their own homes because they had advertised for sex partners, thus forfeiting (in the eyes of the police) their right to privacy.

This is an important lesson. Just when we think we are gaining more freedom from government interference in our private lives, we have to be careful that a change in the law is not used as an excuse to set up an elaborate bureaucracy to enforce more stringently defined standards for acceptable sexual behavior. We have to be careful not to create another group of stigmatized people and make them vulnerable to punishment. We have to make sure we are getting more than we are giving up.

Gay men and lesbians have not learned so much from the history of sex law as they should. Most people who condemn public sex do not seem to know that the legal difference between public and private sex is not a simple matter of choosing either the bushes or your bedroom. There are many zones in between—a motel room, a bathhouse, a bar, an adult bookstore, a car, a public toilet, a dark and deserted alley—that are contested territory where police battle with perverts for control.

The problem is that the state always wishes the zone of privacy to be as narrow as possible. Eric Jay assumes that if we relegated all casual sex to the gay bathhouse, the police would leave us alone. That simply isn't true. American sex laws resemble British law in that a bawdy house, disorderly house, or other legal euphemism for a brothel, is not just a place where sex is exchanged for money. Most state and local laws define such establishments as places where "lewd," "indecent," or "unnatural" acts take place.

Many cops don't like bathhouses any more than they like tearooms. The mayor and the liberal police chief of Minneapolis got into hot water when they called a halt to raids on gay bathhouses late in 1981. One Minneapolis vice squad officer told the press:

> We have a chief [of police] who thinks homosexuals should be kept in the bathhouses so they don't spread it around. When they get out of those bathhouses they are hardcore. They do leather in there. Then they show up in the bathrooms at places like Powers and Penney's. The sick part is that they are involving young kids.[5]

This is a revealing glimpse into what the police think of your right to privacy in a bathhouse (as well as a novel theory of the development of sexual preference). This attitude has sparked a bitter war between vice police and any publicly identifiable place where homosexuals gather. From reading local gay papers, it seems to me that nearly every town large enough to have an adult bookstore is currently experiencing a wave of police surveillance and public pressure to drive the queers, pornographers, and prostitutes out of town.

In San Jose, California, at least 300 men were arrested in a crackdown on adult bookstores that began in September, 1981. Most of those arrested pleaded guilty and received fifteen-day jail sentences and $300 to $500 fines. Other, smaller crackdowns on adult bookstores occurred in Silver Spring, Maryland; San Diego, California; Raleigh, North Carolina; Portland, Oregon; Harrisburg, Pennsylvania; and Houston, Texas (where about 140 men were arrested).

The usual scenario in adult bookstore arrests is a proposition by an undercover vice officer to leave the bookstore and have sex in a private location elsewhere. In Minneapolis police made about 102 arrests in February, 1981, at the Locker Room. No commercial sex was taking place. Nevertheless the Locker Room was charged with being "a disorderly house." This is the most notable of a series of raids on baths and bookstores in Minneapolis. Defense attorney Jeff Anderson said flatly, "The issue in the trial was not whether there were sexual acts. They [the defendants] admitted there were. The issue was whether the Locker Room was a public or private place." On May 30, 1981, at the Capital Club in Albany, New York, twenty men were cited for soliciting deviate sexual intercourse and public lewdness—despite the fact that cops had to climb over partitions of private cubicles to arrest people. The police claimed they raided the club because sex was spilling out of the bathhouse and into nearby streets, a parking lot, and a park. However, no arrests were made in any of these more public locations.

Hot Delivery in Denver, Colorado, has repeatedly been harassed for "operating without a license." The owners have been unable to determine what kind of license is required to operate a bathhouse. This is such a "public" place that a vice cop had to join the club to get in and conduct an investigation. The Finlandia Health Spa in Milwaukee, Wisconsin, got busted on October 2, 1981, and seven men were charged with sexual perversion, fourth degree sexual assault, or indecent touching. Club Tampa, a member of the Club Baths chain, was raided on May 12, and sixty-nine customers were cited. Three employees were charged with running a house of ill repute. And—shades of Toronto—the police report focused on the orgy room. Since the raid, the group sex room has been closed. Many more raids have taken place than I have room to describe.

Most gay men and many lesbians would probably agree that bars and bathhouses must be defended during campaigns against public sex. Some people can even stretch that to include adult bookstores. But what about clear-cut cases where the sex is, in fact, public? Is tearoom cruising defensible?

Laud Humphreys's *Tearoom Trade: Impersonal Sex in Public Places* is required reading for anybody who wants to know the answer to that question. Humphreys beautifully documents the sociology of looking for sex in so-called public places, and he demonstrates again and again that public sex is not a free-for-all. It doesn't take place any time, anywhere, where anyone can see it. Like any other sexual minority, tearoom cruisers comprise a subculture with its own mores and codes of behavior. There is almost always some kind of physical barrier—some bushes, a bathroom door, or a car—between the participants in public sex and the outside world. This barrier screens out the uninitiated. If more than two people are present, one of them usually acts as a lookout. Thus, this behavior is more properly called "quasi-public sex."

People sitting behind the closed door of a bathroom or of a movie booth in an adult bookstore can reasonably assume they have privacy. You could make the same assumption if you were sitting in your car in a deserted location late at night. All of these are favored locations for so-called public sex. If people are going to see what is going on in these places, they must intrude. They must actively look for things that will offend them, either by penetrating physical barriers, by setting up covert surveillance, or by posing as potential participants.

At one time, the California courts recognized this problem and put some limits on entrapment arrests for public sex. In *Pryor v. Municipal Court*, Division Two of the Second Appellate District of the State Court of Appeals ruled that the state's lewd conduct law (647a) applied only if a sex act took place when other people were present who might be offended or if an individual explicitly stated she or he wanted to perform sex in a place where other people were present. These limits dramatically reduced arrests for solicitation and indecent acts in tearooms. However, the ruling was later contradicted by the same court. On April 14, 1981, in *People v. McConville*, the judges ruled that 647a applies "where it is likely that members of the public may enter a restroom even though the only witness in the restroom at the time of the conduct acts as if he is not offended." Arrests for public sex seem to be increasing since this ruling. In January, 1981, about seventy-six men were arrested for "soliciting lewd conduct" in San Francisco alone. The average number of such arrests per month had reportedly been sixteen.

The technology of electronic snooping has become so sophisticated that intimate information can be gathered anywhere, including your bedroom. So the question really isn't, "Can people see sexual activity going on?" The question is, "Who has a right to intrude and take a look?"

The police assume that they do. They have several favorite techniques for invading arenas where quasi-public sexual encounters take place. One technique is to alter or disrupt the physical space so as to make protective, camouflaging behavior difficult or impossible. They cut down underbrush or trees that provide a screen, or they put up bright lights. In Indianapolis the vice squad and the local chapter of the Moral Majority got an ordinance passed that required adult bookstores to cut the doors on their movie booths in half. In Los Angeles the bookstores must remove the doors entirely. This has been done deliberately to transform private places into public ones. Police officers set up hidden cameras, climb on the roofs of public toilets and peek through skylights, or secrete themselves in broom closets. Cops pretend they are available for sex, then arrest the luckless and gullible. Dignified, isn't it? And to think that many vice cops are volunteers...

Despite the lengths that police must go to entrap men engaged in "public" sex, they justify these raids and crackdowns by claiming that families, children, and uninterested heterosexual men are stumbling into group gropes or being harassed by gangs of hostile faggots.

Humphreys's study and my own conversations with tearoom cruisers indicate that it is highly improbable that a family would encounter public sex at, say, a highway rest stop unless they chose to picnic in a urinal. Sex probably is not happening all over the rest stop, park, or beach. It's happening behind the bathroom door. The people behind that door usually keep out a sharp eye for intruders; I can't imagine anything more likely to cause everyone to abdicate the throne than a nuclear family plus hamper, thermos, folding lawn chairs, Polaroid camera, and large, nosy dog.

Vice cops' claims that innocent straight men are getting hustled by aggressive queers just don't ring true. San Francisco attorney Matt Coles says, "In four years of practicing law, I've *never* seen a [public sex] case based on the complaint of a citizen (not a cop) who got propositioned when he didn't want to be."[6]

I'm sure that from time to time heterosexual males receive unwanted sexual attention from other men in public places. Who cares? The priorities in this situation should be spelled out: Society will not tolerate the possibility that a straight man might be propositioned if he walks past a group of gay men on his way to use a public john. Yet society will tolerate the possibility that a gay man could be beaten or murdered if he walks past a group of heterosexuals. And no vice squad has ever embarked on a massive campaign to prevent groups of straight men from harassing women and denying us our right to use many public facilities, like public transit late at night and even—oh, horrors—johns in parks. Furthermore, verbal propositions can serve as protective barriers, preventing the truly uninterested from seeing or doing things they don't wish to. The spectacle of some frightened straight boy trying to keep his knees together doesn't fill me with pity. Maybe it will teach him to think twice before he grabs my tits or calls me a dyke.

The threat that children might see men having sex with each other is far and away the most popular excuse for surveillance and arrests. I have yet to see a documented instance of such an incident. However, I am sure that it's happened occasionally—probably by accident. And it's possible that a child or a teenager who saw such an act could be frightened, disgusted, or upset. However, that's not because sex is inherently toxic or traumatic to children. It's because young people are denied information about sexuality and are kept especially ignorant on the subject of gay and lesbian sex. Children aren't damaged for life by seeing naked bodies or by touching. They are damaged by the adults who scare the daylights out of them if they are caught masturbating, who react with hostility or embarrassment to questions about sex, and who withhold information about birth control, abortion, and venereal disease.

Kids who hang around cruising areas are either deliberately spying (remember hiding out by Lover's Lane and shining flashlights into the parked cars?), waiting to bash faggots, or they are gay boys who have discovered this chancy way to meet gay men. Young faggots do need a more supportive, broader-based milieu in which to explore their sexuality, but closing down this fragile form of male-to-male contact won't help them.

Police capitalize on negative attitudes in the gay community toward public sex. When raiding toilets, adult bookstores, bathhouses, or backroom bars, they usually deny that they are conducting antigay crackdowns. Instead they claim that they are responding (perhaps reluctantly) to public pressure. However, they usually decline to specify which individuals or groups brought that pressure to bear (unless the complainants are gay). The hypocrisy of the police is astonishing. They are capable of conducting full-scale street sweeps in gay neighborhoods (in New Orleans, Houston, San Francisco, and other cities within the last year) and denying that they are conducting antigay campaigns, even as the paddy wagons roll in, filled with hundreds of queens and dykes.

The police even claim that they conduct these anti-vice campaigns on our behalf, for our own good. Here's Los Angeles police chief Daryl Gates, responding to questions about police/gay relations posed by the Gay and Lesbian Community Services Center:

> Our efforts aimed at controlling street hustling and other public homosexual conduct serve, at least indirectly, to reduce the victimization rate of gays who are too often victims of robbery, violent assaults and even murder because of their street activity.[7]

I wonder if Gates would also curtail women who work late at night, go out alone, and wear flashy clothing, so as to "indirectly" reduce rape statistics. Why can't the police use the laws against assault, robbery, and murder to prosecute the criminals who commit these violent acts? Gates is essentially saying that the very nature of the sexual activity of prostitutes and tearoom cruisers attracts violence and therefore absolves the police of any responsibility for their protection. His statement also implies that police care more about getting prostitutes and gays off the street than they do about putting away muggers, rapists, and murderers.

This is a lousy way to deal with antigay violence. Can you imagine the police making as many arrests for queerbashing as they do for solicitation? Wouldn't *that* make you feel safer?

Even if you believe that public sex is politically or morally objectionable, do you think that the police should be in charge of regulating it? Is it worth the expense or the time? And do you think the penalties—a fine, time in jail, registration as a sex offender—are just or equitable? Do you like the idea of the police being allowed to gather that much information about known or suspected homosexuals? During a crackdown, police copy down the license numbers of cars parked outside popular tearooms, gay bars, and baths. They stop "suspicious" people walking around in these areas and demand identification. What do you think they do with that information? Put it under their pillows to help them sleep better at night? Police departments in New York, Chicago, Los Angeles, and the state of Michigan have been ordered by the courts to stop spying and keeping files on communists, homosexuals, and other people considered to be potentially dangerous to society. But in California, as in five other states, it is legal to require convicted sex offenders to register with police. According to E. H. Duncan Donovan, vice president of the American Civil Liberties Union of Southern California, "The bulk of registrations are for...sexual activity, or solicitation of sexual activity, in more-or-less public places."[8] So the cops don't have to be covert about it; they just feed you to the computer.

This logic may not make a dent in the prejudice many gay people harbor against devotees of public sex. I'm still not sure I understand the rage I've heard many gay men express about ostensibly heterosexual, married, respectable men who carry on in public johns. Some of this anger seems to stem from the belief that these men get the rewards of gay sex without the penalties of coming out and accepting a full-time, stigmatized gay identity.

Before "being gay" became a political identity as much as a sexual one, anyone arrested in a tearoom was considered just as queer as a drag queen or a hustler. Oddly enough, it is the burgeoning gay movement with its demand for confrontation and the concomitant demand that everybody choose a side which has left these men without a gay *or* a straight identity, vulnerable to the contempt of both cops and activists.

The gay community has less and less tolerance for folks whose sexuality cannot be clearly defined as heterosexual or homosexual or who have eroticized something other than gender. Some tearoom cruisers identify primarily as fathers and husbands and don't place much significance on their sexual proclivities. It's possible that many gay men would make similar choices if society permitted it. Some men prefer oral sex, and given the reluctance of many straight women to perform this act they resort to male partners in tearooms. Or they may enjoy quick encounters with multiple partners and use the tearooms because this sexual pattern is not readily available to heterosexuals. Some of them may be tentatively and awkwardly forming gay identities, preparing themselves to come out. Whatever pleasure these "heterosexual" men receive from quickie, casual public sex, it's no compensation for the double lives they lead or the devastating consequences of being discovered.

And not everybody who cruises public johns is a closet case. It still isn't so easy for gay people to meet each other as it is for their heterosexual counterparts. Gay men who live in small towns may not be able to get to gay bars or bathhouses often enough to satisfy their desires for companionship and sex. Some men couldn't get into a bathhouse even if they lived next door. The baths are notorious for discrimination based on age, weight, race, and other aspects of personal appearance. Besides, nobody charges admission to a tearoom. It's free. Tearooms offer a different type of sex and a different range of men. One guy told me, "You go to the baths to have sex with gays. You go to the tearooms to have sex with men. You know what I've learned in toilets? I've learned that there's no such thing as a heterosexual. They can all be had."

This is a devastating piece of information that cops have taken charge of suppressing. The prevalence of public sex makes it very, very clear that gay sex is attractive to many men, that heterosexuality is neither monolithic nor inevitable, and that no amount of repression or abuse will prevent people from seeking pleasure.

Why is sex supposed to be invisible? Other pleasurable acts or acts of communication are routinely performed in public—eating, drinking, talking, watching movies, writing letters, studying or teaching, telling jokes and laughing, appreciating fine art. Is sex so deadly, hateful, and horrific that we can't permit it to be seen? Are naked bodies so ugly or so shameful that we can't survive the sight of bare tushes or genitals without withering away?

My own experiences with public sex have been instructive and liberating. I've been going to sex parties for five or six years now, and I've seen the complete range of naked male and female bodies. I no longer find nudity frightening or repulsive (nor has my erotic response to partially clothed or unclothed people disappeared). Instead I have become much more accepting of my own unadorned, vulnerable, imperfect flesh. I no longer postpone pleasure until the day when I will be thinner, more muscular, and physically perfect, nor do I torment my partners with this silly snobbery.

Seeing other people having sex is reassuring and enlightening. It calmed the panic I've been carrying around ever since I first heard my parents fucking and thought they must be murdering each other. I like the way other people look when they're getting turned on or coming. That means I must look good, too. That means it's okay for me to relax and let myself enjoy my body. Watching gay men, heterosexual couples, lesbians, and clusters of people of various genders getting off together has taught me more about sexual technique than any sex manual. It's a direct and easy way to learn about sexuality, and I wish it were more accessible, especially to women.

Personally, I wish all the cops hiding in bushes and sneaking around public restrooms would get out there and prevent more serious crimes like littering and dogs' pooping on sidewalks. If they have to spend so much time in the johns, I wish they would go into the ladies' room and make sure there's plenty of toilet paper and paper towels. They could also repair the water fountains and the Tampax machines. These public-toilet problems are the ones I'd like my tax dollars to solve. Public sex is not.

Notes

1. Norton, Clark. "Sex in America: An Outlaw's Guide." *Inquiry*, October 5, 1981, 2.

2. Jay, Eric. "Public Sex and Community Standards: The Real Issue in the Hinson Affair." *Washington Blade*, February 20, 1981, A19.

3. Weeks, Jeffrey. *Sex, Politics and Society: The Regulation of Sexuality Since 1800.* London and New York: Longman Group Ltd., 1981, 242-244.

4. Weeks, Jeffrey. *Coming Out: Homosexual Politics in Britain, from the Nineteenth Century to the Present.* London, Melbourne and New York: Quartet Books, 1977, 177.

5. "Policy on Gays has Fraser, Police Battling on Beaches." Minneapolis *Star*, October 14, 1981.

6. Coles, Matt. "Pryor Restraint: What Every Gay Man Should Know About Public Sex." *The Sentinel*, April 1, 1981, 5.

7. "Reassurances but no Promises from LA Police Chief Gates." *The Advocate*, Issue 318, 10 and 12.

8. "Scarlet Letter Still Brands 'Sex Offenders.' " *Los Angeles Times*, March 11, 1982, 6.

Victims Without a Voice

1985

When AIDS first appeared, it was perhaps a toss-up to determine which of the top three risk groups was in least favor with the mainstream American public: gay men, IV drug users, or Haitian immigrants...gay men and—to a lesser degree—Haitian-Americans quickly mobilized their constituencies to direct medical and media attention to their plights. Hemophiliacs...soon followed suit. Left behind were the IV drug abusers, a group without any organized advocacy in this country. And yet this group may be most at risk for AIDS.

—Michael Helquist, *"The Neglected Risk Group,"* Coming Up!

Sex and Drugs and...AIDS?!? In New York City, Acquired Immune Deficiency Syndrome (AIDS) is now the number-one killer of men between the ages of thirty and thirty-nine and the number-two killer of women aged thirty to thirty-four. If present trends hold, warned Alan Kristal, director of the city's Office of Epidemiologic Surveillance and Statistics, "By 1986, AIDS will be the leading cause of death of males between 15 and 64."[1]

This wasting disease, in which the body's natural defenses against infection gradually cease to function, is a sad, painful, frightening way to die. According to the San Francisco AIDS Foundation, well over half of the people diagnosed as having AIDS prior to a year ago are now dead. We still do not have a complete picture of the etiology or epidemiology of this disease. Researchers are assuming that a virus called HTLV-III or LAV is responsible, but they do not know if other factors (such as infection with cytomegalo-virus, intestinal parasites, repeated bouts of syphilis or gonorrhea, malnutrition, or genetic predisposition) have to be present before exposure to HTLV-III results in AIDS.

Since it appeared, AIDS has been stereotyped as "the gay plague." It first hit print in 1980 as "gay pneumonia" when there was an outbreak of a rare lung infection, pneumocystis carinii (PCP), among homosexual men. A similar outbreak of PCP among New York City junkies in December of 1981 was ignored by the mass media.[2] This is indicative of the way in which intravenous drug users' risk has been ignored or misrepresented in general by the establishment. When it appeared that PCP was only one of many "opportunistic infections" taking advantage of an underlying problem—a failing immune system—the media coined a new term: "GRID" (Gay-Related Immune Deficiency). Although AIDS is a more neutral (and accurate) term, most heterosexuals assume that they are at little or no risk of contracting AIDS. In a Gallup poll recently conducted for Newsweek, 759 people were asked, "How worried are you that you or someone you know will get AIDS?" Only 14 percent were "very worried," 27 percent "a little worried," and 31 percent "not at all worried."[3]

The media are not wholly to blame. The Centers for Disease Control (CDC), the only source of national statistics about AIDS, has much to answer for about how AIDS is (mis)perceived. The CDC issues weekly reports on how many cases have been diagnosed in the U.S., broken down by "patient characteristics." The proportions of these groups in relation to one another have been relatively stable for some time. Gay/bisexual males always head the list, supposedly representing about 73 percent of the total cases, followed by IV drug users (17 percent), hemophiliacs (1 percent), people who contracted the virus through heterosexual contact (1 percent), transfusion recipients (2 percent), and none of the above/other (7 percent).[4] But these groups are "hierarchically ranked"—that is, a gay/bisexual male who is also an IV drug user will be listed only in the first category because it is "most prevalent." Thus the figures the CDC gives for AIDS cases among IV drug users are inaccurate; if gay and bisexual men who used drugs intravenously are included, about 36 percent of the people with AIDS in the U.S. have histories of shooting up.[5]

The New York City Department of Health's reports are more detailed than the CDC's. Their May 29, 1985, AIDS Surveillance Update tables are broken down by sex, sexual orientation, and history of IV drug use, as well as other risk factors. Using this method of calculation, 2,054 (56 percent) of all of New York City's AIDS cases were homosexual/bisexual males with no history of IV drug use. Intravenous drug use is a risk factor in 1,239 (33 percent) of the city's AIDS cases. For pediatric cases, 72 percent had at least one parent who was an IV drug user.

According to the San Francisco Department of Public Health, as of May 30, 1985, 22 percent of women with AIDS in that city reported IV drug use. Among men with AIDS, IV drug use was reported by 13 percent of gay men, 26 percent of bisexual men, and 46 percent of heterosexuals.

As you can see, IV drug use is a much more important risk factor than the tables routinely supplied by the CDC would lead you to believe. There is no excuse for distorting AIDS statistics this way. The CDC has the information but chooses not to report it. Its "hierarchy of risk" is based on antisex ideology, not medical fact. AIDS can be transmitted by both sexual contact and contaminated blood or needles. But we do not know which behavior—sex that involves the exchange of body fluids, or sharing needles—carries the highest risk of contracting AIDS.

When I asked Barbara Faltz of the AIDS Substance Abuse Program in San Francisco what needs to be done to warn IV drug users about the risk of AIDS, she said, "We need a mass-media campaign similar to large-scale education about 'safe sex' that's been done in the gay male community." However, safe sex education materials have run into censorship, and materials about shooting up and AIDS are having similar problems.

In Ottawa a staff member of the AIDS Committee of Toronto told me that his organization got flak for running an ad that shows a muscular man, his arm tied off and needle poised, with the text: "NEEDLES: It doesn't matter if you shoot into a vein or just under the skin. *Never* share needles. If you do you could get AIDS." The Committee was told by the Advertising Standards Commission that it does, too, matter if you shoot up, and to stop advocating IV drug use or else. "How can you educate people about not sharing needles without talking explicitly about shooting up?" he asked me. The organization has no plans to run the ad again.

Los Angeles County and the federal government financed printing of a pamphlet on AIDS and needle use, only to have three county supervisors call for an investigation on the grounds that the pamphlet "gives advice on how to safely inject drugs." Distribution of the pamphlet has been halted.

In a climate like this, it's an uphill battle to get the powers that be to spend public funds on educating people about how to have sex or use drugs without giving themselves and their partners a fatal disease. In the Reagan era, the official attitude seems to be that sex outside monogamous marriage is perverse, and shooting up is self-destructive, and who cares if queers and junkies die? If they want to stay alive, they're going to have to take care of themselves.

The San Francisco AIDS Foundation (SFAF) was one of the first groups to realize the existence of this attitude and produce educational material about IV drug use and AIDS, with the assistance of the Haight Ashbury Free Medical Clinic. This is surprising considering that San Francisco has one of the lowest rates of AIDS cases attributed to IV drug use. According to Holly Smith, SFAF's public information officer, about 12.4 percent of the gay male cases in her city have a history of IV drug use, but only 0.7 percent are attributable to IV drug use alone. The foundation's pamphlet, "Shooting Up and Your Health," is in English and Spanish and is also distributed in New York by the Gay Men's Health Crisis (GMHC). The foundation and the clinic have also done radio public service announcements and posters about AIDS for methadone clinics.

Federico Gonzalez, GMHC's director of education, told me that he estimates 30 percent of his organization's direct clinical services (including counseling, legal assistance, financial aid, and referrals to medical help) go to IV drug users, and 50 percent of educational efforts are directed to this group. Gonzalez said, "There is a problem with AIDS being stereotyped as a gay disease. Some clients find it difficult to call us for direct services. One of the things we stress in education is that the germ does not discriminate." GMHC's only funding is from private sources and, recently, the New York State AIDS Institute. The group has yet to receive the funds from a promised New York City Department of Health grant. Thus far GMHC has reached only the staff and clients of methadone programs and needs to extend its services to folks who are not in treatment, especially the patrons of shooting galleries who rent works.

Gonzalez faulted the SFAF pamphlet for not "emphasizing that AIDS can be transmitted when needles are used in piercing, tattooing, or by weight lifters or body builders who inject steroids." Gonzalez believes it would greatly reduce the spread of AIDS if people could buy sterile works at pharmacies, and he warned that some prepackaged needles sold by street dealers are not, in fact, sterile. When asked if legalizing paraphernalia would not be viewed as advocating drug addiction, Gonzalez's sensible answer was, "Brochures that use scare tactics to get people to stop using drugs won't work any more than brochures that try to get people to stop having sex. We must concentrate on educating people not to share needles. The decision to stop using drugs is a totally separate issue. When I do speaking about AIDS, users don't start listening to me until I tell them I am not there to make any judgments about drugs."

He also mentioned the false stereotype that "junkies are not healthy and don't care, but the fact is they can change their behavior," a stereotype refuted by a recent study which found that increasing numbers of users were buying needles from street vendors who claimed to have sterile wares. Dr. Don C. DesJarlais of the New York State Division of Substance Abuse reported that a field study conducted by former addicts found that eighteen of twenty-two vendors reported an increase in sales of needles from a year ago, and four of the eighteen believed AIDS was the reason.[6]

I. SEXUAL OUTLAWS V. THE SEX POLICE

On the other hand, Faltz told me that she feels very strongly that legalizing paraphernalia would only give users the message that shooting up is okay, and that people will continue to share any needles they have. She says educational efforts which emphasize that "AIDS hurts" are more important. "IV drug users are not afraid of death, but they don't like pain. The fact that AIDS is a slow, debilitating disease scares them."

John Newmeyer of the Haight Ashbury Free Medical Clinic could help resolve this controversy. Newmeyer (the author of "Shooting Up and Your Health") is the chief epidemiologist of a federally funded research and information project on AIDS and IV drug use. He told me data might be available soon on just how amenable addicts are to education about cleaning their works and not sharing them. Newmeyer's research involves evaluating the sex histories and immune status of four hundred IV drug users currently in treatment as well as an ethnographic survey of IV drug users "on the street"—their attitudes and beliefs about AIDS, sharing needles, and how to implement risk-reduction education.

AID Atlanta has gotten a $12,513 grant from the U.S. Conference of Mayors. Some of that money will be spent to develop education for IV drug users. Paul Plate, acting director, told me that he met in early August with representatives of the state Department of Alcohol and Drug Abuse to plan a survey of what needs to be done in Georgia. AID Atlanta has also produced a brochure that soon will be ready for distribution.

A $20,000 U.S. Conference of Mayors grant went to the New Jersey Personal Liberty Fund, to focus educational efforts on the northeastern metropolitan area of New Jersey. I spoke with Robert Goodman, one of the part-time health educators hired by this grant, who told me that he will work with drug rehabilitation, minority community groups, and health care providers to reach black and Third World gays who are IV drug users. According to Goodman, 8 to 9 percent of New Jersey AIDS cases are gay men who are IV drug users. A study recently conducted by the San Francisco AIDS Foundation indicates that this group is especially important to reach. Eighty percent of the five hundred gay or bisexual men surveyed indicated they had adopted risk-reduction sexual activities. However, the 3 percent of men in the study who admitted to IV drug use accounted for 38 percent of all high-risk sexual behavior.[7]

Since New Jersey has the heaviest caseload of AIDS cases attributed to IV drug use, I spoke with Patricia Nisler, principal training technician, Communicable Disease Operations Program, New Jersey State Department of Health, to find out what her agency is doing about this health crisis. The department's pamphlet has a hierarchy of warnings about IV drug use. "We tell people that even occasional shooting of speed, cocaine, and heroin is risky. The best way to reduce your risk is to stop shooting drugs. If you continue to use IV drugs, try to reduce your use to reduce your risk of AIDS, hepatitis, and other infections. And *never share your works.* If you have to share, clean your set by soaking it for a half hour in a mix of one part bleach to ten parts water. But rinse your set in water before use—don't inject bleach!"

She reported a minor triumph in overcoming the stigma surrounding IV drug users. The first printing of twenty-five thousand brochures was produced without the state health department logo, because it was "too controversial, and could possibly be interpreted as advocating IV drug use. But now they don't care, it's gotten to be too big a problem. So our next printing will include the logo. I hope when people know where this information is coming from they'll take it more seriously."

Nisler's agency does an outreach program to seven methadone clinics, thanks to a CDC cooperative education grant. Eight former addicts have been hired to go to housing projects or wherever users hang out, to distribute a general brochure about AIDS and a sheet of suggestions for cutting down risk, and to talk about the information. One worker in Newark got questioned by police who saw him lecturing a group of addicts, and when he explained what he was doing, the officers asked for their own copies of the brochures. Nisler was very enthusiastic about the success of this program. "It doesn't cost that much to do," she said. "Most of these people were earning minimum wage. They get involved in the work, they are good at it and glad to do it. We hope our program will be imitated elsewhere."

The facts about AIDS and IV drug use are especially crucial for women. According to a CDC Surveillance Report dated June 3, 1985, 374 (50.7 percent) of women with AIDS in the U.S. were IV drug users. The next most common route of transmission is heterosexual contact (88 cases, 11.9 percent of the total). Yet a March, 1985, survey of students at San Francisco State University found that 47 of 100 women did not know they could contract AIDS. A total of 64 percent did not know any risk reduction measures.[8] A very large group of women with AIDS—167, 22.65 percent—have no apparent risk factor, and the route of transmission in these cases remains unknown. (For men, "unknown" cases of AIDS make up only 5.6 percent of the total.) One health worker wrote dryly, "There may be a sophistication in surveillance with male cases, which came about as the numbers grew, that has not fully developed in the surveillance of female cases."[9]

Even if there were lots of encouragement from the state to do AIDS education for women who inject IV drugs or have sex with large numbers of men, it would be a difficult task. As Associate Director for Clinical Medicine Division of Clinical Research at the National Institute of Drug Abuse (NIDA), Harold M. Ginzburg points out that IV drug users "prefer to remain anonymous" and "are generally identified in one of two circumstances: as they seek treatment or when they are arrested. Thus, the drug abuse treatment community and the criminal justice system have traditionally been the primary sources of information on persons with serious drug abuse problems." Many people who do drugs intravenously are not heavy, regular users or never wind up in drug treatment programs or jail for other reasons, making these traditional sources of health care and education inadequate.[10]

They are even more inadequate for women. There are few residential drug-rehabilitation programs for women. I was able to locate only one instance of AIDS education provided to women through the criminal justice system. "Presentations to women at risk through IV drug use and/or multiple sexual contacts were prepared in cooperation with the San Francisco Pre-trial Diversion Program and a San Francisco Jail Medical Service social worker. The first workshop, held in May 1985 at the County Jail, utilized a slide presentation, brochures, Hotline flyers, and a question-and-answer format for an audience of 20 female inmates."[11]

None of the organizations I contacted has produced any literature specifically for prostitutes. The closest thing is a flyer entitled "Women and AIDS," produced by the San Francisco Aids Foundation. At Gay Men's Health Crisis, Gonzalez recalled one instance in which a general information brochure on AIDS was distributed in Times Square. That's it.

Because of our society's punitive attitude toward pleasure, both prostitutes and IV drug users are members of the outlaw classes and, as such, get poor health care. But what about the people unfortunate enough to have been put away for their "crimes"? Dr. Armond Start, medical director for the Texas Department of Correction, said prison is "the worst place in the world" for AIDS patients. "People don't care about the health of these rejected people, and trying to get additional money out of legislatures to properly treat inmates with AIDS is going to be tough sledding."[12]

According to *The New York Times*, "The Federal Centers for Disease Control took note of the explosive potential of AIDS in a prison setting two years ago, but it has not established any Federal program to combat that risk." A telephone canvas of prison medical directors in ten states revealed that "intravenous drug users represent a majority of prisoners who have AIDS."[13]

I spoke with Annette Johnson from the New York State AIDS Institute to find out what is being done to educate inmates and prison workers about AIDS. She told me that they have held two-hour seminars (in conjunction with the Department of Correctional Services) to tell staff members what the symptoms of AIDS are, how it is spread, how people with AIDS should be taken care of, and to answer any questions they have. A videotape has been prepared to supplement written materials. The Department of Correctional Services has prepared a brochure for staff. Similar seminars have been held for inmates in the state prison system and also on Rikers Island. The inmates do not see the videotape; they receive a brochure prepared by the New York State Health Department for the general public. This brochure states that homosexual males and people who share needles to inject drugs can get AIDS, but it contains no information about safe sex or how to clean works. I asked Johnson if inmates were told to use condoms, given condoms, or told not to share needles or given information about how to clean them. She said no.

Needles are, of course, contraband in prison and must be smuggled in. The small supply of needles makes it likely that they will be shared. However, prison administration policy is that inmates with AIDS contracted it prior to incarceration, and nobody in their facility is shooting up—much less having sex! This has seriously hampered preventive health education for inmates.

Gradually, local efforts to fight AIDS are gathering momentum. But what's being done on a national level? Ginzburg explained to me that "one of the problems is the size of the problem." AIDS among IV drug users has the potential to be even more explosive than among gay men. Given the reported rates of how many IV drug users test positive for exposure to HTLV-III, Ginzburg said, "Sharing needles just once a week is a significant risk factor. People who chip on weekends are at as much risk as daily users, especially in New York City, Newark, San Francisco, Los Angeles, Miami, and Washington, D.C."

The National Institute of Drug Abuse is currently developing a national strategy to reach IV users. Ginzburg feels more research is needed to understand the history of the disease among addicts, how to do intervention and education, and how the drugs themselves impact on the immune system. He believes that research has already demonstrated that heroin has immuno-suppressive properties, as do marijuana and inhalants (poppers) to some extent. But the effect of adulterants—what the drugs are cut with—and bacteria introduced when

90

chemicals are produced under nonpharmaceutical conditions is poorly understood. NIDA is also conducting a study on whether or not the decriminalization of drug paraphernalia makes a difference in sharing needles, by examining the using patterns in four states with no laws banning possession of syringes or needles. "Anecdotal data says when needles are freely available they are still shared," he said. However, he still hopes education can change behavior. "A drug user expects infections and abscesses from shooting up, but he does expect to live. AIDS changes that."

The federal government, "following intense pressure capped by the threat of a congressional subpoena," has moved to allot an additional $45.7 million for AIDS-related programs in 1985 and 1986. About one-third of the increase for 1986 is earmarked for education and risk-reduction efforts. Gary MacDonald, lobbyist and head of the AIDS Action Council, noted, "It's probably just enough to get a good beginning on a comprehensive, national public-education and risk-reduction campaign. It's roughly 10 times what's being spent this year on those activities." But funds for research (especially investigation of treatment) lag far behind the need.[14]

Some yo-yo propositions are coming down the pike from right-wing, born-again types who want to use AIDS to push their repressive agendas. Jerry Falwell, head of the Moral Majority, wants the U.S. Senate to pass legislation that would allow civil lawsuits against AIDS carriers, require mandatory testing of blood during all routine physical examinations, give state health departments the authority to quarantine people with AIDS, require mandatory prison sentences for people with AIDS who continue to have sex, and charge with involuntary manslaughter anyone who gives another person AIDS if that person dies from the disease.[15]

Don't laugh. At a May 20 meeting in Washington, D.C., Dr. James Mason, then director of the Centers for Disease Control, revealed that the Reagan administration was considering a quarantine of people with AIDS.[16] Forced hospitalization of people with AIDS is already allowed in Britain.[17] And public health officials in California, South Carolina, and other states have publicly admitted they have at least considered quarantine as a possible response.[18] In New Haven, Connecticut, a twenty-nine-year-old woman who was arrested for possession of drug paraphernalia and suspected of being a prostitute was also suspected of having AIDS. She left the hospital without permission and later turned herself in to the police. Her name was published in local papers, branding her as an AIDS victim even though no official diagnosis had been made.[19] She has since died of AIDS, and Connecticut has enacted a quarantine law specifically in response to this case.[20]

A wide-scale quarantine would raise troublesome civil-liberties issues, especially in the absence of a diagnostic test for AIDS. The blood tests now available can only determine if an individual has been exposed to HTLV-III and produced antibodies to the virus. The most commonly used test, ELISA, is preferred by blood banks who need to screen huge amounts of blood cheaply and quickly. However, ELISA has a very high rate of false positives. About 60 to 75 percent of all positive results are negative when the sample is retested using a more accurate method, the Western Blot assay. More accurate tests are in production in Britain and France. But even an accurate test result is difficult to interpret. Of course blood that contains antibodies to HTLV-III should not be used for transfusions. But no one knows if a positive test means you have AIDS, will eventually develop AIDS, can give AIDS to other people, or are immune to AIDS.[21]

Despite these puzzling problems, the CDC enthusiastically suggested a national registry of blood donors who tested positive on ELISA.[22] A howl of protest scotched this plan, but you should still beware of ELISA. If you are a member of a high-risk group, don't donate blood. If you want to be tested for HTLV-III antibody, call a local AIDS hotline and ask for the nearest "alternate test site," where you can be tested anonymously. Even having your private physician enter this information into your medical records could make you vulnerable to discrimination in employment, health insurance, and life insurance.

The Pentagon has persuaded civilian blood banks on military bases to turn positive ELISA results over to military doctors.[23] On August 30, 1985, the Defense Department announced that all prospective military recruits will be screened for HTLV-III antibody, and those who test positive will be rejected. A proposal to screen everybody currently in the service is being considered.[24] The Navy is already giving everyone diagnosed with AIDS a dishonorable discharge on the assumption that they could only have gotten the disease by violating the United Code of Military Justice.

Nobody wants to think about taking precautions against AIDS before hitting up. It's tempting to ignore the whole mess and wait for the miracle of modern science to come up with a vaccine. That's probably going to be a long wait. HTLV-III appears to mutate at an astonishing rate. Scientists at the National Cancer Institute examined samples of the virus obtained from eighteen different people. Each "isolated virus showed a different variation in its genetic structure...To develop a vaccine, researchers say they need to find a common protein region, preserved in all variations of the virus, that brings an immunologic response." The rueful conclusion was, "developing a preventive vaccine may prove very difficult, if it can be done at all."[25]

AIDS has made even skin-popping a potentially fatal hobby. And it has made it easier for the narcs to justify stepped-up enforcement of our antiquated and unjust drug laws. It will be surprising if new laws and other repressive measures are not imposed on us. But you don't have to get AIDS. You don't have to die. Why give the bastards in charge that satisfaction?

Notes

1. Weiss, Kenneth. "Scary AIDS Stats." *New York Daily News*, August 15, 1985, 3.

2. Helquist, Michael. "The Neglected Risk Group." *Coming Up!*, January 1985.

3. "Public Fears—And Sympathy." *Newsweek*, August 12, 1985, 23.

4. Beldekas, John, Ph.D. "Int'l Conference on AIDS Attended by 2,300 Scientists and Health Care Workers." *New York Native*, May 6-19, 1985, 10.

5. Lauritsen, John. "CDC's Tables Obscure AIDS/Drug Connection." *Coming Up!*, April 1985, 6-7.

6. Altman, Lawrence K. "Drug Abusers Try to Cut AIDS Risk." *The New York Times*, April 18, 1985.

7. Helquist, Michael. "S.F. Survey." *The Advocate*, September 3, 1984, 11.

8. Shaw, Nancy S., Ph.D., Women's Project Development Coordinator, San Francisco AIDS Foundation. "California Models for Women's AIDS Education and Services" fact sheet, 23.

9. *ibid.*, 5.

10. Ginzburg, Harold M. "Intravenous Drug Users and AIDS." *PharmChem Newsletter*, Vol. 13, No. 6, November-December 1984.

11. Shaw, "California Models for Women's AIDS Education and Services," 14.

12. Nordheimer, Jon. "AIDS Among Prisoners Poses National Problem." *The New York Times*, August 11, 1985, 22.

13. *ibid.*

14. Walter, Dave. "Administration—Under Pressure—Asks Additional $45 Million in AIDS Funds." *The Advocate*, September 3, 1985, 10-11.

15. Poggi, Stephanie. "Falwell Launches (Another) Anti-Gay Campaign." *Gay Community News*, July 27, 1985, 2.

16. Ortleb, Charles L. "Reagan Administration Considering AIDS Quarantine." *New York Native*, June 17-30, 1985, 11.

17. Stadler, Matthew. "British Issue New Rules Regarding AIDS Victims." *New York Native*, April 8, 1985, 8.

18. Jones, Brian. "Health Officials Discuss AIDS Patient Quarantine." *New York Native*, June 3-16, 1985, 14. Also, *The Advocate*, June 11, 1985, 25.

19. Guilfoy, Christine. "Media Indicts Woman Rumored to Have AIDS." *Gay Community News*, March 24, 1984, 7.

20. Guilfoy, Christine. "Boston AIDS Conference Discusses Quarantine Issue." *Gay Community News*, May 4, 1985, 1.

21. Fettner, Ann Giudici. "CDC Optimistic About Blood Screening." *New York Native*, August 12-25, 1985, 9.

22. D'Eramo, James Ph.D. "CDC Proposes Nat'l Blood Donor List." *New York Native*, August 27-September 9, 1984, 9.

23. Fettner, Ann G. "Blood Banks vs. the Pentagon." *New York Native*, August 26-September 1, 1985, 11.

24. Poggi, Stephanie. "Military to Screen Recruits for HTLV-III." *Gay Community News*, September 14, 1985, 1.

25. "Variety in AIDS Virus Hindrance to Vaccine." *The New York Times*, August 16, 1985, A11.

The Obscene, Disgusting, and Vile Meese Commission Report

1986

Our Teflon President and his Attorney General, Edwin "There Is No *There* There" Meese III, have thrown a big, juicy bone to the mad dog packs of the New Christian Right. The Justice Department recently appointed a Commission with the mandate to overturn the 1970 Presidential Commission on Pornography's finding that there is no evidence of a link between sexually explicit materials and delinquent or criminal behavior. The final report of this new Commission, published in July, 1986, holds out the hope that by using draconian measures against pornography we can turn America into a rerun of "Leave It to Beaver." The Commission's findings should placate the lowest common denominator of the citizenry who made a drugstore cowboy our Chief Executive—those folks who believe the Bible should be taken literally, but the First Amendment should not.

In a press conference to announce selection of Commission members, Meese claimed that since 1970, "the content of pornography has radically changed, with more and more emphasis upon extreme violence." He also claimed that his Commission "has not come to their task with minds made up. Their job is to approach the issues objectively...In any recommendation the commission makes, it will carefully balance the need to control the distribution of pornography with the need to protect very carefully first amendment freedoms."[1]

This statement was not reassuring, coming from a man who thinks the Supreme Court should not compel the states to abide by the Bill of Rights, a man who has said, "Miranda only helps guilty defendants. Most innocent people are glad to talk to the police." Under his direction, the Justice Department has become an Orwellian ministry that wages war on affirmative action, tried to halt funding for the National Coalition Against Domestic Violence on the grounds that it was a "pro-lesbian" group,[2] and ruled that employers can discriminate against people with AIDS (or people who have been exposed to HTLV-III) if they believe they are preventing the spread of the disease.[3]

The most powerful commissioners—Chairman Henry Hudson, Vice-Chairman Tex Lezar, Executive Director Alan Sears, and Edward J.

Garcia—are law-enforcement professionals. When he was the commonwealth's attorney for a suburb of Washington, D.C., Hudson received a presidential commendation for closing down every adult bookstore and massage parlor in the county. The Commission's constitutional expert, Frederick Schauer, a professor of law at the University of Michigan, takes the position that pornography is not protected by the First Amendment since it is a form of sexual activity, not speech.

The two social scientists on the Commission included Park Elliott Dietz, an associate professor of law at the University of Virginia. Dietz has a visiting appointment as a consultant and guest lecturer at the Behavioral Science Unit of the FBI Academy. He believes that masturbating to deviant images supports and maintains (if not causes) deviance, and he has published research on the dangers of detective magazines. The other researcher, Judith Veronica Becker, an associate professor of clinical psychology at Columbia University, is the director of the Sexual Behavior Clinic in New York. It was probably thought that her work with rape victims would make her sympathetic to efforts to wipe out smut.

Three of the commissioners are moral crusaders. Reverend Bruce Ritter, a Franciscan priest and ardent foe of Times Square, is the founder of Covenant House, a crisis center for runaways. As the vice-mayor and a council-member of Scottsdale, Arizona, Diane D. Cusack urged citizens to photograph patrons of the town's only adult movie theater, copy down their license-plate numbers, and turn over this "evidence" to police. And Dr. James C. Dobson is a fundamentalist pediatrician with a syndicated right-wing radio program, "Focus on the Family."

Deanne Tilton-Durfee, the president of the California Consortium of Child Abuse Councils, was probably expected to join this trio in supporting all proposals to regulate child pornography and hopefully adults-only material as well.

The closest thing the Commission had to a representative of the publishing industry or the arts was Ellen Levine, a vice president of CBS and editor of *Woman's Day*.[4]

This "objective" body was given one year and half a million dollars to come up with a solution to pornography. The 1970 Commission had two million dollars and two years. It funded over eighty independent studies of porn.[5] The new Commission couldn't do that, so it held public hearings—lots of them. From June of 1985 to January of 1986, the Commission held two-day hearings in Washington, D.C., Chicago, Houston, Los Angeles, Miami, and New York City. Their 1,960-page, two-volume *Attorney General's Commission on Pornography, Final Report* was thrown together during work sessions in Washington, D.C., and Scottsdale, Arizona.

Despite its bulk, this is a quick and dirty piece of work. It is also the harbinger of a new wave of sexual McCarthyism. Porn is about to become the "red menace" of the '80s. The report even makes a metaphorical connection between the two: "That the Communist Party is a lawful organization does not prevent most Americans from finding its tenets abhorrent, and the same holds true for a wide variety of sexually-oriented material."[6]

Reading the report is about as much fun as listening to the Mormon Tabernacle Choir. Bizarre examples of doublespeak keep cropping up. "The right to privacy" is a right that is violated when adults appear in sexually explicit material or view such material; "public entertainment" is a married couple watching the Playboy Channel after they have put the kids to bed in another room; "community standards" are the opinions of a bunch of zealots whose politics are slightly to the right of the Old Testament and whose sense of truth and beauty comes from K-Mart; "consent" is something "every adult needs special safeguards against" if they choose to appear in porn;[7] and "protecting the First Amendment" is something you do by fighting porn because its "plausibility" is "jeopardized when the First Amendment too often becomes the rhetorical device by which the commercial trade in materials directed virtually exclusively at sexual arousal is defended."[8]

The report also makes generous use of feminist antiporn rhetoric. New York Women Against Pornography (WAP) helped the Commission staff locate witnesses who testified as "victims of pornography," but at some point it occurred to WAP leaders that it was time to duck the charge of being tools of the state. Dorchen Leidholdt (along with several other WAP leaders) had been willing to testify before the Commission in Washington, D.C., but on the first day of the New York hearings, she led a demonstration against them—the critical edge of which was blunted a little when an officer of the court opened the gate and escorted the WAPettes to a microphone at the witness stand. Chairman Henry Hudson even asked for a copy of her remarks to enter into the record!

When the *Final Report* was issued, WAP called a triumphant press conference. In a joint statement, Andrea Dworkin and Catharine MacKinnon crowed over the Commission's endorsement of their ordinance, which defines and bans pornography as a violation of women's civil rights. They never mentioned the minor hitch that the ordinance had already been declared unconstitutional by the Supreme Court because it would proscribe material that is protected by the First Amendment.[9] Perhaps they had not read the full text of the Commission's recommendation of their ordinance, which contains the demurrer that, of course, "The only constitutionally permissible approach...is to reach material containing sexually violent or...degrading material when it is legally obscene."[10] It takes more than a press conference to hide the fact that WAP was hoodwinked, coopted, and used.

The Commission's proposals for dealing with porn are hair-raising. They want stepped-up enforcement of existing obscenity laws; increased cooperation between local, state, and federal law enforcement personnel and the IRS; and a computerized national database. They want forfeiture statutes, so that any proceeds from production of pornography can be confiscated. They want Congress to enact a statute that the distribution of obscene material "affects" interstate commerce. This would eliminate the necessity to prove transportation in interstate commerce in obscenity cases. According to the Commission, hiring individuals to participate in commercial sexual performances should be made an unfair labor practice. Transmission of obscene matter over cable TV and telephone lines should be proscribed. Obscenity should be made a predicate act for a group to be investigated under the frighteningly powerful Racketeer Influenced and Corrupt Organizations Act (RICO), and states should enact their own versions of RICO. All state legislatures should adopt the lower standard of proof of obscenity found in *Miller v. California*.[11] Pandering laws should be used against porn producers. Conditions within adult bookstores should be investigated and health violations prosecuted. Peep show booths should not be allowed to have doors or holes in the walls between the booths. Use of performers under the age of twenty-one should be forbidden by act of Congress, and producers, retailers, and distributors of sexually explicit material should be required to maintain records containing consent forms and proof of performers' ages.[12]

It was only by a very narrow margin that the Commission did not vote to recommend legislation that would have made vibrators and dildos obscene. Although the report admits that sexually explicit material which is text only (words) should usually be exempt from prosecution, Chairman Henry Hudson says in his individual statement that this exemption "is disturbing."[13]

The Commission's staff was formulating these recommendations from the very first day of hearings, before they heard social-science data about whether or not porn caused harm, before they even *defined* pornography. In the *Final Report*, "pornography" is distinguished from the legal term "obscenity" and defined as material that "is predominantly sexually explicit and intended primarily for the purpose of sexual arousal." This is an extremely broad category which could include almost anything that deals with human sexuality. The report attempts to sidestep this problem by going on to say, "Whether some or all of what qualifies as pornographic under this definition should be prohibited, or even condemned, is not a question that should be answered under the guise of definition."[14]

But the report does in fact assume that none of this material should be available. Since the First Amendment prevents the government from going after everything, the *Final Report* provides a detailed manual on how citizens' action groups can combat "non-obscene but offensive pornographic material." Furthermore, "If a decision is reached to establish such a group, its members should become involved in advocating, establishing and maintaining community standards related to pornography."[15] So much for pluralism.

What is the justification for recommending such sweeping measures? The evidence compiled by the Commission is embarrassingly biased and lightweight, and eventually led three of the women—Levine, Becker, and Tilton-Durfee—to write individual statements that dissent from many of the Commission's findings.

Of 208 witnesses, at least 160 (77 percent) urged tighter control of sexually explicit material. Dozens of these people were self-described "victims of pornography" who claimed that porn had brought adultery, battery, drug abuse, and other miseries into their lives. Only 40 witnesses (19 percent) urged repeal of existing laws or suggested that things should be left as they are. The remaining 8 witnesses were social scientists or academics who tried to explain that the existing evidence doesn't prove porn causes violence or other antisocial behavior.[16] While antiporn activists and "victims of pornography" were rarely cross-examined, anticensorship witnesses were treated with asperity. They were asked if they received funding from the Playboy Foundation. Did they advocate kiddy porn or snuff films? Were they aware that porn is controlled by organized crime?

Commissioners Judith Becker and Ellen Levine complained, "While there is little doubt about the proliferation of pornography since 1970, no serious effort has been made to quantify the increase...We do not even know whether or not what the Commission viewed during the course of the year reflected the nature of most of the pornographic and obscene material in the market; nor do we know if the materials shown us mirror the taste of the majority of consumers of pornography. The visuals, both print and video, were skewed to the very violent and extremely degrading. While one does not deny the existence of this material, the fact that it dominated the materials presented...may have distorted the Commission's judgment."[17]

Highly touted "new research" that was to show a link between pornography and violent crime simply doesn't exist. The Commission hired Canadian sociologist Edna F. Einsiedel to review and summarize existing studies that might have a bearing on their findings. She reported, "No evidence currently exists that actually links fantasies with specific sexual offenses; the relationship at this point remains an inference." She also noted that pornography has been of value to some therapists who use it to treat patients. For writing this report, Einsiedel was placed under a gag order obtained by Alan Sears, and her summation does not appear in the Commission's *Final Report*.[18]

The experts who testified have expressed dismay over how their testimony was used. Edward Donnerstein, a psychologist at the University of Wisconsin whose research shows some connection between viewing certain types of violent pornography and aggressive behavior, said the Commission's "conclusions seem bizarre to me...It is the violence more than the sex—and negative messages about human relationships—that are the problem. And these messages are everywhere." Murray Strauss, a sociologist at the University of New Hampshire, has said that the Commission misinterpreted his work. "I do not believe that this research demonstrates that pornography causes rape," he wrote to them.[19]

Two feeble attempts were made to provide research that was tailor-made to support the Commission. The Justice Department had given antiporn activist Judith Reisman a grant for $734,000 to study the cartoons in *Playboy*, *Penthouse*, and *Hustler*. Reisman is known for attacking Kinsey, whom she says got all his evidence about child sexuality from a man who molested over eight hundred children. Her knowledge of child sexuality probably comes from her experience as a scriptwriter for "Captain Kangaroo." Her grant was so poorly written and its budget so inflated that it drew criticism from the Senate Juvenile Justice Subcommittee. It emerged that Reisman's "peer review" had been conducted by three vice cops, an FBI agent, and fellow antiporn activist and beneficiary of Justice Department funding, Ann Burgess. Reisman testified at the hearings, but her warning that "The cartoon scenario is the common setting in erotica/pornography within which the breaking of sexual taboos first appears," was not exactly what the Commission needed to put itself over the top.[20]

A long list (over one hundred pages) of the magazine, book, and movie titles found in a dozen or so adult bookstores in six cities was compiled for a content-analysis study by staff members trained in "the distinctions necessary to complete the forms (e.g., the distinction between whipping and spanking)."[21] Incidentally, both *The Advocate* and *Advocate Men* are on this list. Unfortunately, "Full formal results were not completed at the time of printing of this final report."[22] Nevertheless, the list of titles appears in the *Final Report*.

The Commission tries to gloss over the lack of conclusive social-science data by calling for further research, but if more research is needed, why make such dramatic recommendations for changes in policy and law? Because, huffs the *Final Report*, "The Commission has examined social and behavioral science research in recognition of the role it plays in determining legal standards and social policy. This role, while notable, is not, nor should it be, the sole basis for developing standards or policy."[23]

Nevertheless, when it came time to write up their conclusions, the commissioners faced quite a dilemma: how could they justify recommending allocation of scarce funds and police time to shutting down the immensely popular adult entertainment industry if they couldn't prove pornography is bad for anybody? Hudson presented his commissioners with a *deus ex machina*. Until the end of their fact-finding mission, pornography had been considered as a single body of material. Now, it was divided into four categories—sexually violent material; explicit sexual activity which depicts submission, humiliation, dominance, or degradation; explicit sexual activity without submission, humiliation, dominance, or degradation; and mere nudity. The key terms *violence, submission, sexual activity,* etc., were not defined. The commissioners were then asked to evaluate each category based on three distinct bases: social-science research, totality of the evidence (e.g., the claims of the "victims"), and moral, ethical, and cultural considerations.[24]

This intellectually bankrupt scheme allowed commissioners who were so inclined to vote that all of the categories of porn were harmful. Materials which show adults only engaging in consensual vanilla sex— even *mere nudity*—were not exonerated. Sadly, the press ignored the fallacious basis of the Commission's findings and simply reported that a link had been found between pornography and violence.

The *Final Report* comes down hard on child pornography, and its treatment of this issue has also been underexamined. It thunders for intensification of efforts to wipe out child pornography, despite the testimony of two law-enforcement officials that the huge bureaucracy already in place to do so has succeeded. Sergeant. W. D. Brown of the Houston vice squad said, "Presently, there is no child pornography that is being sold readily over the counter,"[25] and retired FBI agent William

Kelly told them, "The laws against child porn could not be better. It never constituted more than 1 percent of the total market, but still gets 99 percent of the attention."[26]

The Commission made skillful use of a vague and ever broader definition of "child pornography" to smear material that depicts and is intended only for the use of adults. Any sexually explicit material which adults might show to children to teach them about sex or seduce them into sexual activity was referred to as "child porn." This term also came to include cartoons or drawings of children, photographs of adult models made up to look like children, or the contents of Dial-A-Porn or cable television if children have gained access to these media. Commissioners coined a new phrase—"children between the ages of 18 and 21"—who presumably need as much protection as prepubescents.[27]

The Commission would like to use the current child-pornography law as a precedent to control a wider range of adults-only material. *New York v. Ferber* allows images of actual children to be banned even if they are not obscene.[28] The *Final Report* suggests new categories of material that could be proscribed in a similar fashion—for example, "sexually violent material." All images of S/M activity will almost certainly vanish over the next year as it becomes a category as verboten as kiddy porn. You may not care if there are no more magazines full of whip-wielding ladies in leather corsets, but don't forget that WAP used *Ferber* to justify its civil-rights antiporn ordinance and would like to ban many kinds of nonobscene, sexually explicit images on the grounds that they endanger women.

As shoddy as it is, the chilling effect of the Commission's report is already being felt. The Commission had originally planned to publish a list of distributors of pornography. Sears sent a letter to the twenty-three companies on the list informing them of this plan and warning that failure to reply would be taken as acquiescence. The companies were also sent anonymous excerpts from the testimony of Mississippi minister Reverend Donald Wildmon, whose newsletter targets corporations that he feels sponsor "filth," such as CBS, Time Inc., Coca-Cola, and Simon & Schuster. Southland Corporation, which had been under attack by Wildmon and Jerry Falwell for three years, dropped *Playboy, Penthouse,* and all *Penthouse* publications from its 4,500 7-Eleven stores.[29] *Playboy,* the American Booksellers Association, and the Council for Periodical Distributors Association filed a lawsuit that blocked publication of the list, but many other chains of food, drug, and convenience stores banished these magazines from their premises.[30] This is nothing less than the return of the blacklist.

The Meese Commission has highlighted the failure of most civil libertarians to deal directly with porn. The typical anticensorship witness argued that we can't ban porn because the *next* things to go would be important—art, literature, theater, legitimate film, political protest. But this claim rings hollow. Silencing artists and radicals is not on the Commission's agenda. Most of the commissioners are quite plain about the fact that they just don't like people having sex out of wedlock or looking at porn and not feeling guilty about it.

The flaws of pornography make it difficult to defend. Much of it is sexist, made under poor working conditions, overpriced, and controlled by the Mafia. But you can't fix any of these problems by making it even more illegal and harder to get. The more marginal, the more persecuted porn is, the worse it will become. And the new producers who are gambling with nonsexist, challenging material will be squeezed out of business.

More of us have to start saying that we use porn, like it, and want it to be accessible. Even given the constraints under which it is currently produced, pornography is valuable. It sends out messages of comfort and rebellion. It says: Lust is not evil. The body is not hateful. Physical pleasure is a joyful thing and should not be hidden or denied. It is not true that women have no sexual hunger. There are other people who think about and do the things you dream about. Freedom is possible. There is a choice.

Even those of us who are deviants or sex radicals or both can't seem to stop apologizing for the shabby forms our society often forces Eros to assume. Meanwhile, war has been declared against the sexual imagination, and I'm afraid we're all going to lose.

Notes

1. U.S. Justice Department press release, June 19, 1985.
2. Walter, Dave. "Grant for 'Pro-Lesbian' Group Finally Approved." *The Advocate*, September 17, 1985, 16.
3. Saul, Stephanie. "Opinion Would Permit Firing of AIDS Victims." *New York Newsday*, June 24, 1986, 3.
4. Wooster, Martin Morse. "Reagan's Smutstompers." *Reason*, April 1986, 26-33. Philip Nobile and Eric Nadler, "Ed Meese Gives Bad Commission." *Penthouse*, July 1986, 50-58, 66, 119.
5. *Attorney General's Commission on Pornography, Final Report.* (hereafter referred to as the *Final Report*), July 1986, Vol. I, 225, 903.
6. *ibid.*, 419.
7. *ibid.*, 899.

8. *ibid.*, 266.

9. *Hudnut v. American Booksellers Association*, 54 U.S.L.W. 3560, February 24, 1986.

10. *Final Report*, Vol. I, 394.

11. *Miller* establishes a lower standard of proof of obscenity by requiring only proof that material alleged to be obscene does not have *significant* artistic, scientific, or literary merit. An earlier standard simply required that the material possess *some* artisitc, scientific, or literary merit. Attempts to make *Miller* part of the definition of obscenity in state constitutions are also usually accompanied by attempts to substitute local standards for statewide ones, since individual cities and towns are often more conservative than the population of a state taken as a whole.

12. *ibid.*, 433-458.

13. *ibid.*, 32.

14. *ibid.*, 228-229.

15. *ibid.*, Vol. II, 1318-1319.

16. Lynn, Barry. Legislative Counsel, American Civil Liberties Union. "The New Pornography Commission: Slouching Toward Censorship." *SEICUS Report*, May 1986, 1-6.

17. *Final Report*, Vol. I, 198-199.

18. Scheer, Robert. "Inside the Meese Commission." *Playboy*, July 1986, 162.

19. *Final Report*, Vol. I, 206.

20. Wooster, "Reagan's Smutstompers."

21. *Final Report*, Vol. II, 1500.

22. *ibid.*, 1503.

23. *ibid.*, Vol. I, 901.

24. Lynn, "The New Pornography Commission."

25. Scheer, "Inside the Meese Commission."

26. From my notes from the questioning of William P. Kelly, January 21, 1986, New York City hearings.

27. Lynn, "The New Pornography Commission."

28. McHarry, Mark. "Pornography and the Law." *NAMBLA Journal Six*, 1983, 1, 25-27.

29. Press, Aric and Ann McDaniel. "Hard-Core Proposals." *Newsweek*, April 28, 1986, 39.

30. "Porn Panel Can't Name Vendors." *New York Newsday*, July 4, 1986, 15NY.

II.
Among Us, Against Us:
Right-Wing Feminism

II.
Among Us, Against Us:
Right-Wing Feminism
1980

Soon after the Sex Wars began to rage within feminism, calls were heard for moderation and compromise. Both antiporn activists and sex-positive feminists were labeled "extremists," and several authors suggested that the correct position on this issue must lie somewhere between the positions of these two opposing camps. Interviewers sometimes clear their throats and invite me to admit that antiporn leaders like Andrea Dworkin and Catharine MacKinnon are not the enemy—that we are all just politically active, aware women who want to make the world a better place.

When pigs fly.

The problem is that a book does not exist in the abstract realm of theories and ideas. A book is an object that can be seized and destroyed, or bought and read. Either a book is allowed to cross a border or it is not. Either it can be safely put on a shelf in a bookstore where a customer can select it and take it home or it cannot. Customs officials and vice cops do not compromise with books they don't like. They just stack them up in warehouses where nobody can read them. Or they burn them.

If you'd like to know what it would be like to live in an antiporn utopia, you don't have to go very far. In 1992 the Canadian Supreme Court issued the so-called Butler decision. Butler replaced a morality-based community-standards definition of obscenity with one taken from a legal brief submitted by American antiporn activist and attorney MacKinnon. Pornography is now regulated in Canada because of the ostensible harm it does to women. The decision says in part, "If true equality between male and female is to be achieved, we cannot ignore the threat to equality resulting from exposure to audiences of certain types of violent and degrading materials."

Canadian Customs officials were already notorious for their arbitrary seizures of American books bound for gay and feminist shops in Canada. Since Butler there has been mass confiscation of every sort of lesbian and gay book, magazine, and newspaper. Although much of the material seized deals with all kinds of sexual topics, Customs flunkies seem most concerned about halting the flow of merchandise into alternative bookstores. Scholarly work by bell hooks, David Leavitt's *A Place I Have Never Seen,* and even Dworkin's tomes have been detained. One source estimated that Inland Books, a major distributor of small-press work, had 73 percent of its total 1993 shipments to Canada seized.[1] Inland says that it has had trouble with about three hundred titles and now won't even try to ship certain books to Canada because they are certain to be seized.

Often Customs officials detain books—such as *Macho Sluts*—which have been tried for obscenity in Canada and found to be perfectly legal to distribute. But these decisions are arbitrary, and there is little or no process for appealing them. Even if Customs decides to release a book for sale, there is no guarantee that they will not seize the next shipment of the same title. When bookstores finally do receive their goods from Customs, the materials are often in damaged condition. And some materials become obsolete before they reach their destinations; for example, a six-month-old copy of *The Advocate,* even in pristine condition, is of little value to a bookstore. Because they never know which or how many books they will receive from their distributors, the shops suffer from major problems with cash flow.

Little Sister's bookstore in Vancouver has filed a legal challenge against these seizures, claiming they form prior restraint which prevents the courts from making decisions on whether or not particular books or magazines are obscene. The suit also charges that the law is enforced in a discriminatory and homophobic fashion. Canada has no First Amendment. Words and pictures are equally at risk of being prosecuted for obscenity there. And Customs regulations specifically prohibit any written or visual depiction of anal penetration from entering the country. In Canada it is not illegal to commit sodomy, only to read about it or to look at pictures of it.

This lawsuit has been adjourned twice, supposedly because Customs was not yet ready to proceed. The delays have escalated the cost of a legal battle that was already prohibitively expensive. This matter will probably not return to court until fall of 1994. In the meantime, Customs goes on its merry way, happily confiscating books by John Preston, Susie Bright, John Rechy, Tee Corinne, Kathy Acker, David Wojnarowicz, Laura Antoniou, and others. *Hothead Paisan, On Our Backs, RFD, The Lesbian and Gay Studies Reader,* even a reprint of the 1962 lesbian pulp *Return to Lesbos* have been detained. *The Devil's Dictionary,* a classic by Ambrose Bierce, was seized along with a Bierce reader. The ever-vigilant smutbusters also cordoned off *Hot, Hotter, Hottest*—a cookbook about chili peppers.

The Butler decision has had almost no visible impact on the straight-porn industry. Instead, it has been used to impede the circulation of gay literature. It is part of a legal apparatus that seems bent on closing down gay and feminist bookstores in Canada. *Hustler, Playboy, Penthouse,* and other straight erotic magazines are still available for sale in Canada. *The Joy of Sex,* which has more information about butt-fucking in it than *Advocate Men,* is allowed to circulate, but *The Joy of Gay Sex* was initially banned. The first obscenity case under Butler was a prosecution of Glad Day Bookstore, a gay business in Toronto, for selling the lesbian S/M magazine, *Bad Attitude.* Madonna's *Sex,* however, heated up Canadian cash registers with impunity.

For more than ten years now, antiporn feminists have been telling us that pornography is the cornerstone of woman-hating, sexism, violence against women, and discrimination. They have been telling us that with their antiporn legislation they have a blueprint that will wipe out these social ills. The only way the Canadian porn law could be more consistent with the antiporn movement is if the Canadian government had handed MacKinnon a quill and let her scribble it into the codes herself. Dworkin has said, "the Butler decision is probably the best articulation of how pornography, and what kinds of pornography, hurt the civil status and civil rights of women." But, funniest damned thing, not only are women in Canada still suffering from rape, unequal pay, domestic violence, sexist images in the mass media, and a host of other ills—MacKinnon's law can't even seem to wipe out its nemesis, heterosexual smut!

My belief is that antiporn "feminists" have been obsessed from the very beginning with attempting to eliminate a sexually frank discourse of lesbian and gay male desire. They have always been happy to work with homophobes, anti-abortion politicians, and right wingers. In a recent interview about Canadian censorship of gay literature, Dworkin called lesbian porn "an expression of self-hatred." According to her, lesbian S/M is "based on a deep and sexualized hatred of women." Women who do not support her antiporn politics "have their own agenda that is not necessarily the same as the agenda of lesbians who care about lesbians and lesbian rights."[2]

She does not explain how the confiscation of books written and published by women constitutes "lesbian rights." Nor does she explain why giving another woman pleasure is "self-hatred" and "hatred of women." In the bizarre world of Dworkinthink, the fact that a lesbian-bookstore employee could actually go to jail or pay a fine for selling lesbian sex writing in Canada is just one tiny part of a big plan for the liberation of women. Could I skip the fun part where we win the revolution, and just move straight into the gulag? Can I take a few pencils along?

In this distorted world view, gay male pornography is just as bad as straight smut because it contains a "consistent sexualization of hierarchies of power." That's right, those two surfer boys kissing each other and then engaging in 69 are in fact secret operatives committed to upholding the rule of patriarchal straight men. In fact, Dworkin goes on to say, "The gay and lesbian community has to understand that pornography hurts women as a class...The gay and lesbian community is as reactionary and rearguard and as woman-hating as any other community when it insists on trafficking in those materials...If they traffic in those materials, they are responsible for the harm those materials cause. In my view they need to be held legally accountable." Has this woman ever read how censorship laws in this country were used to obstruct the circulation of birth-control information and early gay-liberation material? Does she care? She seems woefully ignorant of the life-affirming impact that gay sexual imagery has on people who must live in a culture that tells us we are wrong, bad, sick, immoral, or nonexistent. I wonder what her response would be to the implementation of explicit safer-sex education. Bet it wouldn't differ that much, line for line, from Jesse Helms's.

Dworkin is so fixated upon her crusade to save the world from dirty books that she doesn't get the message implicit in Canadian Customs' seizure of her own work. Much as it tickles me to know there are bluenosed bureaucrats out there who can't tell us apart, I'm outraged by this attempt to prevent her dogma from circulating in Canada. After all, that's the whole point of civil liberties—to protect unpopular people and ideas. Let's spell this out: So-called "feminist" porn laws will not be enforced by feminists. They will be enforced for the most part by straight white men who think lesbianism is more degrading and more threatening to women than date rape or sexual harassment. To these minions of Comstockery, cocksuckers are a bigger threat to society than the Hillside Strangler. The cops would much rather rip down safer-sex posters in the subways than patrol them to prevent women from being stalked and assaulted.

When right-wing feminists have their way with the body politic, they only give weapons to the same authorities who hate us and want us to die or at least keep our mouths shut, our heads down, and our hands to ourselves. There's nothing new about the idea that women need to be protected from sex or the dire prophecy that more sexual choices for women will result in their being degraded and victimized by out-of-control men. This is rhetoric straight out of the 1890s. Frankly, I wish antiporn activists would indulge their Victorian fantasies in a little more harmless fashion, by wearing tightlacing corsets or distributing bounty to the deserving poor.

But please don't get the idea that I want to see Customs or the vice squad taken over by antiporn feminists. If that were to happen, the only change would be that *everything*, from *Bad Attitude* to *Playboy*, would disappear from the shelves. How can any sane person imagine that a world free of sexual imagery and erotic fiction would be a better place for women? Do you think it's possible to effectively teach women how to do self-exams for breast cancer, monitor their cervical mucus so they can get pregnant, discuss safer sex with their partners, stand up to sexual harassment, use birth control, tell their daughters about puberty and menstruation, and insist that the cops arrest rapists, in a social climate where sex has become unspeakable and largely invisible? You can't write a law that will remove a porn book from the shelves and leave *Our Bodies, Ourselves* unscathed.

I am scheduled to appear in court in Vancouver later this year to speak on behalf of my books, most of which have been seized at one time or another by Canadian Customs. When we thought this matter would be heard last year, I had to compile written testimony for presentation to the opposing counsel. It took me days to write a mere handful of pages. I do not write for a heterosexual audience, although I am pleased if my work also speaks to people outside of my own community. Not only was I being asked to justify my work in terms a straight reader might understand, but that putative straight reader was a law-enforcement professional—either a judge or an attorney. I felt as if I had to learn another language before I could complete that document. The effort of translating my goals as a writer into something that might pass muster in a Canadian court was sickening. I couldn't think about or write anything else for months. It reminded me that the term "sexual outlaw" is literally true.

No. There is no middle ground. It is not possible to compromise with bigots and fanatics. Under that unlovely rubric, I include the antiporn crusaders as well as the uniformed nosy parkers who put their dirty hands and dirty minds all over my books. I am amazed that these women have any credibility whatsoever with other feminists or with intelligent, freedom-loving queers. Under the guise of ending violence against women, these women have done a great deal of violence to lesbian literature and gay publishing. All their pieces of model legislation, friend-of-the-court briefs, impassioned speeches before television cameras and Congress, and "Take Back the Night" marches are naked bids for personal power which foster nothing but sex phobia, especially among young, impressionable women. The leaders of the "feminist" antiporn movement are the kind of people who stood elbow-to-elbow with Savonarola and threw priceless oil paintings onto the *Auto-da-fé*. Frankly, I think we ought to be marching to take back the night from *them*.

Notes

1. Kingston, Tim. "Queer Censorship: Canada's Bigoted New Custom." *San Francisco Bay Times*, Vol. 15, No. 3, November 4, 1993.
2. *ibid.*

Among Us, Against Us—The New Puritans: Does Equation of Pornography with Violence Add Up to Political Repression?

1980

Superhero comic books were the porn of my childhood. My first fist-fucking magazine was not so thrilling as those brightly colored, fantastic adventures on sleazy newsprint. The images of capture, helplessness, and torture were the most exciting: Superman drained of his strength by Kryptonite; Aquaman dying slowly in a net hung over a swimming pool; Sheena tied upside down and threatened with a hot spear point. In bed I dreamed of flying through space, gifted with strange powers that required me to do battle with evil. I dreamed of being imprisoned and tortured by enemies who were somehow near and familiar to me, then magically and inevitably being released.

When I got older, and my reading skills improved, I discovered more explicit material in Zane Grey (a woman tied to a horse, her blouse ripped off, the horse sent galloping into a forest fire), Pearl Buck (rough soldiers raping a graceful and beautiful boy; the Imperial Woman carried to her curtained bed by her childhood sweetheart), and Henry Miller (a woman reaching under a banquet table to fondle another woman's genitals). There were also psychiatric textbooks and historical accounts of Indian torture and the Spanish Inquisition. Upon discovering indecencies in these circumspect volumes, I blushed and wondered if I were the only person to find anything titillating about them. If not, how on earth did they manage to stay on the shelves?

I turned to the library because none of the adults I knew would talk to me about sex beyond sketching the anatomy of reproduction. I needed to know much more than that; I needed to know about pleasure. I was tormented by lust, which had taken on a new and bittersweet urgency with adolescence. I had little idea what people did about these tempests of need, and I was very sure that the least move to still my frustration would have disastrous consequences. My gleanings of erotica and frequent, guilt-ridden masturbation were all that kept me sane until I escaped parental supervision.

Even then, it was a long time before flesh could be discovered and schooled to yield the bliss of fantasy. I found that sex is a dry lesson in anatomy unless infused with the erotic imagination. The inner voice of

Eros is arbitrary, bizarre, impeccably honest, bountiful, and so powerful as to be cruel. It takes courage to hear its demands and follow them. Because I sensed a connection between private fantasy and good sex, I did not abandon my smutty "home movies" as I learned how to persuade others to join me in sensual exploration; when to persist and when to abandon hope and choose again; how to be bedded and to bed another. I continued to enrich, diversify, and embroider my fantasies. Today, reading porn (or erotica, if you enjoy euphemisms) and plying my vibrator are as important to me as the sex I have with lovers, friends, and tricks. I prefer partners who are willing to risk their dignity in pursuit of delight and who do not make hard and fast distinctions between masturbation and lovemaking, between what we can think of and what we can do. Consequently, I have a small but select collection of prose and visual material that brings out the libertine in me.

Until recently I was under the misapprehension that the Supreme Court had guaranteed my right to enjoy this material in the privacy of my home. When I started doing research for this article, I read Planned Parenthood's book, *The Sex Code of California.* According to that document, this is the legal definition of obscenity:

> *Obscene matter* means matter taken as a whole, the predominant appeal of which to the average person, applying contemporary standards, is to prurient interest, i.e., a shameful or morbid interest in nudity, sex, or excretion; and is matter which taken as a whole goes substantially beyond customary limits of candor in description or representation of such matters; and is matter which taken as a whole is utterly without redeeming social importance.[1]

Just for us "deviant sexual groups," the following paragraph was added:

> The predominant appeal to prurient interest of the matter is judged with reference to average adults unless it appears from the nature of the matter or the circumstances of its dissemination, distribution or exhibition, that it is designed for clearly defined deviant sexual groups, in which case the predominant appeal of the matter shall be judged with reference to its intended recipient group.[2]

Material which exists for the sole or primary purpose of turning someone on is illegal. There is no freedom of sexual speech. As I read the rest of the state and federal laws governing obscenity, I found that it is illegal to buy porn from outside the country or outside the state and to distribute it by mail. In California it is illegal to show pornography to a minor if you are not the parent or guardian. The real clincher is this: it is illegal to "exhibit" obscene matter. "Exhibit" is legally defined simply as "to show."[3]

The Alcoholic Beverage Commission has its own regulations regarding pornography. A liquor license cannot be held by places which:

> show films, still pictures, electronic reproductions, or other visual reproductions depicting: Acts or simulated acts of sexual intercourse, masturbation, sodomy, bestiality, oral copulation, flagellation or any sexual acts which are prohibited by laws. Any person being touched, caressed, or fondled on the breast, buttocks, anus or genitals. Scenes wherein a person displays the vulva or the anus or the genitals. Scenes wherein artificial devices or inanimate objects are employed to depict, or drawings are employed to portray, any of the prohibited activities described above.[4]

Obscenity laws are selectively enforced. The police are fond of using them to harass gays, as in Toronto. In 1979 *The Body Politic* was busted under antipornography laws for printing an article about boy-love. Its mailing list and books from the Pink Triangle Press (including *The Joy of Gay Sex* and *The Joy of Lesbian Sex*) were confiscated. The books and subscription lists have not yet been returned, and the newspaper faces a second trial even though in its first trial it was acquitted of the charges. Individuals who get involved in unpopular political activities are often arrested under obscenity statutes or for other sex offenses. Antipornography laws can also be used to close down any gay or lesbian bar with erotic art on its walls or that shows sexy movies. During a wave of repression, the police will use any excuse to close down the bars and silence our leaders.

Do you own any "obscene matter"? If you're hoping for the development of a more liberal atmosphere, don't hold your breath. In every major city of this country, groups are organizing to pressure the police to enforce current laws against obscenity, and to agitate for the passage of even more severe legislation. The irony is that women who are ostensibly feminists, many of them lesbians, are the leaders of this antipornography movement.

One of the most influential groups in this movement is Women Against Violence in Pornography and the Media (WAVPM). The group is headquartered in San Francisco, so I have had an excellent opportunity to read its literature, attend its public presentations, and see the effect it has had on the lesbian community. WAVPM grew out of a 1976 conference called "Violence Against Women." Friends of mine who attended came back from it almost incoherent with rage. Suddenly, no other issue but violence against women was important. But this did not result in more volunteers' signing up at Women Against Rape or the Casa de las Madres, a shelter for battered women. It resulted mostly in a lot of vituperation about pornography. The conference had included a display of visual images of violence against women, many of them "kinky" pornographic images. Presented in that context, they incensed almost every woman who saw them.

At the time, I was leading lesbian sexuality discussion groups. Some of my friends were producing lesbian erotica and educational material about female sexuality. All of us began to get flak. It became an act of courage to assert that women could talk about or portray their own sexuality without cooperating with the enemy. It was suicidal to suggest that lesbians could enjoy the good parts of some commercial erotica (like David Hamilton's photographs or the movie, *Emmanuelle*) without being contaminated for life by sexist ideology. This trend has continued. A perfect example is a letter which appeared in a recent issue of *Lesbian Connection* criticizing women artisans for selling jewelry that depicts vulvas and breasts.[5]

WAVPM's basic position is that pornography causes violence against women. The organization's definitions of pornography and violence are circular and vague. In addition to films showing various sex acts, pornography can include nonsexually explicit pictures, such as that of a woman whose body is smeared with honey, a woman stabbing a man in the back, or a woman dressed in leather and towering over two men.[6]

WAVPM's definition of violence is equally broad. It includes any kind of sex with a minor, consensual sadomasochism, bondage, watersports, prostitution, fist-fucking, casual and anal sex, as well as rape and assault.[7] After seeing the slide show where this connection is allegedly explicated, my head swam. No distinction was made among a photograph of a woman's genitals, the act of gang rape, an advertisement for spike heels, the act of child abuse, a photograph of a woman who was tied up, and the act of wife-beating. Thus I was not surprised to read in WAVPM's *Newspage* that the organization opposes *all* pornography, not just the genres it labels violent.[8]

Since, within WAVPM's broad definitions, any image that is objectifying or demeaning to women is called pornographic, WAVPM can claim that by fighting against pornography it is fighting against sexist stereotypes of women, not sexually explicit material. But it can then go on to claim that misogyny is more prevalent and pernicious in pornography than in any other type of media.

Many women I know who are upset about pornography have not seen much of it. They are vulnerable to WAVPM's inflammatory descriptions.[9] Commercial pornography is not uniformly sex-positive nor aesthetically pleasing. But WAVPM uses the worst examples (for instance, the cover of *Hustler* that showed a woman being fed into a meat grinder or the movie, *Snuff*) as if they were representative of the entire genre.

It is not true, as Andrea Dworkin claimed in her speech before an antipornography rally, that "The eroticization of murder is the essence of pornography."[10] Dworkin and many other members of the antipornography movement define violence as a male phenomenon and maleness as violence. As Dworkin said in her speech, "sex and murder are fused in the male consciousness, so that the one without the imminent possibility of the other is unthinkable and impossible...the annihilation of women is the source of meaning and identity for men."[11] Thus the fact that pornography is aimed at a male audience is sufficient to justify calling it violent. In fact, pornography depicts a wide variety of sexual acts. Very little of it shows violence or implies that any physical damage is being done to the models. Only if one thinks of sex itself as a degrading act can one believe that all pornography degrades and harms women. It is true that pornography is marketed for a male audience, but there are women who enjoy it. I do not think it sufficient to say these women are brainwashed by the patriarchy, since women are socialized *not* to use erotic materials.

Exaggerations like Dworkin's are questionable bases for political action. Dworkin wound up her speech by warning that "Every woman walking alone is a target. Every woman walking alone is hunted, harassed, time after time harmed by psychic or physical violence." I resent attempts like this to distort my perceptions of reality and make me unduly afraid. I do not get assaulted or verbally harassed every time I walk out my front door—and I have a crewcut. I do not live in a state of siege. My life is hard, and I have been the target of violence more than once, but I cannot suspend all normal activities as if I lived in a war zone. There is an enormous difference between encountering pornographic magazines on display in a store or on a street corner and being beaten up. If I don't like the magazines, I can look away. If I want to see something different (and I do), I can create my own.

WAVPM tries to blame the whole of women's oppression on pornography and convince women that a state of emergency exists that justifies extreme actions. Dworkin says, "the values expressed in it [pornography] are the values expressed in the acts of rape and wife-beating, in the legal system, in religion, in art and in literature, in systematic economic discrimination against women, in the moribund academies."[12] It is absurd to suggest that women will be liberated from discrimination by the closing down of adult bookstores. I wish with all my heart that it were so easy. But it is not so simple to restructure patriarchal society. The chief result of closing down the porn industry would be the enhancement of sexual repression. People would have even less access to erotic material and information about sex than they do now. Homosexuals and other sexual minorities would lose a vital source of contact—the sex ads. It would be even more difficult for women, lesbians, and other disenfranchised groups to circulate accurate information about their sexuality and create their own erotica. And yet, with its success in linking pornography to violence against and stereotypes of women, WAVPM's biggest accomplishment has been to convince lesbians that they do not need the First Amendment.

If you think WAVPM possesses concrete evidence that pornography causes violence against women, you are wrong. Susan Brownmiller feels that "the opinion of law enforcement agencies around the country" is sufficient; these agencies "claim their own concrete experience with offenders who were caught with the stuff has led them to conclude that pornographic material is a causative factor in crimes of sexual violence."[13] The *Newspage* cites an old, ambiguous study on the relationship between violent television programs and aggressive behavior in children.[14] But WAVPM really doesn't believe it needs to demonstrate this so-called causal connection with objective fact. At the 1978 conference on Feminist Perspectives on Pornography, Kathy Barry told the audience that women don't need research to demonstrate the effects of pornography because "We know instinctively what is killing us."

Gut reactions are notoriously unreliable, leading people to such actions as mounting crusades against homosexual school teachers. The truth is that nobody knows why a man becomes a rapist. Rape is a terrible crime. Women have a just and heartfelt need to defend themselves against it and (if possible) put a stop to it. But will our best interests be served by devoting our slender resources and limited time to wiping out pornography? Surely no one believes that all or most of the people who use pornography commit crimes of sexual violence. The number of individuals susceptible to that sort of influence must be very small. So many other factors aside from pornographic material must contribute to rape or other assault. It is the rape, the act itself, that is a crime—not reading a pornographic book. It is not a crime to fantasize committing a rape (or to fantasize being raped). Only violent *behavior* should be the concern of the law. Any legislation intended to control people's thoughts and motivations—like the laws against inciting riots—becomes political repression when enforced. Do we want to give the police any more power than they already have to control our private fantasy lives?

WAVPM is basically a group with a right-wing philosophy masquerading as a radical feminist organization. This can be demonstrated by its positions on sexual issues, by whom it chooses as allies, and by who supports WAVPM and its cause.

The antipornography movement espouses a traditional view of women's sexuality, including the belief that women do not enjoy pornography, casual sex, genital sex, or sex outside the context of a romantic relationship;[15] women are so different from men that there can be no such thing as pornography created by or for women.[16] Women are thus elevated above the realm of kinky sex and perhaps even sexual need. This Victorian image—pure women controlling the vile, lustful impulses of men—is one of the feminine stereotypes the women's movement should be working against. Instead WAVPM seems determined to bring it back into style. At the 1978 conference, Judith Reisman attacked pornography on the grounds that it was destroying the family, invalidating spirituality, and eroding relationships between the sexes. She defended institutionalized religion and the nuclear family as civilizing and controlling influences on male sexuality. But if anyone is responsible for promulgating the double standard, persecuting homosexuals, promoting puritanism, and denying women their right to sexual pleasure, it's religion and the family.[17]

WAVPM confuses sexual variation with violence. The organization is unable to distinguish pissing on, tying up, spanking, and fucking someone with a dildo from torture and murder. WAVPM also reads any kinky sex act as being degrading and demeaning to women, whether or not a woman is depicted. WAVPM cannot seem to digest the concept of male masochism or male homosexuality and believes that gay male pornography encourages violence against women because homosexual erotica shows a man being used and degraded *like* a woman. This concept of male homosexual eroticism could have come straight out of Freud, Socarides, or Bieber.

WAVPM's position on prostitution is especially awful. When asked if they are attacking the women who work in the sex industry—models, photographers, artists, writers, actresses, and whores—WAVPM spokeswomen reply that pornography is a crime against *all* women.

Hence, the solution to these women's problems is not to improve their working conditions or to decriminalize the industry. The notion that a woman might prefer hooking or nude modeling to being a secretary or cleaning hotel rooms is beyond WAVPM's ken. The literature sometimes grants that these women may not have any other choice of employment, but that's all WAVPM can say about them. No suggestions are offered regarding how these women would support themselves if the police rigorously enforced vice laws.

To justify this inhuman attitude toward sex workers, WAVPM trots out the specter of white slavery, claiming that most women in the sex industry were "forced" into it. The definition of force is the usual mishmash. It can include a woman's hooking out of economic necessity or because a man she loved talked her into it, as well as her being kidnapped and sold into a brothel in a foreign country. Thus WAVPM does not have to document the existence of actual traffic in women and leads people to believe that prostitution is a simple matter of innocent women being coerced into selling sex. This view of sex workers rests on the Victorian ideology of the asexual, pure woman. It is a simplistic analysis that does not take into account the marginal status of all women workers in Western society. Harsher laws against prostitution will simply make it harder for these women to make a living and more difficult for them to change professions. Despite this situation, WAVPM passed Resolution Number Six, denouncing "the selling of sex in any form."[18] The organization's New York offshoot, Women Against Pornography (where did the word "violence" go?), is involved in a campaign to clean up Times Square.

In its literature and public presentations, WAVPM repeatedly stresses the fact that eliminating pornography is an action that all women can support and specifically includes right-wing women under the banner of that sisterhood.[19] The antipornography movement has no problem with taking money from right-wing or conservative groups. The "Feminist Perspectives on Pornography" conference was funded by church groups. The New York group, WAP, has received large contributions from Con Edison, Off-Track Betting, and the League of New York Theaters and Producers. WAP's campaign to clean up Times Square is very popular with the vice squad and real-estate companies who would like their property to increase in value. But WAVPM has no program for preventing the antipornography crusade from turning into a full-scale sexual repression movement. Gay bars can be closed as easily as adult bookstores; they often *are* closed by the same set of laws, cops, and "concerned citizens." I think that WAVPM, WAP, and similar groups are being used by much more powerful segments of our society to create a sex-negative social climate that will facilitate the suppression of all forms of sexual dissent.[20]

WAVPM has yet to make any public statements in support of gay rights, sex education in schools, birth control and abortion, children's right to sexual information and freedom, decriminalization of prostitution, or the civil rights of sexual minorities. The organization continues to grow larger, more powerful, and more procensorship and antisex. Few members of the liberal press will risk opposing or criticizing WAVPM because it travels under the protective, self-applied label, "feminist." It is obvious that no one in the conservative press will oppose WAVPM, either— unless it gets too public about having a large lesbian membership.

I see no reason why WAVPM should not accomplish its goals. Still, I'm not going to throw out my fist-fucking magazines, tear out the cunt portraits in *Liberating Masturbation*, turn my Leonor Fini poster to the wall, or cease ordering copies of *What Lesbians Do* from out of state and allowing underage friends to look at it—but I am going to get a good lawyer. I suggest you do the same.

Notes

1. Clevenger, Norma K., ed. *The Sex Code of California*. Sacramento: Planned Parenthood Affiliates of California, 1977, 119.
2. *ibid.*
3. *ibid.*
4. *ibid.*, 122-123.
5. "Celebration or Fixation?" Letter to the Editor, *Lesbian Connection*, Vol. IV, issue 7, November 1979, 10.
6. These examples are taken from a WAVPM slide show.
7. These examples are taken from assorted WAVPM slide shows, Diana E.H. Russel's article, "On Pornography" (*Chrysalis*, No. 4, 1977), and assorted issues of WAVPM's official publication, *Newspage*.
8. A passage in WAVPM's November 1977 *Newspage* reads:"Q: But not all pornography is violent. Do you object to pornography in which there is no violence? A: Yes. Not all pornography is violent, but even the most banal pornography objectifies women's bodies. An essential ingredient of much rape and other forms of violence to women is the 'objectification' of the woman."
9. On-the-street interviews conducted by the *San Francisco Examiner* for its May 2, 1977, article, "A March to Protest Violent Porn," revealed that participants knew little about the realities of pornography: " 'I'm especially incensed at the abuse of children.' said Helen...She conceded that she hasn't actually seen any child porn, but has been reading about it recently. Susan also said she knows little about porn."

10. Dworkin, Andrea. "Pornography and Grief." Speech given before the "Take Back the Night" march in San Francisco, November 18, 1978. The march concluded the WAVPM conference, "Feminist Perspectives on Pornography." The speech was included in a WAVPM literature packet.

11. *ibid.*

12. *ibid.*

13. Brownmiller, Susan. *Against Our Will.* New York: Simon & Schuster, 1975, 395.

14. Bronfbrenner, Urie. *Two Worlds of Childhood: U.S. and U.S.S.R.*, Russel Sage Foundation, 1970, 109-115.

15. This traditional view of women's sexuality is demonstrated in the following quotations, taken from Diana E.H. Russell's article, "Pornography: A Feminist Perspective," which was included in the third edition of the WAVPM literature packet: "In spite of the *widely known fact* that few women buy pornography in any of its various forms, and that it is part of an almost exclusively male culture, the Commission (on Obscenity and Pornography) also felt able to conclude that: 'Women are virtually as interested in erotica as are men.' " "In the less sadistic (pornographic) films women are portrayed as turned on and sexually satisfied by doing anything and everything that men want or order them to do, and *for the most part what this involves is totally contrary to what we know about female sexuality,* that is, it is almost totally penis-oriented, often devoid of 'foreplay,' tenderness, or caring, to say nothing of love and romance." "In all the research on the effects of pornography, they never once try to ascertain...whether it encourages men *to impose upon their wives and lovers* what the women in the movies appear willing to do." [Emphasis added].

16. Brownmiller, *Against Our Will*, 394.

17. Reisman ended her talk by asking the audience to imagine what a world without pornography would be like. "Just think—for the first time in human history, truly loving relationships between the sexes would be possible," she crooned, and flashed a slide of a heterosexual couple walking hand in hand on a beach. I couldn't believe a room full of dykes was going to sit still for this. They didn't—they applauded!

18. WAVPM *Newspage.* February 1979, 4.

19. Walsh, Linda. "Women Protest Brutal Images in Pornography." *Zengers*, a publication of the Associated Students at San Francisco State University, May 4, 1977. In this article, San Francisco NOW president Shelley Fernandez is quoted as saying, "Violence has become a household word...I can see us in coalition with many women on this issue. I could see a Pro-Lifer (a Catholic who is anti-abortion) coming together with us on these issues."

20. They are also given to red-baiting. See Andrea Dworkin's essay, "Why So-Called Radical Men Love and Need Pornography," and Kathy Barry's book, *Female Sexual Slavery* (Englewood Cliffs, New Jersey: Prentice-Hall, Inc., 1979) pages 39 and 132-133.

See No Evil: An Update on the Feminist Antipornography Movement

1985

*When American feminists began to organize against pornography...
we were immediately greeted by a backlash of staggering proportions...Civil libertarians denounced us as censors, despite our rejection of government censorship and our decision to fight pornography
through education and private actions instead of legislation.*[1]

—Dorchen Leidholdt of New York's Women Against Pornography

Nevertheless, in 1985 two antiporn activists, Catharine MacKinnon and
Andrea Dworkin, published a piece of model legislation that would
define pornography as sex discrimination and outlaw it as a violation of
women's civil rights. A form of this law has been introduced in several
cities. Language has been lifted from it for a federal antiporn bill, and
proponents have testified at federal hearings on pornography. Still, Leidholdt is reduced to claiming that this type of legislation is "not a
ban...not censorship."[2]

Does this ordinance have anything to do with ending sex discrimination? Would its effects be limited to "violent pornography"? It is
important to know exactly how this bill is phrased; it is not enough to
rely on its supporters' promises.[3]

The legislation says pornography should be eliminated as a matter
of public policy because the "bigotry and contempt it promotes...dimin-
ish opportunities for equality of rights in employment, education, property, public accommodations and public services"; because pornographic materials "promote...rape, battery, child sexual abuse, and
prostitution and inhibit just enforcement of laws against these acts," and
"undermine women's equal exercise of rights to speech." Thus responsibility for discrimination is shifted to porn rather than the individuals and
institutions that actually commit such acts, and women's anger and
fear of violence are directed away from rapists and batterers and shifted
to dirty magazines. But discrimination and violence are caused by many
things; they will not stop just because sexist, sexually explicit material
becomes unavailable. This bill is no more than a comforting placebo.

The term *pornography* is generally thought to mean sexually explicit material that can be purchased only by adults. However, this bill's definition is a lot broader than that: "Pornography is the graphic sexually explicit subordination of women through pictures and/or words that also includes one or more of the following: (i) women are presented dehumanized as sexual objects, things, or commodities; or (ii) women are presented as sexual objects who enjoy pain or humiliation; or (iii) women are presented as sexual objects who experience sexual pleasure in being raped; or (iv) women are presented as sexual objects tied up or cut up or mutilated or bruised or physically hurt; or (v) women are presented in postures or positions of sexual submission, servility, or display; or (vi) women's body parts—including but not limited to vaginas, breasts, or buttocks—are exhibited such that women are reduced to those parts; or (vii) women are presented as whores by nature; or (viii) women are presented being penetrated by objects or animals; or (ix) women are presented in scenarios of degradation, injury, torture, shown as filthy or inferior, bleeding, bruised, or hurt in a context that makes these conditions sexual."

This definition is vague and subjective. Who knows what exactly is meant by *subordination, sexual objects, sexual submission,* or *degradation?* Feminists use these terms differently from fundamentalists, who believe that lesbianism, work outside the home, abortion, and extramarital sex degrade women. The bill proscribes numerous nonviolent images— simple nudity, penetration, being tied up. And it does not include sexist (but nonsexual) images of women that contribute to our being taken less seriously than men, such as situation comedies and commercials for laundry detergents.

Among the "unlawful practices" the bill forbids is "coercion into pornography." Defending oneself against such a charge would be practically impossible, since defenses do *not* include: "that the person actually consented to the use of the performance that is changed into pornography...that the person knew that the purpose of the acts or events in question was to make pornography...that the person showed no resistance or appeared to cooperate actively in the...events that produced the pornography...that the person signed a contract, or made statements affirming a willingness to cooperate in the production of pornography...that no physical force, threats, or weapons were used in the making of the pornography; or...that the person was paid or otherwise compensated."

This provision would be to women what age-of-consent laws are to minors—a presumption that sexual activity (especially for money) is so harmful that whether or not we want to do it (or have any other way to make a living) is irrelevant. It threatens years of feminist struggle to win the right of adult women to enter into contracts.

Another new unlawful act is called "trafficking in pornography": "It shall be sex discrimination to produce, sell, exhibit, or distribute pornography, including through private clubs." This would leave vulnerable to legal charges groups of sexual minorities who publish educational or erotic material. Libraries "in which pornography is available for study" are exempt, as long as they do not have "special display presentations" of pornography. Since this is not defined, "there is, in reality, no exemption whatsoever," according to a brief submitted in a lawsuit filed against the legislation's adoption in Indiana.[4]

The bill makes it illegal to "force pornography on a person...in any place of employment, education, home, or public place." "Force" is not defined. Will it become a crime to have a sexually explicit magazine on your desk, where a fellow worker might see it? What if your roommate doesn't like your porn collection? What if the lady sitting next to you on the bus doesn't like what you are reading? Can they accuse you of "forcing" pornography on them?

The legislation also makes actionable assault "that is directly caused by specific pornography," but the criteria for proving causation are not defined. Therefore, this offense is unprosecutable and only serves to reinforce a conflation of pornography and violence. Our real problem is persuading police and the courts to enforce existing laws against rape and battery when children, women, gay people, and people of color need protection.

"Any woman who has a claim hereunder as a woman acting against the subordination of women" can enforce this ordinance either by filing a complaint with a local Civil Rights Commission or a suit in civil court. No criminal charges are involved. The bill's claim that pornography "differentially harms women" is watered down by inclusion of the clause, "Any man, child, or transsexual who alleges injury by pornography in the way women are injured by it also has a claim."

This bill first surfaced in the fall of 1983. Minneapolis was trying to devise a new zoning law to regulate adult bookstores and massage parlors. (Previous attempts had been struck down by the courts.) MacKinnon, a professor of constitutional law at the University of Minnesota, and Dworkin, a visiting professor, were invited to testify. They argued against the proposed zoning law, saying it condoned the existence of pornography, and urged the city to ban porn as a form of sex discrimination.[5] The City of Minneapolis paid them $70 an hour to write such a law and organize testimony for hearings. (Their assistants, incidentally, were paid $3.50 an hour, which is enough to make any woman look for a job in the sex industry.)[6]

The hearings were conducted by MacKinnon, Dworkin, and City Council member Charlee Hoyt, a sponsor of the legislation. Dworkin and MacKinnon testified, along with Linda (Lovelace) Marchiano (who alleges she was forced as a "sexual slave" to make the movie, *Deep Throat)*; sociologist, professor, and antiporn activist Pauline Bart; counselors to sex offenders and abused children who testified that pornography is usually involved in child abuse; rape victims and battered women who felt that their assailants were influenced by pornography; and experimental psychologist Edward Donnerstein whose studies of the effects of violent and/or sexually explicit material on the attitudes of college students toward rape are widely quoted by antiporn activists.

In an article reporting on these proceedings, David Rubinstein of *In These Times* wrote, "Opponents [of the legislation] were cut short, put at the end of the list and interrupted...it all happened before a crowd of partisans."[7] Yet this body of doctored testimony has frequently been referred to as "evidence" that pornography causes sex discrimination and violence against women. Of opponents to her bill who called themselves feminists (including two female city council members, one of whom testified about her experience as a rape victim), MacKinnon later said, "Someone should explain to me how one can be a feminist and be pro-pornography...yes, they're mutually exclusive."[8] Apparently, MacKinnon has sympathy for rape victims only if they subscribe to her theories about why rape exists.

The council passed the new law on December 30, 1983, by a seven to six vote. But it was vetoed by Mayor Don Fraser, who felt uneasy about its definition of porn, "so broad as to make it impossible for a bookseller, movie theater operator or museum director to adjust his or her conduct in order to keep from running afoul of its proscriptions."[9] The council passed another, similar version, which Fraser also vetoed on July 13, 1984. However, with this veto he made a speech that assailed "the scourge of pornography that is dangerous to women." (Three days earlier, a supporter of the ordinance had doused herself with gasoline, set herself afire in an adult bookstore, and was hospitalized with burns over 65 percent of her body)[10] He also signed a revision of the city's existing obscenity ordinance to include material depicting bondage, S/M scenes, and sexually violent material, and to require sealed, opaque covers on sex magazines. And he signed a resolution stating he would reverse his veto if a similar ordinance in Indianapolis was upheld by a federal district court.[11] This was apparently not strong enough for antiporn demonstrators, who reportedly hanged Fraser in effigy and vandalized porn shops.[12]

Although other right-wing forces kept a low profile during hearings on the ordinance, anti-abortion demonstrators joined antiporn feminists during the August 27, 1984, "Take Back the Night" march.[13]

Right-wing involvement was more pronounced in the next city where this ordinance was introduced—Indianapolis. Mayor William H. Hudnut III, a Republican who has refused to meet with local gay leaders, heard about this new approach to combat smut and persuaded city-county Council member Beulah Coughenour (an anti-ERA activist) to look into it. Coughenour hired MacKinnon as a consultant to the city, and she got Reverend Greg Dixon, a former Moral Majority official, to lobby city council members to bury their doubts about the expense of possible litigation and pass the bill. (Coughenour's children go to school at Dixon's Baptist Temple.) Dixon put his Coalition for a Clean Community to work on it. Nearly three hundred of his supporters appeared at the April 23, 1984, final vote on the bill. It passed, twenty-four to five (with every Republican on the council voting for it and every Democrat, including black council members, voting no) and was signed into law by the mayor on May 1, 1985. A coalition of bookstores, video retailers, press trade associations, and a cable television station filed a challenge the same day.[14]

On November 19, 1984, Judge Sarah Evans Barker of the United States District Court, Southern District of Indiana, found the ordinance to be unconstitutional on the grounds that it would restrict speech protected by the First Amendment, was overbroad and vague, and constituted prior restraint. It would be hard to imagine a more stinging rebuttal than Judge Barker's decision. The City of Indianapolis has doggedly appealed it to the United States Circuit Court of Appeals, Seventh Circuit. Estimated cost? $250,000.[15]

Even Dworkin had to acknowledge the support that the Indianapolis law had received from right-wing women. But she claimed that this alliance was a rare opportunity for women of different political beliefs to work together, united by a common fear of male violence.[16] Such alliances look very different to right-wing men like state Representative Coy C. Privette, director of the Christian Action League of North Carolina, "an anti-liquor and anti-pornography group." Privette smacked his lips over the chances for the religious right's agenda in the state legislature, "noting that liberal feminist organizations were also lobbying for such measures. 'When you've got this kind of coalition, that is a politician's dream,' he said."[17]

The "civil rights" approach to fighting porn was completely coopted by the right on August 23, 1984, when Republican Michael D'Andre (who opposes the ERA, gay rights, and abortion) proposed a similar bill for Suffolk County, New York. He made a couple of major changes: Complaints would not be filed with an antidiscrimination commission but would go directly to court. To be proscribed, materials had to meet three, rather than just one, of a list of "pornographic" criteria. And the "legislative intent" section of the law stated that pornography causes "sodomy" and "destruction of the family unit," as well as rape, child abuse, and other conditions "inimical to the public good."

Frances Patai, a WAP spokesperson, and other WAPettes appeared at September 25 hearings to congratulate D'Andre and the legislature for this effort. Patai criticized the bill for not being strong enough (specifically for requiring too many criteria before material could be labeled pornographic) but did not mention its antigay language.[18] Other testimony was primarily from fundamentalists, who said things like, "God does not promote, nor does he condone deviant sex behavior," and, "True, people want to live decadent and perverted lives, and they will do so. But you members of the legislature don't have to legitimate their silly escapades by allowing pornography to be sold in Suffolk County. Sodom and Gomorra were judged when the stench of their immorality became too much for God. When you cast your vote, ask yourself how God would have you vote."[19] When hearings resumed on October 9, several feminists, including members of the newly formed Feminist Anti-Censorship Taskforce (FACT), rose to criticize the bill. A FACT member told me that D'Andre had contacted her prior to her testimony and asked her if she was a lesbian.

In part because of Judge Barker's ruling, the bill was defeated on December 26 by a vote of nine to eight. However, D'Andre's legislative aide said the bill would be reintroduced if it fared better with higher courts. Just before the vote, WAP withdrew its support for D'Andre's *Local Law to Limit Violence Against Women*. It contended that the bill was in fact an antiobscenity measure rather than *civil rights* legislation, but WAP still did not condemn the bill's homophobic language.[20] An undaunted D'Andre jauntily told *The New York Times*, "I'm willing to think for the majority. The majority rules. I don't want to tell anybody what to do as long as they live by the Ten Commandments. I'm telling people what they can print only if it's immoral, only if it's filth, only if it's dehumanizing."[21] What a friend of feminism!

Dworkin and MacKinnon's model law also flunked out in Madison, Wisconsin, and Los Angeles. Thus far its most noticeable effect has been to cost city governments a lot of money, get Dworkin, MacKinnon, and assorted politicians a lot of publicity, and embarrass its authors in the courts.

Why should we worry about a law that is so poorly written, so blatantly unconstitutional, a law that would only affect a particular city or county even if it did survive judicial review?

We should worry because this model porn bill creates moral panic wherever it goes. In its wake, it becomes easier to pass more traditional obscenity laws. It takes time and energy away from other crucial issues and makes it more difficult for us to combat homophobia.

During 1984 gay men and lesbians in Minneapolis experienced a much more concrete threat to their civil rights than pornography. The city's Gay and Lesbian Rights Ordinance was endangered by a court ruling that implied the city did not have the right to protect groups or classes of people not protected under state law.[22] Where was WAP?

While MacKinnon was fighting X-rated videocassettes in Indianapolis, the police were downtown in the gay district, videotaping whoever came through. I'm sure MacKinnon never heard about it; the police had only been doing this for *three years*, claiming they were fighting juvenile prostitution. After unprecedented numbers of complaints of police brutality were filed, hundreds of protesters gathered week after week until the police chief was ordered to meet with gays.[23] He is stalling on requests for education for new police recruits. Undercover officers are still arresting men in adult bookstores and parks.[24]

In Suffolk County, New York, several arrests of members of the North American Man/Boy Love Association (NAMBLA) were made on October 1, after introduction of D'Andre's bill. A bill has been introduced that would require opaque covers on books and magazines sold to adults only. The Suffolk County legislature has also approved a $100,000 grant to set up a chapter of Teen-Aid, Inc., a group that encourages teenagers to avoid premarital sex and opposes birth control and abortion.[25]

In Los Angeles two "weakened anti-porn proposals" were enacted in the wake of Dworkin and MacKinnon, and await state funding to put them into effect.[26] Meanwhile, frustrated by the community's lax obscenity standards, the Los Angeles Police Department has taken to busting actors and actresses who appear in adult flicks and charging them with prostitution. Producers are charged with pandering.[27]

The Dworkin-MacKinnon bill has not been restricted to the city and county levels. There are several antiporn bills pending in the California state legislature, and according to the Bay Area chapter of FACT, some of them are clearly influenced by the civil-rights strategy. Unfortunately, the strategy has drawn the attention of the Reagan Administration.

November 1984 hearings of the Senate Judiciary Subcommittee on Juvenile Justice, chaired by Republican Senator Arlen Specter of Pennsylvania, produced legislation that creates a new category of speech—child pornography—which will not be protected by the First Amendment even if it is not obscene.[28] Antiporn advocates (including Judy Goldsmith, national president of NOW, which has endorsed these ordinances) used these hearings to showcase their demand that women be given similar protection.[29] None of these worthies objected to Specter's making use of Giovanni's Room—a gay bookstore that got itself into hot water by carrying pedophile literature—as grist for his mill.

On May 21, when President Reagan signed Specter's *Child Protection Act of 1984* into law, he mandated creation of a national commission on pornography. It will run for one year and cost taxpayers approximately $500,000. Henry Hudson, commonwealth's attorney for Arlington County, Virginia, will chair it.[30] Attorney General Edwin Meese III, who appointed many of the members of the Commission, claims that "reexamination of the issue of pornography is long overdue. Its impact upon society was last assessed fully 15 years ago" (by the 1970 Commission on Obscenity and Pornography, which concluded that sexual materials do not have a harmful effect on adults or adolescents). "Since then, the content of pornography has radically changed, with more and more emphasis upon extreme violence...With the advent of cable TV and video recorders, pornography now is available at home to anyone—regardless of age—at the touch of the button...The formation of this commission reflects the concern a healthy society must have regarding the ways in which its people publicly entertain themselves." Meese calls his Commission "a balanced group," and doesn't "know any of them that have a particular opinion" about pornography.[31]

Oh, yeah? Three of the eleven members have backgrounds in law enforcement, and there are no representatives from the media the creative arts, or the civil liberties community (unless you count Ellen Levine, editor-in-chief of *Woman's Day*). In 1983 Hudson urged Reagan to begin a "Clean Up America" campaign against pornography. He is also well known for claiming that Arlington is one of the few counties near Washington that "does not have an adult book store or massage parlor" because his "strong law enforcement and prosecution" had prevented sex-related businesses from opening.[32]

The Commission held its first hearings in Washington, D.C., on June 19 and 20, 1985. Much of the rhetoric and content appeared to be derived from the feminist antiporn movement. Testimony was heard from anonymous "victims of pornography," who spoke from behind a screen. These victims were supplied by WAP and by Straight, Inc., a drug treatment program. A vice-squad detective from Fairfax County had a slide show which took the Commission on a "tour" of an adult bookstore with individual "peep show" booths. His show emphasized gay male pornography (especially magazines depicting fisting) and cruising outside the booths. Surgeon General C. Everett Koop told the members that pornography is a "clear and present danger" to American public health, and that it "clearly and viciously degrades women." When Isabelle Pinzler, director of the American Civil Liberties Union's Women's Rights Project, testified, she was asked if her project was funded by the Playboy Foundation, and if so, what strings were attached.[33] FBI agent Kenneth Lanning gave a forty-minute slide show which claimed to trace "the evolution of pornography." Lanning distorted the content of pornography by showing material which cannot be found in an adult bookstore (including pictures of mutilated bodies and snapshots confiscated from sex offenders).[34] A similar tactic is used in every slide show made by feminist antiporn groups. Right-wing Senator Jeremiah Denton said, "In my belief, pornography destroys liberty. So it is a governmental matter and we shouldn't be bashful about addressing it as such."[35] Assistant Attorney General Lois Herrington said, "Pornography has many facets. It can be the record of a crime being committed against children. It can be the depiction of women as sexual objects to be used, abused and tossed aside. It can be an anesthetic, desensitizing people to violence and sexual deviance in society."[36] These "many facets" apparently don't include the many times that pornography is used for sex education, to comfort a lonely person, to rekindle a couple's sex life, or simply to entertain a horny adult who wants to enrich a masturbation session.

New York FACT's written request to testify at these hearings was never answered. The closest thing to opposition (other than the ACLU) came from Feminists Against Pornography (FAP), a Washington, D.C., group that supports the civil-rights approach to fighting pornography. However, FAP expressed concern "about the political agenda that may have prompted the formation of the Commission...and the possibility that its work may be used...to justify repressive measures." FAP also stated, "The proliferation of sexually explicit material *per se* is *not* the problem." The group condemned censorship and concluded, "The only solution to the problem of pornography is full equality for women: equal pay, equal education, equal political power, and equal social standing in a non-sexist society."[37] FAP was cut off after five minutes.

What recommendations will this commission make? Note how concerns about "sexual deviance" are being wed to feminist language about violence. Will the commission produce a bill with a feminist gloss that is worded (unlike MacKinnon and Dworkin's version) so that it *will* pass judicial review? S/M porn is especially vulnerable, but more mainstream gay and lesbian materials are probably threatened as well. Ironically, these new approaches to censorship come at a time when women are beginning to produce sexually explicit magazines and videos specifically for a female audience. Can this fledgling industry survive such hostility?

We have a hint about the use the feds will make of WAP's bill in Specter's *Pornography Victims Protection Act of 1985*, which incorporates MacKinnon and Dworkin's list of nondefenses to "coercion into pornography." This bill would make it impossible for sex workers to plead self-incrimination if they were asked to testify against their employers. It makes producers of sexually explicit material vulnerable to unreasonable lawsuits, even if they treat their employees well. It is also unclear whether any pornography actually has to be produced, or if intent alone is enough to win a conviction.[38]

Luckily, the reaction to the newest antiporn crusade has not been completely positive. WAP itself has split, and former members like Florence Rush are giving speeches explaining that they still hate pornography, but they also hate this ordinance. WAP has even lost some of its knee-jerk support from the feminist press. *Ms.* magazine gave the ordinance mixed reviews.[39] Antiporn stalwart Alice Henry of *off our backs* has published a tart critique of Donnerstein's research.[40] (MacKinnon's response to this criticism was that "whatever you call it, I suspect it isn't feminism.")[41] New York FACT managed to get people like Betty Friedan, Phyllis Lyon and Del Martin, Kate Millett, and Adrienne Rich to sign their *amicus* brief opposing the Indianapolis ordinance. (MacKinnon calls this brief "a crime against women.")[42] U.S. Prostitutes Collective has denounced the ordinance, saying it is racist and "will increase the violence, coercion and repression of women who will be first affected by the ordinance—sex industry workers."[43]

I think it's time we all asked ourselves what antiporn leaders are really after. If you just listen to Andrea Dworkin long enough, her intentions become quite clear: "If personal, private sexual practice involves the use of pornography,...the question then is, do they have a right to that product no matter what...? No, you don't."[44]

Dworkin and her ilk hate pornography so much that they are prepared to run roughshod over our right to privacy and the First Amendment. These constitutional rights are fragile and incomplete, but we can't afford to toss away the little bit of protection that we have from government intrusion and control. Don't be deceived by claims that the WAP law is good for women's rights or anybody else's rights. It's just a new ploy to make it possible for the state to censor free expression under the guise of "protecting" a vulnerable class. While trumpeting against the evils of S/M and pornography, Dworkin is trying to distract us while she tamps a gag into our mouths.

Notes

1. Leidholdt, Dorchen. "Lesbian S/M: Sexual Radicalism or Reaction." *New Women's Times*, July/August 1982, 17.
2. Herlihy, Sean. "Porn Debate Continues: Dorchen vs. Civil Liberties Union." *Gay Community News*, May 24, 1985, 6, 10. During this debate with Natasha Lisman, president of the Massahusetts Civil Liberties Union, Leidholdt also argued that the sex education manual, *Show Me!*, is child pornography, and that feminist artist Judy Chicago's show, *The Dinner Party*, might qualify as porn under the proposed law.
3. Dworkin, Andrea and Catharine MacKinnon. "Model Civil Rights Anti-Pornography Law." *WAP Newsreport*, Vol. vii, No. 1, 4-5. (All subsequent quotations from the legislation taken from this document.) This model law differs slightly from versions proposed in various cities. For example the Indianapolis bill deletes the phrase, "women are presented as whores by nature."
4. Brief for *Amici Curiae* American Library Association, Indiana Library Association, and Indiana Library Trustee Association, *ABA et al v. William B. Hudnut III et al*, in the United States Court of Appeals for the Seventh Circuit, 9.
5. Dworkin, Andrea. from her testimony before the City of Minneapolis Zoning Commission, October 18, 1983, 1. "I think you should say that what this statute does is to permit pornography...you are allowing hate literature directed at women...you are allowing the celebration of rape, the promotion of rape, the advocacy of rape...you are going to permit the exploitation of live women, the sadomasochistic use of live women, the binding and torture of real women and then have the depictions...sold in this city."
6. "Agreement for Services as Consultants to the Minneapolis City Council," January 18, 1983.
7. Rubenstein, David. "Pornography Law Splits Minneapolis." *In These Times*, January 18-24, 1984, 5-6.
8. Page, Sharon. "Radical Feminists v. Civil Libertarians: Minneapolis Mayor Vetoes Anti-Porn Law." *Gay Community News*, January 14, 1984, 1, 6.

9. *op cit.*, 1.

10. "Anti-Porn Ordinance Vetoed Again." *Gay Community News*, July 28, 1984, 2.

11. "Mayor Vetoes One Out of Three Anti-Porn Laws." *New York Native*, August 13-26, 1984, 7-8.

12. Page, Sharon. "Limitations of a Mistaken Strategy: City Council Scuttles Anti-Porn Amendment." *Gay Community News*, February 4, 1984, 3.

13. "Take Back the What?" *Gay Community News*, September 8, 1984, 3.

14. Duggan, Lisa. "Censorship in the Name of Feminism." *Village Voice*, October 16, 1984, 14-17, 42.

15. Kearney, Robert P. "Porn and Civil Rights: II." *Playboy*, July 1985, 56.

16. Eckhaus, Phyllis. "Censorship or Civil Rights? Feminists Split Over Indy Porn Law." New York *Womanews*, January 1984, 7.

17. Raleigh, North Carolina *News and Observer*, January 28, 1985.

18. "Minneapolis-Style Bill: Anti-Porn Fever Strikes Long Island." *Gay Community News*, October 13, 1984, 1.

19. "Civil Rights, or Morality Crusade?" Undated press release of the Feminist Anti-Censorship Task Force.

20. "Porn Panic Panned: Anti-Porn Bill Dies; Indianapolis Law Cited." *Gay Community News*, January 19, 1985, 1-2.

21. "News Notes." *Gay Community News*, November 24, 1984, 2.

22. Halfhill, Robert. "Minneapolis Appeals Court Upholds Ruling Threatening Minneapolis Gay Rights Ordinance." *New York Native*, January 14-27, 1985, 12.

23. Jackson, James. "Fascist Surveillance: Indianapolis Gay Protests Bring Concessions." *Gay Community News*, September 15, 1984, 1, 7.

24. Freiberg, Peter. "Gays and Police: Old Problems, New Hope." *The Advocate*, June 11, 1985, 10-11, 19.

25. Chew, Sally. "Anti-Porn Legislation Defeated." *New York Native*, January 14-27, 1985, 112.

26. Woodyard, Chris. "Porn Ordinance Rebuffed Again." *Los Angeles Herald*, June 5, 1985.

27. Welkos, Robert. "Hard-Core Sex Films—Does Casting Constitute Pandering?" *Los Angeles Times*, May 20, 1985.

28. "Child Pornography Law Enacted." *The New York Times*, May 22, 1984, A20. Also, the age of those covered was raised from sixteen to eighteen; minimum fine for a first offense was raised from $10,000 to $100,000; and it deletes an earlier law's provision that restricted prosecution to cases involving commercially sold literature. Reproduction of such material, in addition to distribution, is now a crime.

29. "Feminists Fighting Pornography." *The Backlash Times*, Winter 1984, 9. On page five, this issue features a photo from an S/M magazine, showing a man standing next to a woman in bondage, suspended upside down. The caption

reads, "Notice the gun in his hand." The "gun" turned out to be the shadow of a ping-pong paddle.

Leidholdt, Dorchen. "Senate Hearings Prompt Pornography Victims Act." *WAP Newsreport*, Vol. vii, No. 1, 1, 18. In this story, Leidholdt refers to Specter as "a liberal Republican" and proudly describes her own testimony about the dangers of material that uses models who only *appear* to be under eighteen.

30. "Unit on Pornography to Begin Hearings." *Publishers Weekly*, June 12, 1985.

31. U.S. Justice Department press release, July 19, 1985, 1-2.

32. Sniffen, Michael J. "Panel Is Named to Study Effects of Pornography." *The Philadelphia Inquirer*, May 21, 1985, 3A.

Shenon, Philip. "Meese Names Panel to Study How to Control Pornography." *The New York Times*, May 21, 1985, A21.

33. Robinson, Bob. "Pornography Called a 'Clear Danger.' " *The Washington Times*, June 21, 1985, 5A.

34. "Pornography Hearings Open." *The Washington Post*, June 20, 1985, A14.

35. Robinson, Bob. "Court Limits Obscenity Law." *The Washington Times*, June 20, 1985, 1A.

36. "U.S. Opens Inquiry into Pornography." *The Philadelphia Inquirer*, June 20, 1985, 5A.

37. Langelan, Martha J. and Deborah M. Chalfie. "Prepared Statement of D.C. Feminists Against Pornography before the Attorney General's Commission on Pornography," June 20, 1985.

38. U.S. Senate. *Pornography Victims Protection Act of 1985*, 99th Cong., 1st sess. S. 1187, presented by Senator Arlen Specter, Chairman of the Senate Judiciary Committee's Subcommittee on Juvenile Justice, May 22, 1985.

39. Blakely, Mary Kay. "Is One Woman's Sexuality Another Woman's Pornography? The Question Behind a Major Legal Battle." *Ms.*, April 1985, 37-47.

40. Henry, Alice. "Porn Is Subordination?" *off our backs*, November 1984, 20, 24.

41. MacKinnon, Catharine. "Pornography, the Law, the Laboratory..." *off our backs*, February 1985, 25.

42. Wallsgrove, Ruth. "Feminist Anti-Censorship Taskforce: The Case Against Indianapolis." *off our backs*, June 1985, 13.

43. Poggi, Stephanie. "U.S. Prostitutes Collective Organizing Against L.A. Anti-Porn Ordinance." *Gay Community News*, June 22, 1985, 2.

44. Blakely, "Is One Woman's Sexuality Another Woman's Pornography?" 38.

Feminism, Pedophilia, and Children's Rights

1992

In 1980 I published a two-part article in *The Advocate*, critiquing American age-of-consent laws. While extremely controversial, the articles did hit print and spur discussion about the sexuality of young people, intimate relationships between men and boys, and the dangerous implications of banning all erotic images of minors. Eleven years later, I am writing this piece. It will be translated into Dutch and published abroad in a special issue of *Paidika* on women and pedophilia. I support *Paidika* and enjoy working with the editors of this special issue. I also know I probably could not get anything on this topic published today in the American gay and lesbian press.

Doc and Fluff, my recent science-fiction novel, has been banned by some women's bookstores because it supposedly depicts a cross-generational lesbian relationship, and I've been attacked as "an advocate of child molestation" in the feminist press. This happened despite the fact that I made it clear that the younger character, Fluff, had reached the legal age of consent. She initiates all the sexual activity. If I had made Fluff eleven or even sixteen, instead of eighteen, the book probably would not have been published at all.

The American government's campaign against the sexual rights of young people has been so successful that most gay men, lesbians, and feminists are convinced that the movement to repeal age-of-consent laws was nothing more than an attempt to guarantee rapacious adults the right to vulnerable child victims. The North American Man/Boy Love Association (NAMBLA) has been banned from so many annual gay pride marches that people are astonished when the organization does appear.

The adult gay community here has cut off its next generation. We are afraid to reach out to young men and women who are coming out. A teenager who has suffered abuse from parents, peers, and teachers for being homosexual often finds that adult gay men and lesbians will not offer her or him sanctuary from homophobia. We do not because we dare not. We have been terrorized and made ashamed.

And yet I know very few lesbians, and even fewer gay men, who waited until they were eighteen to come out. Most of us were aware well before puberty that we wanted to be close to or sexual with members of our own sex. I've heard countless stories from women about their attempts to seduce their high school gym teachers or camp counselors. Not all of these attempts were unsuccessful. Our real-life experiences do not jibe with our politics on this issue. In this case, at least, the personal does not seem to be political.

It's impossible to sum up thirty years of American politics in a short article. But a sketchy chronicle of this background is important for anyone who wants to understand the suspicion and hatred that most American gay-rights activists and lesbian-feminists display toward pedophilia.

During the '60s, the military draft which sent young men to war in Vietnam proved to be the impetus for the formation of several popular radical movements. Because the draft was age-linked, the campaign against it used age as a rallying point, protesting the government's "sending young men to fight an old men's war." Movements for the liberation of blacks, women, and homosexuals emerged. And there was a nascent movement for the liberation of young people. High school students fought for the right to publish underground newspapers, wear their hair long, and join in antiwar protests by wearing armbands and other political symbols to school. They contested searches and seizure of their property conducted by school officials.

In the early days of the women's movement, feminists criticized all the institutions of male-dominated society. The traditional family was under siege. It was common to talk about how young women were oppressed by the public schools and received an inferior, feminized education. There was agitation for reproductive rights for all women, including teenagers.

The antiwar movement collapsed when the draft was repealed, and the war in Vietnam ended. Few of the movement's members had developed a comprehensive or sophisticated critique of the American state. The feminist movement was deflated by the Supreme Court decision *Roe v. Wade*, which granted American women the right to abortion in 1973. Ironically, because of this major victory, American feminism lost its intense, radical focus. It was also divided by bitter struggles over the presence of lesbians in the women's movement and their eventual departure from it. Mainstream feminism became bogged down in a doomed campaign to pass the Equal Rights Amendment. Litigation against sex discrimination in the areas of employment and education made significant gains for women, but it was difficult to use this issue as a rallying point for a mass movement.

The Antiporn Movement

Feminism did not regain its fervor until the antiporn movement emerged in the late '70s. This campaign almost immediately won a large number of adherents. Antiporn activists were successful in attracting both lesbian and heterosexual feminists. All women could unite against misogynist violence. Because the antiporn movement quashed discussion of private sexual practices that might conflict with its critique of sexually diverse imagery, it became much easier for women with differing sexual orientations to work together. Their leaders were excellent public speakers who allowed followers to be titillated by pornography without giving up their righteous indignation about it.

This social-purity movement promised to do away with discrimination and violence against women by simply eliminating porn. It also made street action and protests viable once more, instead of focusing on boring legal cases. Closing adult bookstores is much easier than changing the power relations between the sexes. And it allowed women to take action within the private sphere, politicizing something we were already accustomed to doing—regulating other people's sexual conduct.

The feminist antiporn movement routinely trashed its feminist critics by attacking them as perverts and advocates of rape, battery, and child abuse. Members of the antiporn movement have been so successful that most people—including the press—today assume that they represent the only feminist position on issues of sexuality, censorship, pornography, violence against women, and the sex industry.

The feminist antiporn movement mirrored a growing conservatism in American society about all sexual matters. As economic conditions here got worse, people began to look toward "traditional values" to provide a feeling of security and safety. It became much harder for women to survive economically outside the nuclear family or to criticize it. Plenty of evidence exists to show that the traditional family is not a particularly nice place to grow up. Sexual abuse is a common experience for girls (and not so uncommon for boys) in the family. Federal law-enforcement figures indicate that five children per day (mostly infants and young children) are murdered by their parents in the United States. Yet the nostalgia for this ideal, safe, loving, nurturing, patriarchal family persists.

The panic over child pornography and pedophilia that has racked American society since the '70s is an inseparable part of our society's denial of the shortcomings and failures of the family. Moral crusades have also been used to attack both feminism and gay rights, and neither of these progressive movements has been very successful at defending itself against such attacks or at presenting a complete analysis of them.

Child Pornography

Child pornography has been a special category in American law since 1977. This was the year that Anita Bryant began her campaign against gay rights legislation in Dade County, Florida, and Congressional hearings were held on the sexual exploitation of children. The most flamboyant agitators against kiddy porn included Judianne Densen-Gerber, manager of a chain of drug rehabilitation centers, and Los Angeles cop Lloyd Martin, who had received city funding to head the Sexually Exploited Child Unit. Since the hearings concluded, Densen-Gerber's Odyssey House drug-rehabilitation centers were the subject of a two-year investigation conducted by then New York State Attorney General Robert Abrams. The investigation found that federal, state, and city grants had been diverted to pay for her private expenses. Densen-Gerber had to agree to repay the money, and Odyssey House was placed on probation to avoid criminal charges. Lloyd Martin was eventually transferred out of the Sexually Exploited Children Unit to a less visible and less powerful position. Activists speculated that this transfer was the result of remarks Martin had made alleging that the Big Brother program and the Boy Scouts of America did not screen their volunteers carefully enough and were full of pedophiles. After this transfer was announced, Martin went on "psychiatric sick leave" and finally resigned from the police department.

Witnesses' claims that the child-porn industry grossed billions of dollars and involved the abuse of millions of children were never substantiated. In fact, even in its heyday, child porn was not a popular genre of sexually explicit material. One expert has estimated that no more than five thousand to ten thousand copies of each magazine were sold worldwide.

In 1978 a federal law took effect that made it a felony to photograph anyone under the age of sixteen in the nude, engaged in sexual activity with another person, or masturbating. By that time, most distributors and bookstores had stopped handling the controversial material. The only child pornography left was produced by amateurs, usually for private use. Since 1978 the law has been amended to make penalties more severe, and the definition of a minor now includes any person under the age of eighteen. Subsequent court decisions have determined that material depicting minors does not have to meet the same strict criteria that

adult material has to meet to be defined as obscene and therefore proscribed. If a boy-lover has a nude photograph of his seventeen-year-old
boyfriend in his wallet, that photograph—even though it is not commercially distributed and does not depict sex—is child pornography. It is
illegal to transport it across state lines, and in many states it is even illegal to possess it.

In 1990 the Supreme Court upheld an Ohio state law which crimi-
nalized the possession and viewing of child pornography. Many other
states then passed similar legislation. In the U.S. it is illegal to be in the
business of producing or distributing obscene matter, but it is not illegal
for a private citizen to possess obscene material to view in her or his own
home—unless it depicts minors.

Despite the fact that child pornography is no longer commercially
available, law-enforcement efforts against it have escalated. Special task
forces to combat it have been set up by U.S. Customs, the FBI, the Justice
Department, and state and local police. In order to justify their swollen
budgets and manpower rosters, the cops have created a series of expensive entrapment schemes. Ironically, the only kiddy porn now produced
in the U.S. is paid for by taxpayers' dollars and hawked by the guardians
of our legal system.

Between 1978 and 1984, only sixty-seven defendants were indicted
for federal child-porn crimes. But since May 1984, about six hundred
defendants have been indicted as a result of sting operations conducted
by U.S. government agencies.

This is how it works: The Post Office targets people who are unlucky
enough to have landed on mailing lists compiled by U.S. Customs. These
lists come from many sources. When adult-porn businesses are raided,
the authorities also confiscate their mailing lists, even if their customers
have committed no crimes. The Post Office and Customs keep track of
people who order sexually explicit material through the mail. Police
have even confiscated the membership list of a gay computer bulletin
board that was shut down because its operator was accused of violating
age-of-consent laws. The Post Office then conducts direct-mail campaigns soliciting orders for child porn. Some of the government
brochures are vaguely worded and do not make it clear that the customer is ordering contraband. Law enforcement officials sometimes
become pen pals, pretending to be pedophiles or sexually active children, and solicit their correspondents to send or receive child porn
through the mail. If targeted individuals seize the bait, they are
arrested, and the odds are overwhelmingly in favor of conviction even
if they have never ordered this type of material before.

One such operation, Project Looking Glass, conducted in 1986, involved more than two hundred U.S. Customs inspectors and state and local cops. The government paid millions of dollars to obtain a mere one hundred indictments.

Strict child-porn laws have created a chilling effect upon any discussion of child sexuality. After the passage of the 1978 law criminalizing nude photographs of minors, the excellent sex education book, *Show Me!*, was withdrawn by its publisher, St. Martin's Press. Art photographers like Robert Mapplethorpe and Jock Sturges who display nonerotic, nude portraits of children have been threatened with prosecution. Since film developers are required to notify police any time they see negatives that feature nude minors, parents have been charged with and even convicted of child-porn offenses for taking nude pictures of their own children at play or in the bathtub. There have been so many wrongful accusations regarding pornography and sexual and physical child abuse that wrongfully accused child care workers and parents formed Victims of Child Abuse Laws (VOCAL).

The government has also tried to use child-porn laws against adult material. American magazines that publish nude photographs are required to keep files on their models, showing proof of each model's age and legal name. These files have to be kept available for inspection by law-enforcement personnel.

When most people think of child pornography, they imagine full-color movies and magazines that show adults raping prepubescent children. In fact, most of the material consisted of black and white photo magazines. The bulk of the imagery was of nude children or teens. A minority of images showed young people being sexual with each other, and a very tiny proportion of it showed adults engaged in sexual conduct with minors. Since the pictures were so hard to obtain, they were usually pirated by rival magazines and reprinted.

It's certainly true that some of the young people who appeared in this material were coerced into modeling and were damaged by that experience. But it would be a mistake to characterize all child porn as "a record of child abuse." Sometimes it was a record of children's exhibitionism and free erotic play with one another. Sometimes it was a record of adolescent vanity, pride, and budding sexuality. Sometimes it preserved a moment of exceptional trust and pleasure between partners whose ages would normally have kept them apart.

To simply speak this truth is very dangerous today. But we do not serve ourselves—or children—very well when we interpret all sexual experiences in the most negative terms possible. Sex is not simply a matter of violence or danger. And issues of consent, autonomy, and power are never simple to sort out, especially in the realm of the senses. Adult panic or disgust about young people's seeking pleasure for themselves is responsible for much of the trauma that minors experience when they are caught behaving "inappropriately" for their ages, even in a consensual context.

Missing Children

The campaign against child pornography was fueled by related moral hysteria over missing children. During the early '80s, the American media was full of melodramatic accounts of the "millions" of children who were kidnapped and then sexually abused by strangers. A representative article appeared in the women's magazine *Family Circle* in 1986, headlined, "Every Mother's Fear: Abduction," with the subhead, "An estimated 1.8 million children will be reported missing this year. What can you do to protect your child?" Photos of missing children who were supposedly in grave danger appeared everywhere—on grocery bags, milk cartons, billboards, and flyers. Public fear about missing children grew to such a pitch that in 1984 the Justice Department awarded a $3.3 million grant to set up the National Center for Missing and Exploited Children.

It took a while for the facts to emerge, still longer for the panic to fade. An alarming 1983 U.S. Department of Health and Human Services statistic that there were 1.5 million missing children reported each year was widely quoted. But this huge number was hardly ever broken down into appropriate categories. About 95 percent of those children were runaways, most of whom returned voluntarily within days; throwaways (children abandoned by their parents); or children who had been kidnapped by parents or guardians involved in custody battles. Jay Howell, executive director of the Justice Department-funded center, often told the press that he estimated that 4,000 to 20,000 children were kidnapped by strangers each year. But other child advocates such as Bill Treanor, executive director of the American Youth Work Center, put the figure closer to one hundred, and the F.B.I. logged only 67 stranger-abduction reports annually.

Even after the scare about missing children had begun to abate and its credibility to wane, it continued to color public policy. The U.S. Justice Department's Office of Juvenile Justice and Delinquency Prevention released a report entitled *America's Missing and Exploited Children: Their Safety and Their Future* in March of 1986. While acknowledging that many so-called missing children were actually abandoned by their parents, had run away "to flee from intolerable conditions of emotional or physical abuse at home," or were "victims of family abduction," the report still called up the specter of:

> paedophiles, serial murderers, or those who want to sell abducted children on the black market...They photograph children engaged in sordid, explicit sexual activity and sell the photos on the international market that is available for the exchange of such pictures.

Rather than analyze why young people might prefer precarious lives on the street to the dangers of remaining in their homes, the advisory board recommended giving police the authority to detain anyone under the age of eighteen. The report says primly that minors "do not have a right to freedom from custody." Both runaway and throwaway children should be returned to their parents as soon as possible. The report blames "violent and sexually explicit facets of the popular culture such as art, rock music lyrics, and video games" and "preadolescent peer culture" for young people's desire to escape from the family, and asks

> Would children be less vulnerable to running away, to sexual exploitation, to sex rings, and destructive cults if they were more sheltered from lurid, everyday depictions of perversion?

In other words, teenagers who voluntarily leave home or who are thrown out have been tainted by sexual deviance.

In fact, the sexuality of young people often provokes violence within the family—whether it's a child's demand for birth control or sex education; a need for treatment of a venereal disease; pregnancy; coming out as bisexual or homosexual; or a parent's discovery of a minor's sexual activity. But the Justice Department report does not suggest that adults need to accept the reality of youth sexuality and give young people the information they need to cope with it, including access to birth control and abortion. No mention is made of alleviating poverty, providing better health care or mental health services, or making it easier for families to deal with substance-abuse problems. It's much easier to jail the young man whose father beats him up for being a fag and then buy him a bus ticket home. It's much tidier to ship the pregnant high school junior back to the hometown where her mother does not want her to be seen in public.

The Attack on Feminism

In the late '80s, a series of scandals about child abuse which supposedly occurred in day care centers represented a major assault on feminism and the increasing numbers of American women with children who worked outside their homes. These scandals also created the myth that organized rings of Satanists were preying on America's youth.

What one author has called "the ritual sex abuse hoax" began in 1983, when Judy Johnson noticed that her two-year-old son's bottom was red. Her son attended the McMartin preschool in Los Angeles. She told police her son had indicated a man at the center, named Ray, but it wasn't clear what Ray had done. In the next few weeks, Johnson's accusations grew more complex and colorful. Eventually she accused Raymond Buckey, whose family owned the school, of making her son ride naked on a horse, of wearing a Santa Claus suit while abusing him, of jabbing scissors into his eyes, and of putting staples in his ears. She accused Peggy Buckey, Ray's mother, of killing a baby and making her son drink the blood. She also said that an AWOL marine and three models in a health club had raped her son, and that her family's dog had been sodomized. Johnson was eventually diagnosed as psychotic, and defense attorneys would claim her son had been abused by his own father. But her wild stories set in motion the most expensive criminal case in U.S. history.

Police sent about two hundred letters to families whose children attended the McMartin preschool, asking if their children had been molested. The letter suggested that families take their children to Children's Institute International (CII), an abuse therapy clinic, for therapy. There, children were questioned by social workers plying anatomically correct puppets. The therapists at CII assumed that children who denied being abused must be lying and encouraged them to prove they weren't "stupid" by telling "the yucky secret." The children began to tell stories about being assaulted in hot-air balloons and on the shoulders of busy freeways, and about being used in Satanic rituals in tunnels beneath the school. Teachers supposedly mutilated and killed animals in front of the children to persuade them to keep silent about the abuse. Eventually, several members of the Buckey family, including a seventy-seven-year-old, wheelchair-bound grandmother and three female teachers, were accused of committing hundreds of acts of sex abuse against children.

The case wasn't resolved until 1990. None of the defendants were convicted, mostly because it became apparent that the child witnesses had been coached, and there was a lack of hard, physical evidence to support their claims. For example, no tunnels were ever found below the school. But many people caught up in ritual-abuse cases have not been that lucky.

From 1984 to 1989, some one hundred people nationwide were charged with ritual abuse crimes against children. About half of them were tried and half of those convicted, usually with no evidence except testimony from children, parents, experts who testified the children seemed traumatized, and doctors who were willing to make definitive diagnoses of sexual abuse even though this is very difficult to detect in any victim, regardless of age. These convictions were made possible in part by many state laws enacted around 1986, which were intended to make it easier for child victims to win justice. In some states, it wasn't necessary for the children even to be in court—parents could testify as hearsay witnesses, or the children could appear on videotape or closed-circuit TV. Of course, this also makes it more difficult to confront one's accusers and present a defense.

FBI agent Kenneth Lanning, who initially believed allegations of Satanic abuse, today says, "If the cults were real, they would constitute the greatest conspiracy in history." Yet law-enforcement personnel continue to receive government funding to attend conferences where experts tell them how to detect Satanic child-pornography and prostitution rings, and government-funded publications warning parents about the phenomenon have been published in several states.

These cases have been used, not very subtly, to make parents who need day care feel guilty for leaving their children in other people's hands. For the first time, women are being labeled as pedophiles. This increases the public's paranoia. If children aren't safe with female caretakers, there must not be any safe place for them except home with Mommy.

This moral panic conveniently locates the source of child abuse outside of the home. It also precludes demands for increased government subsidization of child care and more frequent state safety inspections, since neither measure can prevail against child-hating witches who can kill babies without leaving bodies around for the cops to find, and covens that skewer toddlers' private parts with swords, film the ritual for sale on the international pedophile market, and leave no telltale negatives or wounds behind. People can wax indignant about the "selfishness" of mothers who endanger their children by placing them in day care and ignore the economic reality that most mothers have to work if their children are going to have shelter and food.

Cross-Generational Relationships

American society has become rabidly phobic about any sexual contact between adults and minors. In this social climate, very few lesbians will admit to having cross-generational relationships or defend even the abstract idea of them. Within the lesbian community, other forces exist that prevent girl-lovers and underage lesbians from telling their own stories. We encourage incest survivors to break the silence and tell family secrets about violence and sexual abuse. But this sisterly support turns to outrage and cries for silence if a woman wants to talk about being a sexually active child or even a teenager who was not traumatized by the experience. Lesbian-feminism supposedly empowers women, but we are reluctant to see young women's sexual experiences as anything but victimization.

Lesbians work constantly to undo their racism, classism, able-bodyism, looksism, coupleism, and all other forms of prejudice. We give lip service to confronting ageism, but we do not really include underage lesbian and bisexual women in our community. The simple truth is that we are afraid to. We are afraid the state will come down on us, brand us as child molesters, and put us in jail.

Why should a woman have to wait until she turns eighteen or twenty-one to be sexually active with other women? You may argue that adolescent dykes should experiment sexually and romantically with each other. But when they are trapped in schools, neighborhoods, churches, and families where being called queer targets them for harassment and assault, how many young lesbians can afford to come out or seek out others like themselves? The adult lesbian community is much easier to find than gay peers. True, not all younger dykes are interested in older women. But if a woman is interested in having a cross-generational lover, I cannot think of one good reason—apart from the threat of persecution—why she should deny herself such a relationship. Each generation of lesbians winds up to some extent recreating the wheel—rediscovering the possibilities of women's sexuality, relationships, and culture. We could save each other so much time and pain if we were not so deeply divided.

Opposing the state is a fearful thing. Nobody wants to go to jail, be blacklisted, or experience the violation of a tapped telephone and mail opened by strangers. But sometimes the injustice is too huge to ignore. I cannot blot out the memory of my own adolescent struggle to become a lesbian, how hard it was to persuade adult dykes to move over just a few inches and let me stand with them at the bar, how few of them were willing to talk to me, much less sleep with me. I cannot forget how freakish and alone I felt because other deviants were afraid to acknowledge me, how guilty I felt because I seemed to threaten them and make their marginal lives even more perilous. I understand now why those gray-haired women and the younger women in their twenties turned their heads away from me, but it was wrong. Self-hatred and cowardice often conceal themselves as self-preservation. I wish I could believe that fewer adult dykes would make those mistakes today.

Our government is happy to spend millions of dollars to put pedophiles in jail and keep the bogeyman of kiddy porn before the public eye to justify inflated law-enforcement budgets and increasingly draconian enforcement of obscenity laws. But the government is not willing to make sure people have enough money to support their children or to create safe and affordable day care. Funds for education still take a back seat to defense. The state is not willing to take the radical action that would be necessary to protect child victims of abusive adults. That would mean challenging parents' ownership of their children. It would mean providing viable alternatives to the family. Minors who are given the power to say "no" to being sexually used by an abusive parent or relative are also going to assume the right to say "yes" to other young people and adults whom they desire. You can't liberate children and adolescents without disrupting the entire hierarchy of adult power and coercion and challenging the hegemony of antisex fundamentalist religious values.

III.
Sluts in Utopia:
The Future of Radical Sex

III.
Sluts in Utopia:
The Future of Radical Sex

Most plans for creating a more just society focus on ameliorating human misery. They address unemployment, hunger, illiteracy, class-based inequity, unequal access to medical care, pollution, overpopulation, and discrimination based on sex, race, age, or membership in other devalued groups. While I care about all of those problems, I also wonder why so many of the proposed solutions make me shudder with dread. Perhaps it's because people who take on such enormous political chores are usually suffering from burnout. There's no room in their brave new worlds for fun, creativity, ornamentation, play, and desire. I am skeptical of utopian schemes that don't take into account the human need for adventure, risk, competition, self-display, pleasurable stimulation, and novelty.

In fact, many theoretical utopias are dreamed up by people who are afraid of diversity and deeply conservative about sex. Furthermore, they seem to think they can create tolerance by wiping out or minimizing differences. They envision worlds where men and women could barely be told apart—so of course there would be no sexism. Since gender would no longer be a social category, there would be no such thing as transvestitism or transsexuality. After all, how can you crossdress if both sexes are wearing the same clothes? Why would anybody envy or want to emulate the opposite sex if the distinctions between them had been blurred? The same argument is applied to homosexuality. If children were reared in an atmosphere of unconditional love without being threatened by corporal punishment or other abusive treatment, no one would eroticize bondage or a slap on the butt. Since there would be no prisons, restraint or captivity would cease to titillate. People would care more about ecology than about almost anything else, so Spandex, latex, spiked heels, and costume jewelry would go the way of the dinosaurs. Everyone would wear baggy clothing made out of "green" cotton that had been genetically engineered to grow in various shades of beige. In a "just" society, there wouldn't be anything to rebel against, so there wouldn't be much call for rock 'n' roll or protest poetry. If the state was a benign entity that only served to take care of and nurture the people, why would anyone engage in civil disobedience?

Dreary, isn't it?

In the movie, *Personal Services*, a fictionalized account of the life of one of England's most famous professional dominatrices, a retired RAF officer proud of having flown several missions over Germany during World War II in panties and a bra announces, "The future lies in kinky people!" He was onto something. In a world where men and women were equal, people might choose to exaggerate (rather than abandon) their differences, if only to preserve erotic tension between the sexes. Some people might choose to be neither male nor female. If nobody could be arrested for "impersonating the opposite sex," you'd probably see a lot more drag on the street, not less. In some ways, the scions of the New Right who issue such stern warnings about the dire consequences of feminism and gay liberation are correct. Decriminalizing sex and empowering women and queers would cause an explosion of decadence, perversity, dirty talking, intuition, fetishes, intelligence, sex toys, satire, makeup, promiscuity, blasphemy, celebration, bangles, art, nudity, weird hair, and political upheaval. For the first time we'd get to take a look at what's really inside the Pandora's Box of human sexuality.

Each of us would probably find something different. This wouldn't be a world where anything goes. It would be a world where people got to make sexual choices based on what they liked and needed, not based on what they had been told they should want or what they thought was available. No one would have the right to limit somebody else's options or impose her or his morality upon the rest of us. Monogamy would be just one more choice, not the Gold Standard for every meaningful relationship. People who wanted to could be wild and crazy, but more sedate individuals wouldn't feel that they had to imitate that behavior. There would be license in the context of responsibility: people would not willfully injure one another.

"Sluts in Utopia: The Future of Radical Sex" includes just a few of many possibilities. There are articles about S/M, gender play, crossing the lines of sexual orientation, fetishism, sex and spirituality, nonmonogamy, and sex work. There's also a critical look at the sexual geography of the city. Any attempt to liberate sex must address the literal boundaries of the red-light district and the gay ghetto as well as bring down the barricades within our own psyches.

What is the future of radical sex? That lies as much in your hands as it does in mine. When it comes to sex, most of us are afraid to be truthful even with ourselves. We've been browbeaten into thinking sex isn't that important. (And we're secretly afraid that if we ever got clear about what we really wanted, we wouldn't be able to have it anyway.)

We need to let ourselves dream big. The first duty of a revolutionary may be, as Abby Hoffman said, to survive. But it's pretty difficult to survive without the nurturance of an all-consuming fantasy about where you are headed and what all this hard work is for.

Below are some ways that you can unleash your inner sex radical (a much more fun person to party with than that pesky inner child).

Forty-two Things that You Can Do to Make the Future Safe for Sex

Defend an abortion clinic. Help women get through right-wing pickets and into the building.

Write a sex ad.

When your newspaper says police are cracking down on prostitution, call the police and tell them you don't like them spending your money to bust hookers. Then write a letter to the paper saying the same thing. Urge the government to decriminalize prostitution. Nobody should have to go to jail for trying to make a living.

Write a weekly letter to your congresspeople. Ask them to repeal RICO laws, vote against mandatory sentencing for drug offenses, allocate more money for addiction-treatment services and family planning, fund more research on breast cancer and AIDS, and shut down the Justice Department's antiporn campaign. Remind these rich enemies of the asshole that being poor is not a crime. The money we now spend on building new prisons should be spent to bring jobs to the inner city and to build better schools. The League of Women Voters can tell you who your representatives are and give you their addresses. Be sure to send a copy of your letter to the Presidential Bubba.

Study sex.

Write a weekly letter to your mayor, officials in city government, state representatives, and governor. Tell them you oppose sodomy laws, laws which make solicitation illegal, and laws that force sex offenders to register with the cops. Tell them you vote.

Vote.

Oppose attempts to get states to adopt a lower standard of obscenity (often known as the Miller standard).

Give away some pleasure.

Join a group like the American Civil Liberties Union (Dept. of Public Education, 132 W. 43rd St., New York, NY 10036), Californians Against Censorship Together (1800 Market St., Suite 1000, San Francisco, CA 94102), Feminists for Free Expression (2525 Times Square Station, New York, NY 10108), the National Coalition Against Censorship (275 Seventh Avenue, New York, NY 10001), the National Campaign for Freedom of Expression (1402 Third Ave., No. 421, Seattle, WA 98101), Planned Parenthood Federation of America (810 Seventh Ave., New York, NY 10019), or Coyote (2269 Chestnut St., Suite 452, San Francisco, CA 94123). These groups are fighting for your sexual freedom. Be sure to enclose a stamped, self-addressed envelope with your request for information.

Find a new fantasy.

If a convenience store is being picketed for carrying adult magazines, walk in and buy one. Tell the manager you support her or his decision to carry the materials the customers want.

Make art about how sex feels.

If an antiporn group is photographing the customers of an adult bookstore, turn up with a Polaroid and take pictures of *them.*

Write a love letter to an unlovable part of your body.

Organize a benefit for the Little Sister's Defense Fund and send the money to 1221 Thurlow Street, Vancouver, B.C., Canada V6E 1X4.

Do regular self-examinations for breast or testicular cancer.

Teach somebody how to come with a rubber barrier.

If your city initiates a crackdown on baths or sex clubs, write to your elected representatives and send a copy of your letter to your local newspapers. Tell the powers that be that you want a clean, well-lighted place for random encounters with randy strangers. Don't forget to mention that having safe sex in a public place is much more healthy than having unsafe sex at home in the privacy of your own bedroom.

Seize the moral high ground. Be righteous in your indignation.

If somebody tries to ban a book at a school or public library, go to the hearing. You wouldn't believe how easy it is to win these battles if you just show up and speak up. Keeping books about sex in the libraries is even more important than keeping them in bookstores because they are free and more people see them (especially young people).

Look at a cervix. (Hint: Annie Sprinkle is not the only woman who has one!)

Find out what the sex education curriculum is like in your local schools. If you think it is inadequate, express your concerns to school officials. You don't have to be a parent to do this. Everybody gets taxed to pay for free public education, so we all have a right to shape public policy. Young people need to know about birth control, safer sex, and homosexuality.

Look at your genitals.

Tell record stores that you don't want labels on your music. Tell your state representative you don't want laws that limit what kind of music young people can buy.

Do not be shamed. Do not be stampeded by fear.

If your pharmacy keeps condoms behind the counter, ask that they be displayed where people can buy them without having to ask for them. Tell the manager that she or he will sell more of these items if the customer can avoid embarrassment. Ask for latex gloves. Ask for dental dams. Ask for water-based personal lubricants. Ask for leaflets about AIDS and safer sex.

Write to a prisoner.

Call ABC, NBC, and CBS (both the national offices and your local affiliates). Tell them you want to see condom ads during prime time.

Tell gay organizations that you want them to support the First Amendment and start tracking obscenity cases. Tell them you want to see them supporting needle-exchange volunteers. Tell them you want them to defend sex workers who get arrested. Tell them it's time to put the sex back into homosexuality.

Keep your eyes open the whole time.

Organize a benefit for the Spanner defendants, gay men who were sentenced to prison in England for practicing consensual S/M; write a check payable to the NLA Spanner Defense and Education Fund, Account No. 01-7008237800, Central West End Bank, and mail it to Woody Bebout, Treasurer, P. O. Box 8224, St. Louis, MO 63108.

Crossdress.

Talk to a sex worker, a transgendered person, a celibate, a sadomasochist, a heterosexual—anybody whose sexual identity or practices are different from yours.

Masturbate, and don't hurry.

Tell video stores that you enjoy being able to rent X-rated videos.

Give up the concept of trying to control other people's sexual tastes. It will give you more time to develop your own.

Make or buy a sex toy.

Volunteer for a rape crisis center, a shelter for battered women, or an AIDS hotline.

Hand out clean needles and free condoms. If you can't do this, give money to the people who are doing it for you.

Organize a neighborhood patrol. Let bashers know they can't get away with hate and violence in your little part of the world.

Live a long time and make waves. The name of this ride is "Rock the Boat," not "Pretend You're Dead Already."

A Secret Side of Lesbian Sexuality

1979

Is it true that gay women don't do SM? Generally, this is true. Men often require a high degree of resistance, whereas most women do not. The escalating effect that two men have on each other facilitates all forms of resistance, which is why SM is much more prevalent in gay male circles than it is among heterosexuals. With very rare exceptions, SM simply has no value for gay women.

—R.D. Fenwick, The Advocate Guide to Gay Health

The sexual closet is bigger than you think. By all rights, we shouldn't be here but we are. It's obvious that conservative forces like organized religion, the police, and other agents of the tyrannical majority don't want sadomasochism to flourish anywhere. Sexually active women have always been a threat the system won't tolerate. But conservative gay liberationists and orthodox feminists are also embarrassed by kinky sexual subcultures (even if that's where they do their tricking). "We are just like heterosexuals (or men)," is their plea for integration, their way of whining for some of America's carbon monoxide pie. Drag queens, leathermen, rubber freaks, boy-lovers, girl-lovers, dyke sadomasochists, prostitutes, transsexuals—we make that plea sound like such a feeble lie. We are not like everyone else. And our difference is not created solely by oppression or biology. It is a preference, a sexual preference.

Lesbian S/M isn't terribly well-organized yet. But in San Francisco women can find partners and friends who will aid and abet them in pursuing the delights of dominance and submission. We don't have bars. We don't even have newspapers or magazines with sex ads. I sometimes think the gay subculture must have looked like this when gay life first became urbanized. Since our community depends on word-of-mouth and social networks, we have to work very hard to keep it going. It's a survival issue. If the arch-conformists with their cardboard cunts and angora wienies had their way, we wouldn't exist at all. As we become more visible, we encounter more hostility, more violence. This article is my way of refusing the narcotic of self-hatred. We must break the silence that persecution imposes on its victims.

I am a sadist. The polite term is "top," but I don't like to use it. It would dilute my image and my message. If someone wants to know about my sexuality, she can deal with me on my own terms. I don't particularly care to make it easy. S/M is scary. That's at least half its significance. We select the most frightening, disgusting, or unacceptable activities and transmute them into pleasure. We make use of all the forbidden symbols and all the disowned emotions. S/M is a deliberate, premeditated, erotic blasphemy. It is a form of sexual extremism and sexual dissent.

I identify more strongly as a sadomasochist than as a lesbian. I hang out in the gay community because that's where the sexual fringe starts to unravel. Most of my partners are women, but gender is not my boundary. I am limited by my own imagination, cruelty, and compassion, and by the greed and stamina of my partner's body. If I had a choice between being shipwrecked on a desert island with a vanilla lesbian and a hot male masochist, I'd pick the boy. This is the kind of sex I like—sex that tests physical limits within a context of polarized roles. It is the only kind of sex I am interested in having.

I am not typical of S/M lesbians, nor do I represent them. In fact, because I define myself as a sadist, I am atypical. Most S/M people prefer the submissive, bottom, or masochistic, role. The bulk of porn (erotic, psychoanalytic, and political) that gets written about S/M focuses on the masochist. People who do public speaking about S/M have told me they get a more sympathetic hearing if they identify as bottoms. This makes sense in a twisted kind of way. The uninitiated associate masochism with incompetence, lack of assertiveness, and self-destruction. But sadism is associated with chainsaw murders. A fluffy sweater type listening to a masochist may feel sorry for her but will be terrified of me. I'm the one who is ostensibly responsible for manipulating or coercing the masochist into degradation—all 130 pounds and five feet, two inches of me. Therefore, my word is suspect. It is nevertheless true that my services are in demand, that I respect my partners' limits, and that both (or all) of us obtain great pleasure from a scene. I started exploring S/M as a bottom, and I still put my legs in the air now and then. I have never asked a submissive to do something I haven't done or couldn't do.

In addition to being a sadist, I have a leather fetish. If I remember my Krafft-Ebing, that's another thing women aren't supposed to do. Oh, well. Despite the experts, seeing, smelling, or handling leather makes me cream. Every morning before I go out the door, I make a ritual of putting on my leather jacket. The weight of it settling on my shoulders is reassuring. Once I zip it, turn up the collar, and cram my hands into the pockets, the jacket is my armor. It also puts me in danger by alerting the curious and the angry to my presence when I wear it on the street. I get all kinds of reactions. Voyeurs drool. Queer-baiting kids shout or throw bottles from their cars. Well-dressed hets, secure in their privilege, give me the condescending smile of the genital dilettante. Some gay men are amused when they see me coming. They take me for a fag hag, a mascot dressed up to avoid embarrassing my macho friends. Others are resentful. Leather is their province, and a cunt is not entitled to wear the insignia of a sadomasochist. They avoid my shadow. I might be menstruating and make their spears go dull. When I visit a dyke bar, the patrons take me for a member of that nearly extinct species, the butch. Femmes under this misapprehension position themselves within my reach, signaling their availability but not bothering to actively pursue me. They seem to expect me to do everything a man would except knock them up. Given the fact that I prefer someone to come crawling and begging for my attention and work pretty damned hard before she gets it, this strikes me as very funny. In women's groups, the political clones and the Dworkinites see my studded belt and withdraw. I am obviously a sex pervert, and good real true lesbians are not sex perverts. They are high priestesses of feminism, conjuring up the wimmin's revolution. As I understand it, after the wimmin's revolution sex will consist of wimmin holding hands, taking off their shirts, and dancing in a circle. Then we will all fall asleep at exactly the same moment. If we didn't all fall asleep, something else might happen—something male-identified, objectifying, pornographic, noisy, and undignified. Something like an orgasm.

This is why they say leather is expensive. When I wear it, disdain, amusement, and the threat of violence follow me from my door to my destination and home again. Is it worth it? Can the sex be that good?

If I'm interested in a woman, I call her up and ask if she'd like to go out for dinner. I have never picked up a stranger in a bar. My partners are friends, women who strike up acquaintances with me because they've heard me talk about S/M, and women I know from Samois. (I also have a lover who is my slave. We enjoy conducting joint seductions or creating bizarre sexual adventures to tell each other about later.) If she agrees, I will tell her where and when to meet me. Over dinner I begin to play doctor—Dr. Kinsey. I like to know when she started being sexual with other people; if and when she started masturbating; if and how she likes to have an orgasm; and when she came out as a lesbian (if she has). I give her similar information about myself. Then I ask about her S/M fantasies, and if and how she has acted them out. I also try to find out if she has any health problems, such as asthma or diabetes, that might limit our play.

This conversation need not be clinical. It is not an interview—it is an interrogation. I am taking for granted my right to possess intimate information about my quarry. Giving me that information is the beginning of her submission. The sensations this creates are subtle, but we both begin to get turned on.

I will probably encourage her to get a little high. I don't like playing with women who are too stoned to feel what I am doing, nor do I want someone shedding inhibitions because of a chemical she's ingested. I prefer to deny a bottom her inhibitions. However, I do like her to feel relaxed and a little vulnerable and suggestible.

If there's time, we may go to a bar. Socializing in gay men's leather bars is problematic for lesbians. I prefer bars where I know some of the bartenders and patrons. I rarely have been refused admittance, but I have been made uncomfortable by men who saw me as an intruder. If there were women's bars that didn't make me feel even more unwelcome, I'd go there. Since I am a sadomasochist, I feel entitled to the space I take up in men's bars. I sometimes wonder how many of the men exhibiting their leather in the light from the pinball machines go home and really work it out and how many of them settle for fucking and sucking.

A leather bar provides a safe place to establish roles. I order my submissive to bring me a drink. She doesn't get a beer of her own. When she wants a drink, she asks me for one, and I pour it into her mouth while she kneels at my feet. I will begin to handle her, appraising her flesh, correcting her posture. I fondle or expose her so that she feels embarrassed and draws closer to me. I like to hear her ask for mercy or protection. If she isn't already wearing a collar, I will put one on her, drag her over to a mirror—behind the bar, in the bathroom, on a wall—and make her look at it. I watch her response very carefully. I don't like women who collapse into passivity, whose bodies go limp and whose faces go blank. I want to see the confusion, the anger, the turn-on, the helplessness.

As soon as I am sure she is turned on (something that can be ascertained with an index finger if I can get her zipper down), I hustle her out of there. I especially like to put her in handcuffs and lead her out on a leash. This is one of the gifts I offer a submissive: the illusion of having no choice, the thrill of being taken.

The collar will keep her aroused until we reach my flat. I prefer to play in my space since it's set up for bondage and whipping. I order her to stay two steps behind me, which reassures her that we really are going to do a scene. As soon as the door is locked behind us, I order her to strip. In my room, there is no such thing as casual nudity. When I take away a woman's clothing, I am temporarily denying her humanity with all its privileges and responsibilities.

Nudity can be taken a step further. The bottom can be shaved. A razor removes the pelt that warms and conceals. My lover/slave has her cunt shaved. It reminds her that I own her genitals and reinforces her role as my child and property.

Shedding her clothes while I remain fully dressed usually is enough to shame and excite a bottom. Once she is naked, I put her on the floor, and there she stays until I move her or raise her up. I stand over her, trail a riding crop down her spine, and tell her that she belongs underneath me. I talk about how good she's going to make my cunt feel and how strict I am going to be with her. I may allow her to embrace my boots. After delineating her responsibilities and cussing her out a little for being easy, I haul her up, slap her face, hold her head against my hip while I unzip, and let her feast on my clit.

I wonder if any man could understand how this act of receiving sexual service feels to me. I was taught to dread sex, to fight it off, to provide it under duress or in exchange for romance and security. I was trained to take responsibility for other people's gratification and to pretend pleasure when others pretend to have my pleasure in mind. It is shocking and profoundly satisfying to commit this piece of rebellion, to take pleasure exactly as I want it, to exact it like tribute. I need not pretend I enjoy a bottom's ministrations if they are unskilled, nor do I need to be grateful.

I like to come before I do a scene because it takes the edge off my hunger. For the same reason, I don't like to play when I am stoned or drunk. I want to be in control. I need all my wits about me to outguess the bottom's needs and fears, take her out of herself, and bring her back. During the session, she will receive much more direct physical stimulation than I will. So I take what I need. From her mouth she feeds me the energy I need to dominate and abuse her.

While I am getting off, I usually begin to fantasize about the woman on her knees. I visualize her in a certain position or a certain role. This fantasy is the seed from which the whole scene sprouts. When she's finished pleasing me, I order her to crawl onto my bed, and I tie her up.

Bottoms tend to be anxious. Because there is a shortage of tops, they compensate by playing all kinds of little psychological numbers on themselves to feel miserable and titillated. They also like to feel greedy and guilty, and they get anxious about that. The bondage provides reassurance. She can measure the intensity of my passion by the tightness of my knots. It also puts an end to bullshit speculation about whether I am doing this just because she likes it so much. I make sure there's no way she can get loose on her own. Restraint becomes security. She knows I want her. She knows I am in charge.

Being tied up is arousing, and I intensify this arousal by teasing her, playing with her breasts and clit, calling her nasty names. When she starts to squirm, I begin to rough her up a little, taking her to the edge of pain, the edge that melts and turns over into pleasure. I move from pinching her nipples with my fingers to pinching her nipples with a pair of clamps that makes them ache and burn. I may put clips all over her breasts or on her labia. I will check her cunt to make sure it's still wet and tell her how turned on she is—if she doesn't already know. At some point, I always use a whip. Some bottoms like to be whipped until they are bruised. Or she may be excited by the image of the whip coming toward her and may want to hear the sound of it whistling in the air or feel the handle moving in and out of her. A whip is a great way to get a woman to be here *now*. She can't look away from it, and she can't think about anything else.

If the pain goes beyond a mild discomfort, the bottom will probably get scared. She will start to wonder, "Why am I doing this? Am I going to be able to take this?" There are many ways to get her past this point. I may ask her to take it for me, because I need to watch her suffer. Or I may administer a fixed number of blows as a punishment for some sexual offense. I may convince the bottom that she deserves the pain and must endure it because she is "only" a slave. Pacing is essential. The sensations need to increase gradually. The particular implement involved may also be important. Some women who cannot tolerate whipping have a very high tolerance for other things—nipple play, hot wax, enemas, or verbal humiliation.

When I am playing bottom, I don't use pain or bondage for its own sake. I want to please. The top is my mistress. She has condescended to train me, and it is very important to me to deserve her attention. The basic dynamic of S/M is the power dichotomy, not pain. Handcuffs, dog collars, whips, kneeling, bondage, tit clamps, hot wax, enemas, penetration, and giving sexual service are all metaphors for the power imbalance. However, I must admit that I get bored pretty fast with a bottom who is not willing to take any pain.

The will to please is a bottom's source of pleasure, but it is also a source of danger. If the top's intentions are dishonorable (e.g., emotional sabotage), or her skill is faulty, the bottom is not safe when she yields. Tops compete to be worthy of the gift of submission. Someone who makes mistakes gets a bad reputation very fast, and only inexperienced or foolish bottoms will go under for her.

Why would anyone want to be dominated, given the risks? Because it is a healing process. As a top, I find the old wounds and unappeased hunger. I nourish. I cleanse and close the wounds. I devise and mete out appropriate punishments for old, irrational "sins." I trip up the bottom, I see her as she is, and I forgive her and turn her on and make her come, despite her feelings of unworthiness or self-hatred or fear. We are all afraid of losing, of being captured and defeated. I take the sting out of that fear. A good scene doesn't end with orgasm—it ends with catharsis.

I could never go back to tweaking tits and munching cunt in the dark, not after this. Two lovers sweating against each other, each struggling for her own goal, eyes blind to each other—how appalling, how deadly. I want to see and share in every sensation and emotion my partner experiences, and I want all of it to come from me. I don't want to leave out anything. The affronted modesty and the hostility are as important as the affection and lust.

The bottom must be my superior. She is the victim I present for the night's inspection. I derive an awful knowledge from each gasp, the tossing head, the blanching of her knuckles. In order to force her to lose control, I must unravel her defenses, breach her walls, and alternate subtlety and persuasion with brutality and violence. Playing a bottom who did not demand my respect and admiration would be like eating rotten fruit.

S/M is high-technology sex. It is so time-consuming and absorbing that I have no desire to own anyone on a full-time basis. I am satisfied with her sexual submission. This is the difference between real slavery or exploitation and S/M. I am interested in something ephemeral—pleasure—not in economic control or forced reproduction.

This may be why S/M is so threatening to the established order and why it is so heavily penalized and persecuted. S/M roles are not related to gender or sexual orientation or race or class. My own needs dictate which role I will adopt.

Our political system cannot digest the concept of power unconnected to privilege. S/M recognizes the erotic underpinnings of our system and seeks to reclaim them. There's an enormous hard-on beneath the priest's robe, the cop's uniform, the president's business suit, the soldier's khakis. But that phallus is powerful only as long as it is concealed, elevated to the level of a symbol, never exposed or used in literal fucking. A cop with his hard-on sticking out can be punished, rejected, blown, or you can sit on it, but he is no longer a demigod. In an S/M context, the uniforms and roles and dialogue become a parody of authority, a challenge to it, a recognition of its secret sexual nature.

Governments are based on sexual control. Any group of people that gains access to authoritarian power becomes an accessory to that ideology. These groups begin to perpetuate and enforce sexual control. Women and gays who are hostile to other sexual minorities are siding with fascism. They don't want the uniforms to degenerate into drag— they want uniforms of their own.

As I write this, there is a case in Canada that will determine whether or not S/M sex between consenting adults can be legal. This case began when a gay male bathhouse that caters to an S/M clientele was raided. After that raid, a man in Toronto was busted for "keeping a common bawdy house." The "bawdy house" was a room in his apartment he had fixed up for S/M sex. Yet another man was busted for false imprisonment and aggravated assault. These charges stemmed from an S/M three-way.

In San Francisco, months before Moscone and Milk were assassinated and the cops smashed into the Elephant Walk, half the leather bars in the Folsom Street area had lost their liquor licenses due to police harassment. The Gay Freedom Day Parade Committee tried to pass a resolution that would bar leather and S/M regalia from the parade.

I don't know how long it will take for other S/M people to get as angry as I am. I don't know how long we will continue to work in gay organizations that patronize us and threaten us with expulsion if we don't keep quiet about our sexuality. I don't know how long we will tolerate the "feminism" of women's groups who believe that S/M and pornography are the same thing and claim that both cause violence against women. I don't know how long we will continue to run our sex ads in magazines that feature judgmental, slanderous articles about us. I don't know how long we will continue to be harassed and assaulted or murdered on the street, or how long we will tolerate the fear of losing our apartments or being fired from our jobs or arrested for making the wrong kind of noise during some heavy sex.

I do know that when we start to get angry, walk out, and work for our own cause, it will be long overdue.

Feminism and Sadomasochism

1980

I hope you only do those things in leather bars. If I ever saw women doing S/M in a lesbian bar, it would make me so angry I'd want to beat them up.

—*Anonymous gratuitous comment*

Three years ago, I decided to stop ignoring my sexual fantasies. Since the age of two, I had been constructing a private world of dominance, submission, punishment, and pain. Abstinence, consciousness-raising, and therapy had not blighted the charm of these frightful reveries. I could not tolerate any more guilt, anxiety, or frustration, so I cautiously began to experiment with real sadomasochism. I did not lose my soul in the process. But in those three years, I lost a lover, several friends, a publisher, my apartment, and my good name because of the hostility and fear evoked by my openness about my true sexuality.

Writing this article is painful because it brings back the outrage and hurt I felt at being ostracized from the lesbian-feminist community. I've been a feminist since I was thirteen and a lesbian since I was seventeen. I didn't lose just a ghetto or a subculture—lesbian-feminism was the matrix I used to become an adult. Fortunately for my sanity and happiness, I managed to construct a new social network. My friends and lovers are bisexual women (some of whom do S/M professionally), gay and bisexual men, and other outlaw lesbians. If I were isolated, I would not be strong enough to speak out about something that makes me this vulnerable.

I describe my feelings about this issue because sadomasochism is usually dealt with in an abstract, self-righteous way by feminist theorists who believe it is the epitome of misogyny, sexism, and violence. In this article, I shall examine sadomasochism in a theoretical way and attempt a rapprochement between feminism and S/M. I am motivated by my concern for the people who are frightened or ashamed of their erotic response to sadomasochistic fantasies. I don't want to hear any more tragic stories from women who have repressed their sexuality because they think yearnings for helplessness or sexual control are

165

politically unacceptable. I don't believe that any more than I believe homosexuals should be celibate so they can continue to be good Catholics. The women's movement has become a moralistic force contributing to the self-loathing and misery experienced by sexual minorities. Because sexual dissenters are already being trampled by monolithic, prudish institutions, I think it is time the women's movement started taking more radical positions on sexual issues.

It is difficult to discuss sadomasochism in feminist terms because some of the slang S/M people use to talk about sexuality has been appropriated by feminist propagandists. Terms like *roles, masochism, bondage, dominance,* and *submission* have become buzzwords. In a feminist context, their meanings differ sharply from their significance to S/M people. The discussion is rendered even more difficult because feminist theorists do not do their homework on human sexuality before pronouncing judgment on a sexual variation. Like Victorian missionaries in Polynesia, they insist on interpreting the sexual behavior of other people according to their own value systems. A perfect example of this is the "debate" over transsexuality. So in its present form, feminism is not the best theoretical framework for understanding sexual deviation, just as unmodified Marxism is an inadequate system for analyzing the oppression of women.

Since the label *feminist* has become debased coinage, let me explain why I still call myself a feminist. I believe that the society in which I live is a patriarchy with power concentrated in the hands of men, and that this patriarchy actively prevents women from becoming complete and independent human beings. Women are oppressed by being denied access to economic resources, political power, and control over their own reproduction. This oppression is managed by several institutions, chiefly the family, religion, and the state. An essential part of the oppression of women is control over sexual ideology, mythology, and behavior. This social control affects the sexual nonconformist as well as the conformist. Because our training in conventional sexuality begins the minute we are born, and because the penalties for rebellion are so high, no individual or group is completely free from erotic tyranny.

I am not a separatist. I believe that men can be committed to the destruction of the patriarchy. After all, the rewards of male dominance are given only to men who are willing and able to perpetuate and cooperate with the system. I am not "woman-identified." I do not believe that women have more insight, intuition, virtue, identification with the earth, or love in their genes than men. Consequently, I cannot support everything women do, and I believe the women's movement could learn a lot from politicized or deviant men. On the other hand, I do not find it easy to work with men, partly because male feminist theory is pitifully underdeveloped. I do not think separatism is worthless or bankrupt. It can be useful as an organizing strategy and to teach women valuable survival skills. The taste of autonomy that separatism provides is intoxicating and can be a powerful incentive to struggle for real freedom.

I think it is imperative that feminists dismantle the institutions that foster the exploitation and abuse of women. The family, conventional sexuality, and gender are at the top of my hit list. These institutions control the emotional, intimate lives of every one of us, and they have done incalculable damage to women. I cannot imagine how such drastic change can be accomplished without armed struggle, the appropriation and reallocation of wealth, and a change in the ownership of the means of production. When women are liberated, women as a class will probably cease to exist since our whole structure of sex and gender must undergo a complete transformation.

The term *sadomasochism* has also been debased, primarily by the mass media, clinical psychology, and the antipornography movement. After all, homophobia is not the only form of sexual prejudice. Every minority sexual behavior has been mythologized and distorted. There is a paucity of accurate, explicit, nonjudgmental information about sex in modern America. This is one way sexual behavior is controlled. If people don't know a particular technique or lifestyle exists, they aren't likely to try it. If the only images they have of a certain sexual act are ugly, disgusting, or threatening, they will either not engage in that act or be furtive about enjoying it.

Since there is so much confusion about what S/M is, I want to describe my own sexual specialties and the sadomasochistic subculture. I am basically a sadist. About 10 percent of the time, I take the other role (bottom, slave, masochist). This makes me atypical, since the majority of women and men involved in S/M prefer to play bottom. I enjoy leathersex, bondage, various forms of erotic torture, flagellation (whipping), verbal humiliation, fist-fucking, and watersports (playing with enemas and piss). I do not enjoy oral sex unless I am receiving it as a form of sexual service, which means my partner must be on her knees, on her back, or at least in a collar. I have non-S/M sex rarely, mostly for old times' sake, with vanilla friends to whom I want to stay close. My primary relationship is with a woman who enjoys being my slave. We enjoy tricking with other people and telling each other the best parts afterward.

Because sadomasochism is usually portrayed as a violent, dangerous activity, most people do not think there is a great deal of difference between a rapist and a bondage enthusiast. But sadomasochism is not a form of sexual assault. It is a consensual activity that involves polarized roles and intense sensations. An S/M scene is always preceded by a negotiation in which the top and bottom decide whether or not they will play, what activities are likely to occur, what activities will not occur, and about how long the scene will last. The bottom is usually given a *safe word* or *code action* she can use to stop the scene. This safe word allows the bottom to fantasize that the scene is not consensual and to protest verbally or resist physically without halting stimulation.

The key word to understanding S/M is *fantasy*. The roles, dialogue, fetish costumes, and sexual activity are part of a drama or ritual. The participants are enhancing their sexual pleasure, not damaging or imprisoning one another. A sadomasochist is well aware that a role adopted during a scene is not appropriate during other interactions and that a fantasy role is not the sum total of her being.

S/M relationships are usually egalitarian. Very few bottoms want full-time mistresses. In fact, masochists are known within the S/M community to be stubborn and aggressive. Tops often make nervous jokes about being slaves to the whims of their bottoms. After all, the top's pleasure is dependent on the bottom's willingness to play. This gives most sadists a mild to severe case of performance anxiety.

The S/M subculture is a theater in which sexual dramas can be acted out and appreciated. It also serves as a vehicle for passing on new fantasies, new equipment, warnings about police harassment, introductions to potential sex partners and friends, and safety information. Safety is a major concern of sadomasochists. A major part of the sadist's turn-on consists of deliberately altering the emotional or physical state of the bottom. Even a minor accident like a rope burn can upset the top enough to mar the scene. And of course a bottom can't relax and enjoy the sex if she doesn't completely trust her top. The S/M community makes some attempt to regulate itself by warning newcomers away from individuals who are inconsiderate, insensitive, prone to playing when they are intoxicated, or unsafe for other reasons. Unfortunately, the suppression of S/M isolates novice sadists and masochists from this body of information which can minimize danger and make playing more rewarding.

For some people outside the subculture, the fact that S/M is consensual makes it acceptable. They may not understand why people enjoy it, but they see that S/M people are not inhumane monsters. For other people, including many feminists, the fact that it is consensual makes it even more appalling. A woman who deliberately seeks out a sexual situation in which she can be helpless is a traitor in their eyes. Hasn't the women's movement been trying to persuade people for years that women are not naturally masochistic? Originally, this meant that women do not create their own second-class status, do not enjoy it, and are the victims of socially constructed discrimination, not biology. A sexual masochist probably doesn't want to be raped, battered, discriminated against in her job, or kept down by the system. Her desire to act out a specific sexual fantasy is very different from the pseudopsychiatric dictum that a woman's world is bound by housework, intercourse, and childbirth.

Some feminists object to the description of S/M as consensual. They believe that our society has conditioned all of us to accept inequities in power and hierarchical relationships. Therefore, S/M is simply a manifestation of the same system that dresses girls in pink and boys in blue; allows surplus value to accumulate in the coffers of capitalists while giving workers a minimum wage; and sends out cops and soldiers to keep down the disfranchised.

It is true, as I stated before, that society shapes sexuality. We can make any decision about our sexual behavior we like, but our imagination and ability to carry out those decisions are limited by the surrounding culture. But I do not believe that sadomasochism is the result of institutionalized injustice to a greater extent than heterosexual marriage, lesbian bars, or gay male bathhouses. The S/M subculture is affected by sexism, racism, and other fallout from the system, but the dynamic between a top and a bottom is quite different from the dynamic between men and women, whites and blacks, or upper- and working-class people. That system is unjust because it assigns privileges based on race, gender, and social class. During an S/M encounter, roles are acquired and used in very different ways. The participants select particular roles that best express their sexual needs, how they feel about their particular partners, or which outfits are clean and ready to wear. The most significant reward for being a top or a bottom is sexual pleasure. If you don't like being a top or a bottom, you switch your keys. Try doing that with your biological sex or your race or your socioeconomic status.

Some feminists still find S/M roles disturbing because they believe they are derived from genuinely oppressive situations. They accuse sadomasochism of being fascistic because of the symbolism employed to create an S/M ambiance. And some S/M people do enjoy fantasies that are more elaborate than a simple structure of top versus bottom. An S/M scene can be played out using the personae of guard and prisoner, cop and suspect, Nazi and Jew, white and black, straight man and queer, parent and child, priest and penitent, teacher and student, whore and client, etc.

However, no symbol has a single meaning. Meaning is derived from the context in which it is used. Not everyone who wears a swastika is a

Nazi; not everyone who has a pair of handcuffs on his belt is a cop; and not everyone who wears a nun's habit is a Catholic. S/M is more a parody of the hidden sexual nature of fascism than it is a worship of or acquiescence to it. How many real Nazis, cops, priests, or teachers would be involved in a kinky sexual scene? It is also a mistake to assume that the historical oppressor is always the top in an S/M encounter. The child may be chastising the parent; the prisoner may have turned the tables on the cop; and the queer may be forcing the straight man to confront his sexual response to other men. The dialogue in some S/M scenes may sound sexist or homophobic from the outside, but its real meaning is probably neither. A top can call his bottom a cocksucker to give him instruction (i.e., to indicate that the top wants oral stimulation); to encourage him to lose his inhibitions and perform an act he may be afraid of; or simply to eroticize and use shame and guilt to enhance the sex act rather than prevent it.

S/M eroticism focuses on forbidden feelings or actions and searches for a way to obtain pleasure from them. It is the quintessence of nonreproductive sex. Those feminists who accuse sadomasochists of mocking the oppressed by playing with dominance and submission forget that we are oppressed. We suffer police harassment, violence in the street, and discrimination in housing and employment. We are not treated the way our system treats its collaborators and supporters.

The issue of pain is probably as difficult for non-S/M people to understand as polarized roles are. We tend to associate pain with illness or self-destruction. First of all, S/M does not necessarily involve pain. The exchange of power is more essential to S/M than intense sensation, punishment, or discipline. Second, pain is a subjective experience. Depending on the context, a certain sensation may frighten you, make you angry, urge you on, or get you hot. In many situations, people choose to endure pain or discomfort if the goal for which they are striving makes it worthwhile. Long-distance runners are not generally thought of as perverts, nor is Mother Theresa. The fact that our society disapproves of masochism while it lauds stressful athletic activity and religious martyrdom is an interesting demonstration of how sex has been made a "special case." We seem incapable of using the same reasoning and compassion we apply to nonsexual issues to formulate our positions on sexual issues.

S/M violates a taboo that preserves the mysticism of romantic sex because any pain involved is deliberate. Aroused human beings do not see, smell, hear, taste, or perceive pain as acutely as the nonaroused individual. Lots of people find bruises or scratches the morning after an exhilarating session of lovemaking and can't remember exactly how or when they got them. The sensations involved in S/M are not that different. But we're supposed to fall into bed and do it with our eyes closed. Good, enthusiastic sex is supposed to happen automatically between people who love each other. If the sex is less than stunning, we blame the quality of our partners' feelings for us. Planning a sexual encounter and using toys or equipment to produce specific feelings seems antithetical to romance.

What looks painful to an observer is probably being experienced as pleasure, heat, pressure, or a mixture of all these. A good top builds sensation slowly, alternates pain with pleasure, rewards endurance with more pleasure, and teaches the bottom to transcend her own limits. With enough preparation, care, and encouragement, people are capable of doing wonderful things. There is a special pride which results from doing something unique and extraordinary for your lover. The sadomasochist has a passion for making use of the entire body, every nerve fiber, and every wayward thought.

Recently, I have heard feminists use the term *fetishistic* as an epithet and a synonym for *objectifying*. Sadomasochists are often accused of substituting things for people, of loving the leather or rubber or spike heels more than the person who is wearing them. *Objectification* originally referred to the use of images of stereotypically feminine women to sell products like automobiles and cigarettes. It also referred to the sexual harassment of women and the notion that we should be available to provide men with sexual gratification without receiving pleasure in return and without the right to refuse to engage in sex. A concept which was originally used to attack the marketing campaigns of international corporations and the sexual repression of women is now being used to attack a sexual minority.

Fetish costumes are just as unacceptable to employers and advertising executives as women's wearing overalls and smoking cigars. Hardly instruments of the sexual repression of women, fetish costumes can provide the women who wear them with sexual pleasure and power. Even when a fetish costume exaggerates the masculine or feminine attributes of the wearer, it cannot properly be called sexist. Our society strives to make masculinity in men and femininity in women appear natural and biologically determined. Fetish costumes violate this rule by being too theatrical and deliberate. Since fetish costumes may also be used to transform the gender of the wearer, they are a further violation of sexist standards for sex-specific dress and conduct.

The world is not divided into people who have sexual fetishes and people who don't. There is a continuum of responses to certain objects, substances, and parts of the body, and few people can disregard these and still enjoy having sex. However, much fetishism probably passes as "normal" (nonfetishist) sexuality because the required cues are so common and easy to obtain that no one notices how necessary they are.

Human sexuality is a complicated phenomenon. A cursory examination will not yield the entire significance of a sexual act. Fetishes have several qualities which make them erotically stimulating and unacceptable to the majority culture. Wearing leather, rubber, or a silk kimono distributes feeling over the entire skin. The isolated object may become a source of arousal. This challenges the identification of sex with the genitals. Fetishes draw all the senses into the sexual experience, especially the sense of smell and touch. Since they are often anachronistic or draw attention to erogenous zones, fetish costumes cannot be worn on the street. Fetishes are reserved for sexual use only, yet they are drawn from realms not traditionally associated with sexuality. Fetishism is the product of imagination and technology.

Sadomasochism is also accused of being a hostile or angry kind of sex, as opposed to the gentle and loving kind of sex that feminists should strive for. The women's movement has become increasingly pro-romantic love in the last decade. Lesbians are especially prone to this sentimental trend. Rather than being critical of the idea that one can find enough fulfillment in a relationship to justify one's existence, feminists are seeking membership in perfect, egalitarian couples. I question the value of this trend.

There is no concrete evidence that a sadomasochist's childhood contained any more corporal punishment, puritanism, or abuse than the childhoods of other people. There is also no evidence that we secretly fear and hate our partners. S/M relationships vary from no relationship at all (the S/M is experienced during fantasy or masturbation) to casual sex with many partners, to monogamous couples, and include all shades in between. There are many different ways to express affection or sexual interest. Vanilla people send flowers, poetry, or candy, or they exchange rings. An S/M person does all that and may also lick boots, wear a locked collar, or build her loved one a rack in the basement. There is little objective difference between a feminist who is offended by the fact that my lover kneels to me in public and a suburbanite who calls the cops because the gay boys next door are sunbathing in the nude. My sexual semiotics differ from the mainstream. So what? I didn't join the feminist movement to live inside a Hallmark greeting card.

Is there a single controversial sexual issue that the women's movement has not reacted to with a conservative, feminine horror of the outrageous and the rebellious? A movement that started out saying biology is *not* destiny is now trashing transsexuals and celebrating women's "natural" connection to the earth and living things. A movement that spawned children's liberation is now trashing boy-lovers and supporting the passage of draconian sex laws that assign heavier sentences for having sex with a minor than you'd get for armed robbery. A movement that developed an analysis of housework as unpaid labor and acknowledged that women usually trade sex for what they want because that's all they've got is now joining the vice squad to get prostitutes off the street. A movement whose early literature was often called obscene and was banned from circulation is now campaigning to get rid of pornography. The only sex perverts this movement supports are lesbian mothers, and I suspect that's because of the current propaganda about women comprising the nurturing, healing force that will save the world from destructive male energy.

Lesbianism is being desexualized as fast as movement dykes can apply the whitewash. We are no longer demanding that feminist organizations acknowledge their lesbian membership. We are pretending that the words *feminist* and *woman* are synonyms for *lesbian*.

The antipornography movement is the best of the worst of the women's movement, and it must take responsibility for much of the bigotry circulating in the feminist community. This movement has consistently refused to take strong public positions that support sex education, consenting-adult legislation, the right to privacy, the decriminalization of prostitution, children's and adolescents' rights to sexual information and freedom, and the First Amendment. It has encouraged violence against sexual minorities, especially sadomasochists, by slandering sexual deviation as violence against women. The antipornography movement's view of S/M is derived from one genre of commercial pornography (male-dominant and female-submissive) and makes Krafft-Ebing look like a liberal.

Commercial pornography distorts all forms of sexual behavior. There are several reasons for this. One is that it is designed to make money, not to educate people or to be aesthetically pleasing. The other is that it is quasi-legal and thus must be produced as quickly and surreptitiously as possible. Another reason is that erotic material is intended to gratify fantasy, not serve as a model for actual behavior.

S/M pornography can be divided into several types, each designed for a different segment of the S/M subculture. Most of it represents women dominating and disciplining men, since the largest market for S/M porn is heterosexual submissive males. Very little S/M porn shows any actual physical damage or even implies that damage is occurring. Most of it depicts bondage or tops dressed in fetish costumes and assuming threatening poses.

Very little S/M porn is well-produced or informative. But eliminating it will have the effect of further impoverishing S/M culture and isolating sadomasochists from one another, since many of us make contact via personal ads carried in pornographic magazines. The excuse for banning "violent" porn is that this will end violence against women. But this causal connection is dubious. It is indisputably true that very few people who consume pornography ever assault or rape another person. When a rape or assault is committed, it usually occurs after some forethought and planning. But legally, a free society must distinguish between the fantasy or thought of committing a crime and the actual crime. It is not a felony to fantasize committing an illegal act, and it should not be, unless we want our morals regulated by the Brain Police. Banning S/M porn is the equivalent of making fantasy a criminal act. Violence against women will not be reduced by increasing sexual repression. People desperately need better information about sex; more humanistic and attractive erotica; more readily available birth control, abortion, and sex therapy; and more models for nontraditional, nonexploitative relationships.

I am often asked if sadomasochism will survive the revolution. I think all the labels and categories we currently use to describe ourselves will change dramatically in the next one hundred years, even if the revolution does not occur. My fantasy is that kinkiness and sexual variation will multiply, not disappear, if terrible penalties are no longer meted out for being sexually adventurous.

But there is an assumption behind the question that bothers me. The assumption that sadomasochists are part of the system rather than part of the rebellion has already been dealt with in this article. But there is another assumption—that we must enjoy being oppressed and mistreated. We like to wear uniforms? Then we must get off on having cops bust up our bars. We like to play with whips and nipple clamps and hot wax? Then it must turn us on when gangs of kids hunt us down, harass and beat us. We're not really human. We're just a bunch of leather jackets and spike heels, a bunch of post office boxes at the ends of sex ads.

We make you uncomfortable partly because we're different, partly because we're sexual, and partly because we're not so different. I'd like to know when you're going to quit blaming us, the victims of sexual repression, for the oppression of women. I'd like to know when you're going to quit objectifying us.

Genderbending:
Playing with Roles and Reversals
1983

I am in High Gear at the corner of Eighteenth and Castro. Two pairs of Levi's 501s tucked under my arm, I stand in front of a display case of jockstraps and run through them until I find my size. I take everything up to the cash register. The clerk, a sweet muffin with a ginger mustache who's probably made it with about five thousand men (in the dressing room alone) and about two and a half girls (in high school), looks at my tits, looks at the jock, then rings up the sale. He manages to get my purchases into a bag without dropping anything, writes my driver's license number on my check, and thanks me for my business, albeit a bit dryly. That's okay. I'm grateful. Can you imagine trying a stunt like this at Macy's?

Later, at home, I force myself to get dressed in front of a mirror. I'm still not used to doing this, and it makes my hands shake and my palms get wet. But it gets easier as the transformation proceeds. First, the dildo harness, which I made myself out of two leather straps, one that goes around my waist and one attached to it that goes through my crotch. Both pieces attach in front to a rubber cock ring, which holds the dildo that becomes my cock. Once it's in place, I pull all the straps snug (Velcro makes them adjustable; I love technology), put on the jock, and bend over to pull on my boots. I put on my black leather chaps. I shrug into my motorcycle jacket and zip it shut with nothing underneath it—another broken taboo for a woman. But I don't feel like a woman anymore. The semiotics have shifted. For instance my long hair doesn't mean femme; it means hippie biker. And there's my cock. I can grab it, stroke it—and it feels good. It looks good, too, the bulge covered by tightly stretched white cotton, framed by black leather.

Of course the illusion is not complete enough for me to present myself as male on the streets, though it is for some of my friends. But this identity and equipment are going to give me and the woman who will arrive shortly a very intense evening of sexual pleasure. While I'm tucking a couple of Trojans into my jacket pocket, the doorbell rings.

Two hours later, I'm through playing around, and I want to screw her ass off. My cock has been hard for way too long. I reach down and squeeze it, showing her how long it is. She watches, fascinated, in the same position she landed when I tossed her onto the bed. "Do you want it?" I demand. She licks her lips, but she doesn't answer me, so I grab her by the hair and rub her face over my crotch. Her tongue slips out of her mouth as if by accident, and she begins to lick me, at first slowly, tentatively, then more quickly until her pace is frantic, as if she could lick her way through the jock, melt it away with her tongue, and reach my flesh. So hard that I ache, I shove the jock to one side and tell her to suck my dick. It's difficult not to hold her head and fuck her throat, but I've still got a little self-control left, so I just encourage her by talking real dirty. She finally manages to take the whole thing, and it looks incredibly hot, her mouth pressed into my pubes, her throat working convulsively; and I want to come in her cunt, so I take it away from her and order her onto her hands and knees. She piles pillows under her hips, so her ass will stay up in the air later when I start slamming into her. Kneeling behind her, I push apart her naked thighs with my leatherclad ones and look down to see the soft, dark fur of her vulva. The inner lips are so engorged that they have spread themselves apart like little fans, and when I separate the cheeks of her ass and run my thumbs down the groove, it's slippery. Her cunt has gotten so juicy, it's dripped down that far.

"You do want it," I say, and this time I get a groaning acknowledgment, a plea that I continue. My thumbs slide down further, find and plumb the depth of her wet hole. I use one hand to keep it open and the other hand to push the head of my cock down and into her. She slides back onto me with a shout of relief and dread, and I take her by the waist and move her to my pleasure, plunging into her vulnerability, her need. I want to fill her completely and keep her filled forever. She moans that she's scared because it feels so good, she's not sure she can stand it. In response my hips slap into her faster, rougher. We both sound like rutting animals; it's obscene. All our actions become involuntary, unselfconscious. We don't care what we look or sound like, just how it feels. We have to make it keep feeling this good. I pin her, pound into her with new urgency. I am about to come, and I will not let her get away until I have. Deep in my lower belly, there is a feeling of pressure building, intolerable heat, then pulsing, little explosions that build and build until there is one big explosion, a climax that makes me see stars. I collapse on her back, exhausted, sweating like a pig, gasping and drymouthed, my hands still clamped onto her shoulders.

The next time we see each other, I will probably be the one on my knees. Her cock is longer than mine, but I don't have any trouble taking it all the way down my throat if she is *making* me take it. I love to be fucked hard that way until tears run down my face, and I'm dizzy from not being able to breathe. And I love being fucked on my back (will a penchant for the missionary position become a secret feminist perversion?) because that way my partner can see my face, every detail of my response to the cock that is moving inside me. I become pornographic, a slut, a whore—an identity that has been denied me with as much ferocity as the pleasures of masculinity. Pornography is made for men, not women—except in my bed, where I will try to give another woman every pleasure, power, and privilege that men want to keep for themselves, including the pleasure of holding a woman in her arms and penetrating her with a sensitive part of her own body. This is one vaginal orgasm of which Freud would not approve.

The time after that, we might both be men. That gets very interesting, especially if one of us is straight. Believe it or not, though, we have some of our best times as women. Vanilla lesbian sex can seem pretty risqué to us hardened perverts.

Gender. Sex. Boys and girls, men and women. Penises and vaginas. Sperm and eggs. Hairy chests and 38D tits. The fundamental division, polarity, split, separation, difference in the human species. It's biological, has nothing to do with culture or learning. It's in the genes (jeans?), dictated by nature. Some of us are male; some of us are female. That's the way it's been, and that's the way it always will be. We can argue about what our gender implies about our personalities, our capacities and inadequacies, our social responsibilities, but human beings will always be divided into those two categories. They are that fundamental.

Yeah, and the world is flat, and the sun moves around it.

When I was a raging separatist who wanted to kick transsexuals out of the women's movement (oh, well, we all live and learn...), I read up on people like Richard Green and John Money, the social scientists who coined the term *gender dysphoria* and suggested that "sex reassignment" might be an appropriate way to "treat" this condition. Most of the genderbender researchers are conservative to the point of fascism about sexual identity. Ideally, they say, infants are clearly male or female at birth. Infants with ambiguous genitalia should be assigned to one sex or the other (preferably by a medical authority) and raised that way with no ambivalence or qualms on the part of their parents. Little boys should grow up to be masculine, heterosexual men with penises, and little girls should grow up to be feminine, heterosexual women with babies. Adults who deviate from this norm (transvestites, transsexuals, masculine women, feminine men, homosexuals, hermaphrodites) should be "fixed" by whatever means necessary, including surgery, artificial hormones, behavioral therapy, and voice lessons. Despite their "if-it-doesn't-fit-cut-it-off" attitude, these guys permanently shook my firm belief in the reality of biological sex, in the natural and inevitable existence of only two genders.

They made it clear (especially Money in *Man Woman Boy Girl*) that as a society we have made a *decision* to believe in, accept, and allow only two sexes. In fact, human beings come in more models than xx or xy. There *is* variation in gender, even at the most basic, genetic level. And once you start considering anatomical anomalies, hormonal balances and imbalances, self-images, and desire, you get a host of possibilities.

That knocked me out. Why does our society allow only two genders and keep them polarized? Why don't we have a social role for hermaphrodites? Berdaches? Why do transsexuals have to become "real women" or "real men" instead of just being transsexuals? After all, aren't there some advantages to being a man with a vagina or a woman with a penis, if only because of the unique perspective it would give? And why can't people go back and forth if they want to?

I have come to the conclusion that this situation exists because it is eroticized. Strict gender division is so important to the majority of people's sexual pleasure that they want to disguise it as nature or biology, so nothing will threaten to change it. The differences between men and women are seized upon, encouraged, artificially exaggerated, and even lied about to create a distance and a tension that give heterosexuals something to struggle with, a strange territory to explore, a mystery to apprentice themselves to and celebrate. A belief in sex differences and a dependence on them for sexual pleasure is the most common perversion, if we define *perversion* as allowing imagination, intelligence, and choice to create sex for pleasure, as opposed to restricting ourselves to instinct, hormones, and religion, and limiting sex for procreation. Perhaps institutional sexism is so recalcitrant because even people who realize how bad it is are afraid that getting rid of it would mean getting rid of the pleasure they obtain from the dual-gender system.

Homosexuality both challenges and reinforces this system. In the traditional view of sexual identity, all the components are irrevocably welded together (man/penis/masculinity/heterosexuality). A homosexual man or lesbian has rearranged these components, which is a dangerous and difficult thing to do. Despite all the nasty things they have to say about one another, sissies, gay businessmen, androgynous lesbian-feminists, and sapphic fashion models all challenge the system in equal degrees. The homosexual who conforms to her or his sex role (the masculine gay man, the feminine lesbian) is saying, "I am *not* a member of the opposite sex; I simply have a preference for members of my own gender." The homosexual who does not conform to her or his sex role (the effeminate faggot, the bulldyke) is also saying, "These components can be arranged any way I damn well please. Mind your own business."

However, to the extent that homosexuality is based on being able to make distinctions between two sexes, albeit for the purpose of choosing the "wrong" one, gay people, too, have an investment in maintaining a dual-sex system. This dialectic—the fact that homosexuals are challenging and resisting, yet simultaneously dependent upon and deeply attracted to gender differences—may explain why transsexuals and transvestites have a place in the gay community, but an uneasy and sometimes threatened one. It may also explain why there are two different (and ideologically opposed) forms of homosexuality—the narcissistic form (which today means butch-on-butch or clone-on-clone gay male sex and the pairing of androgynous, almost asexual lesbians) and the butch/femme form (which includes queens and their masculine partners as well as the more visible and better-known lesbian role system).

Narcissistic homosexuals tend to have a strong investment in their own "appropriate" gender identity. "I'm a man, and I want another man!" is said with the same tone of self-righteousness as a lesbian-feminist's saying, "I'm a woman, and I want another woman!" Oddly enough, they often accuse butch/femme homosexuals of remaining attached to a repressive system of gender differences. The most commonly voiced criticism of butch/femme homosexuals is, "They're just imitating the hets."

Defenders of butch/femme roles usually deny this accusation and try to point out the differences between their sexuality and heterosexual behavior. So I was initially shocked when I heard Amber Hollibaugh, a long-time gay activist, self-declared femme, and controversial columnist for the *New York Native*, say bluntly that she thought butch/femme was a system of "gay gender." Now I think she's right. The idea has a lot of interesting potential. There's nothing inherently oppressive about getting off on polarized roles during sex. Butch/femme homosexuals can select the things that are rewarding and gratifying about the male/female gender system and leave behind the ugly aspects of institutionalized inequality. "Gay gender" can be a way to critique "heterosexual gender."

In the past, it was neither that simple nor liberating. When I came out, lesbian butch/femme culture was certainly not so bad as heterosexuality, but it didn't feel like a viable alternative, either. There were too many inequalities built into the system. Butches were the "real" lesbians. They did most of the talking and occupied the largest amount of social space. They had most of the prestige and power. They were the heroes. Femmes were suspect. No butch ever completely believed her femme was a genuine lesbian. The fact that high-status femmes tended to be bisexual women currently in a "lesbian phase" or women who had ended heterosexual marriages to be with their butches exacerbated this tension. There was a double standard. A butch was supposed to flirt and carry on. A femme was supposed to belong to one butch and keep her eyes down when the butch was not around. Of course, femmes wielded quite a bit of de facto power because they were scarce. An independent and bitchy femme could keep several butches on a string and competing for her favors for quite a while. Femmes often had just as much or even more money than butches, since they tended to be more employable. But femme power was always covert, and I hated that. I was also uncomfortable with the ideology of inherent differences. There were supposed to be "real" reasons why some women were butch, and other women were femme. A role was supposed to express your "true" nature. This meant you had to construct a personal mythology confirmed by childhood experiences and your entire sex history to justify your role. This got a little embarrassing and cumbersome if you ever wanted to switch.

Even under these conditions, there were important differences between butch/femme and male/female that made it a better system, tailored to give more pleasure to the individuals within it, with more breathing room and flexibility. The butch phallus is very different from the male phallus. The butch phallus does not exist if the femme does not recognize it. The femme reifies its presence—its reality—with her response to it, which ranges from wearing feminine clothing and makeup to cooking dinner to having orgasms. If the butch phallus does not succeed in giving the femme sexual pleasure, it does not exist. This gives femmes a tremendous amount of sexual power (although it is a negative, reactive power). In butch/femme culture, the phallus is at the service of women rather than the service of men.

I am not using the term *phallus* as a synonym for *penis*. Some butches have explicit fantasies about having penises, but many do not. For them, the whole point of sex with a femme is that they can get her off better than a man can, *without* using a penis. Thus they would be offended by the suggestion that they have, or the femme wants them to have, a cock. Instead I use *phallus* to mean male privilege and sexual power, the presence of that privilege and power even in the absence of a penis.

Likewise, the femininity of the femme is different from the femininity of a typical heterosexual woman. This femininity gives comfort and pleasure to other women. In a society where women never have wives, this role is radical. It contains an element of choice. It is a fetish, rather than a dress code that a woman has to obey before she can get a job or go out on the street without experiencing harassment and violence.

■ ■ ■

Today lesbian butch/femme is acquiring more flexibility than it had in the '70s when I came out. This is partly due to the influence of S/M dykes who have introduced the concept of "tops" and "bottoms" into vanilla lesbian sex. Now butch/femme dykes talk about "butch bottoms" and "femme tops" as valid sexual categories. The butches I met in Perky's would have laughed an idea like that right out the door. But then, those women were heavy mothers who would have thought Beebo Brinker was a kiki bra burner. Modern butch/femme lesbians talk more about how these roles can be used to provide sexual pleasure and less about their springing from intrinsic differences in people's personalities or hormones. There's even a new form of transvestitism appearing—butches who like to be "forced" to dress up in feminine clothing. This was unheard of ten years ago. I love it when a new perversion appears.

Transsexuality has even more explosive potential to alter our dual gender system. Imagine what it would mean if everybody knew they did not have to keep the biological sex with which they were born. Unfortunately, the medical and psychiatric establishment has driven this potential underground. Transsexuals are like heroin addicts who have to know exactly what story to tell the doctors to get their methadone. Transsexuals must say just the right thing to receive their hormones. This makes the "research" on the etiology of transsexuality worthless. Transsexuals who don't insist they feel they've had the wrong body since early childhood, or who say they don't hate their genitals and feel fine about pleasuring them during masturbation, or who admit that they get turned on when they wear opposite-sex clothing (instead of just wanting to wear it because it reinforces their identity as members of the desired sex), or who divulge that after sex reassignment they will probably be gay will be diagnosed as transvestites or homosexuals and denied the drugs or surgery that they want. In follow-up studies of "reassigned" transsexuals, one of the criteria for mental health is how well they have "passed." A transsexual in a heterosexual relationship who has no contact with other transsexuals is "normal," a success. Transsexuals who spend time in the gay community, acknowledge their transsexual identity, and maybe even think it's a political issue are failures. How can schizophrenia or amnesia be mentally healthy? Transsexuals have strong feelings of yearning to change their biological sex; no matter how many people eventually come to accept them as members of their preferred sex, that history cannot be erased.

A friend of mine who works as a sex surrogate says he now recommends that his transsexual clients avoid surgically altering their bodies until they've tried to be happy crossdressing and finding partners who will accept them as transsexuals. He feels uncomfortable about the side effects of the artificial hormones, the poor results of surgery to alter the genitals, and the fact that so many of the changes are irreversible.

Of course there will always be some people who won't be happy unless they can be completely reassigned, and I think this process should continue to be available, and doctors should work harder to make it a more humane, practical alternative for folks unhappy with the sex they were assigned at birth. It wouldn't hurt to put a little more slack into the whole gender system.

Those of us who work for a world without gender privilege need to ask ourselves how we want to accomplish this. Do we want a society where the similarities between men and women are emphasized, and people are discouraged from expressing or eroticizing their differences? Or do we want a society of pluralistic gender where people can mix and match the components of their sexual identities? I personally would rather live in a world where every man could be a woman or might have been one yesterday—and vice versa.

Gay Men, Lesbians, and Sex: Doing It Together

1983

I have sex with faggots. And I'm a lesbian. You think *you're* confused? How did this happen to a woman who maintained a spotless record as a militant lesbian separatist for eight years, a woman who had sex with only three men (once apiece) before coming out, a woman who gets called a dyke on the street at least once a week, a woman who has slept (and not stayed to sleep) with hundreds of other women?

To explain, I need to go back to 1977. Those of you who aren't ready for this have my permission to leave the room. But don't slam the door on your way out. Who knows who will be sitting on *your* face in 1984?

In 1977 when I bought my first dog collar, there was no such thing as a lesbian S/M community. There probably were a few isolated dykes who owned rope they never intended to string up for clothesline—but I couldn't find them. So when I heard about a women's S/M support group, I joined it even though most of the members were straight or bisexual. I was surprised to discover that most of them were honest, intelligent perverts—and feminists! One of them, a professional dominatrix, became my lover.

My lover found the straight S/M scene pretty joyless, so she hung out with a small group of gay men who were into fisting and S/M. She was especially attached to Steve McEachern, who ran private hand-balling parties in his extremely well-equipped basement. This club was called The Catacombs. The Christmas after we became lovers, she took me to a party at his house. About fifteen men were present. She and I were the only women. After a huge dinner, everybody just started taking off his clothes. I found myself sitting alone in a corner, wondering if I was going to spend the entire orgy feeling sorry for myself (my girl-friend had wandered off with Steve). A tall, handsome man (albeit a little skinny) sat down beside me and said, "Hi, my name's Joe. How would you like to fist me?"

I took a deep breath and said, "I'd like that, but you'll have to show me what to do." That was fine with him. He got me an emery board and some nail clippers and showed me how to perform the very severe man-icure handballing requires. He took for granted that a novice had to

183

receive detailed instructions, and he didn't expect me to dazzle him with a magic show of sexual expertise. This attitude was very reassuring and completely different from the way anybody else I'd met had approached sex. When Joe approved my hands, we went downstairs, located some towels and Crisco, and climbed onto the waterbed.

Joe lay on his back. He wrapped his arms around his thighs and held them apart. My first handful of grease melted right into his ass. It was like feeding a hungry animal—an animal that talked back. He gave me such careful instructions about when to push and when to pull back that I got into him easily, I can't remember how deep. It seemed like miles. I came to at one point and realized just how vulnerable he was, this big man clutching his thighs and groaning uncontrollably because I was so far into him. The walls of his gut hugged my hand and forearm, smoother and softer and more fragile than anything I'd ever touched before. I think I cried. I know I got wet.

Well, that's how it started. I've lost track of exactly how many men I've put my hand(s) into, and it still puts me in a trance. It's awesome to be that close to another human being. In between cans of Crisco, I've thought a lot about why it's possible to cross the "gender line" in the context of this kind of sex. First of all, in fisting the emphasis is not on the genitals. Men at handballing parties don't usually cruise each other's dicks. They cruise each other's hands and forearms. It is not unusual for fisters to go all night without a hard-on. Tops with small hands are in demand, and my glove size is a popular one. Gay men who are into handballing usually think of themselves as sexually different from other gay men. They get a lot of attitude about being sick, kinky, and excessive. Hence some of them are willing to break a gay taboo and do it with a woman.

As I acquired more experience in the S/M community, I realized this, too, was a sexuality that allowed people to step outside the usually rigid boundaries of sexual orientation. I met lesbians who topped straight men for money (and did that myself for a while). I met straight men who would go down on other men or be fucked by them if their mistresses ordered them to do it. Since the acts took place under the authority of women, they thought of them as heterosexual behavior. (I also met a lot of bisexuals who didn't need any excuses.)

These combined experiences have resulted in a lifestyle that doesn't fit the homosexual stereotype. I live with my woman lover of five years. I have lots of casual sex with women. Once in a while, I have casual sex with gay men. I have a three-year relationship with a homosexual man who doesn't use the term *gay*. And I call myself a lesbian.

Of course, I've modified my sexual pattern in the face of the AIDS crisis. I've become much more conscious of the need to maintain good general health by getting enough sleep, eating a nutritious diet, and reducing stress and recreational drug use. I've also quit having sex with strangers. I have the same amount of sex but with fewer people—and none of them are taking excessive risks with their health, either. I have not dropped fisting from my repertoire, I am simply more selective about whom I do it with. I have yet to be convinced that fisting exposes me or my partners to more danger than other kinds of sexual contact.

Why not identify as bi? That's a complicated question. For a while, I thought I was simply being biphobic. There's a lot of that going around in the gay community. Most of us had to struggle so hard to be exclusively homosexual that we resent people who don't make a similar commitment. A self-identified bisexual is saying, "Men and women are of equal importance to me." That's simply not true of me. I'm a Kinsey Five, and when I turn on to a man it's because he shares some aspect of my sexuality (like S/M or fisting) that turns me on *despite* his biological sex.

There's yet another twist. I have eroticized queerness, gayness, homosexuality—in men and women. The leatherman and the drag queen are sexy to me, along with the diesel dyke with greased-back hair, and the femme stalking across the bar in her miniskirt and high-heeled shoes. I'm a fag hag.

The gay community's attitude toward fag hags and dyke daddies has been pretty nasty and unkind. Fag hags are supposed to be frustrated, traditionally feminine, heterosexual women who never have sex with their handsome, slightly effeminate escorts—but desperately want to. Consequently, their nails tend to be long and sharp, and their lipstick runs to the bloodier shades of carmine. And They Drink. Dyke daddies are supposed to be beer-bellied rednecks who hang out at lesbian bars to sexually harass the female patrons. The nicer ones are suckers who get taken for drinks or loans that will never be repaid.

These stereotypes don't do justice to the complete range of modern faghaggotry and dyke daddydom. Today fag hags and dyke daddies are as likely to be gay themselves as the objects of their admiration.

I call myself a fag hag because sex with men outside the context of the gay community doesn't interest me at all. In a funny way, when two gay people of opposite sexes make it, it's still gay sex. No heterosexual couple brings the same experiences and attitudes to bed that we do. These generalizations aren't perfectly true, but more often than straight sex, gay sex assumes that the use of hands or the mouth is as important as genital-to-genital contact. Penetration is not assumed to be the only goal of a sexual encounter. When penetration does happen, dildos and fingers are as acceptable as (maybe even preferable to) cocks. During gay sex, more often than during straight sex, people think about things like lubrication and "fit." There's no such thing as "foreplay." There's good sex, which includes lots of touching, and there's bad sex, which is nonsensual. Sex roles are more flexible, so nobody is automatically on the top or the bottom. There's no stigma attached to masturbation, and gay people are much more accepting of porn, fantasies, and fetishes.

And, most importantly, there is no intention to "cure" anybody. I know that a gay man who has sex with me is making an exception and that he's still gay after we come and clean up. In return I can make an exception for him because I know he isn't trying to convert me to heterosexuality.

I have no way of knowing how many lesbians and gay men are less than exclusively homosexual. But I do know I'm not the only one. Our actual behavior (as opposed to the ideology that says homosexuality means being sexual only with members of the same sex) leads me to ask questions about the nature of sexual orientation, how people (especially gay people) define it, and how they choose to let those definitions control and limit their lives.

During one of our interminable discussions in Samois about whether or not to keep the group open to bi women, Gayle Rubin pointed out that a new, movement-oriented definition of lesbianism was in conflict with an older, bar-oriented definition. Membership in the old gay culture consisted of managing to locate a gay bar and making a place for yourself in bar society. Even today, nobody in a bar asks you how long you've been celibate with half the human race before they will check your coat and take your order for a drink. But in the movement, people insist on a kind of purity that has little to do with affection, lust, or even political commitment. Gayness becomes a state of sexual grace, like virginity. A fanatical insistence on one hundred percent exclusive, same-sex behavior often sounds to me like superstitious fear of contamination or pollution. Gayness that has more to do with abhorrence for the other sex than with an appreciation of your own sex degenerates into a rabid and destructive separatism.

It is very odd that sexual orientation is defined solely in terms of the sex of one's partners. I don't think I can assume anything about another person simply because I've been told she or he is bisexual, heterosexual, or homosexual. A person's politics may be conservative, liberal, radical, or nonexistent, regardless of sexual orientation. In fact, a sexual orientation label tells you nothing about her or his sex life, for

God's sake. There are lots of "heterosexual" men who have plenty of anonymous sex with other men. There are celibate faggots and dykes. There are lesbians who've been married for thirty years and have six children. There are heterosexual women who frequently have sex with other women at swing parties. For many people, if a partner or a sexual situation has other desirable qualities it is possible to overlook the partner's sex. Some examples: a preference for group sex, for a particular socioeconomic background, for paid sex, for S/M, for a specific age group, for a physical type or race, for anal or oral sex.

I no longer believe that there is some ahistorical entity called homosexuality. Sexuality is socially constructed within the limits imposed by physiology, and it changes over time with the surrounding culture. There was no such thing as a Castro clone, a lesbian-feminist, or a Kinsey Six a century ago, and one hundred years from now these types will be as extinct as *Urnings*.

This is not to say that in a sexual utopia we would all be bisexual. There is nothing wrong with having sex exclusively with members of your own sex (or the opposite sex). I simply question some of the assumptions or attitudes that have grown around the fact that some people have an erotic preference for same-sex behavior. Gay people have responded to persecution and homophobia by creating our own mythology about homosexuality. Whenever desire and behavior conflict with rhetoric, it's time to reexamine the rhetoric. Some lesbians and gay men are having opposite-sex experiences. Why? What are they learning?

Gay male friends and lovers have taught me things that I would never have learned in the lesbian community. I can't exaggerate my admiration for the well-developed technology, etiquette, attitudes, and institutions that gay men have developed to express their sexuality. (Remember, this is from the perspective of a woman who can't go to the baths every night or answer fifty sex ads in the "Pink Pages.") There's a basic attitude that sex is good in and of itself and that people ought to get what they want and treat each other well while they pursue it. That includes taking responsibility for preventing and treating sexually transmitted diseases. There's certainly room for improvement, but gay men are better educated about STDs and deal with them more promptly than typical heterosexual swingers or nonmonogamous lesbians.

Having good sex with men also allowed me to confront some of my fears about what it might "mean" to be a lesbian. You know, all that stuff about dykes being too unattractive to get a man and all the psychobabble about penis envy. I now feel that having sex with women really is a choice for me. I know that sexually active women are in demand in any straight sex environment, and I could walk into most of those joints and take my pick. I just don't want what they have to offer. I no longer feel threatened by sexual come-ons from men. Once you've had vice presidents of large corporations on your leash, straight men lose a lot of their power to intimidate you.

As for penis envy, I often think it would be nice to have a cock. I love fucking people, and because there's all this cultural meaning assigned to getting fucked with a cock (as opposed to fingers or a dildo), I'd like to have that sexual power. But I'm better with a strap-on dildo than most straight boys are at using their own cocks, and besides, I can change sizes. Once you've gotten two hands up somebody's ass, you aren't likely to feel jealous of a penis. Nobody's cock is *that* big. So, while I wouldn't mind having one, I think after I was done using it, I'd want to be able to take it off and leave it on a shelf. I don't want to have to be adjusting it in my pants all the time. And I *like* sitting down to pee. It makes it easier to read, and if you're outdoors, the grass tickles your heinie.

It's been very nice to lose my phobia about cocks. Our culture's phallic mythology has given the male sex organ so much highly charged symbolic significance that anything powerful is a phallic symbol. A lot of feminist antiporn ideology puts out the idea that cocks are ugly weapons that do nothing but defile or murder women. This symbolic system is very harmful. If cocks really have an inherent power to pollute and damage women, the only solution is to forcibly excise them from the male body. Instead I'd like to see women become more phallic (i.e., more powerful). Cocks seem more fragile than thermonuclear to me. There's a vulnerability about getting an erection that I'm really grateful I don't have to experience before I can give someone a night to remember.

The last and most painful thing I've learned from my contacts with gay men is how the war between the sexes looks from the other side. As embarrassing as it is, I finally had to concede that women engage in a lot of behavior that is homophobic or sexist, and that it is women who enforce much of the sexual repression of the children they raise. This doesn't mean that I think women are equally responsible for their own oppression. Men get most of the goodies from the system and have the highest investment in keeping it running. But I no longer feel that all women are innocent victims, and all men are misogynist monsters.

The information flows both ways. I don't remember how many times I've explained to a gay man what rape is and why women, being physically smaller, feel less safety and mobility on the streets than men do. Then there's economics. Many gay men really don't understand what kinds of jobs women can readily obtain and what these jobs pay.

And of course they get to learn a lot about things like menstrual cycles and multiple orgasms. I can still hear the quaver in the voice of the first gay man who ever went down on me. "Let's see," he said bravely, as he gently spread my labia apart, "where's that famous clitoris I've heard so much about?"

In the midst of the craziness, hostility, ignorance, and angst that plague human relations and sexuality, I feel entitled to whatever comfort or gratification I can find. I'll be looking for some more tonight, in the company of a girlfriend of mine. We have a date to tie up a furry little number and show him a good time. If it bothers you to envision the details, consider it in the abstract. Think of it as a fine example of lesbian/gay solidarity...just queers doing queer things together!

Beyond Leather:
Expanding the Realm of the Senses to Latex

1984

I don't know what it is about rubber that excites Englishmen so much...I have seldom seen a foreigner who gets excited over macs, and never a woman. Black leather, which is the next closest thing to black rubber, gets a lot of people excited...Leather symbolizes strength and virility, mastery and control and so on, and people can fantasize themselves into being at either the giving or the receiving end. Men and women who've never given a thought to leather can be turned into devotees once they're exposed to it, but rubber lovers apparently are born—by the thousands—and not made.

—Sheila Foster, Soho Whore: The Making of a London Prostitute

I always knew I was sexually turned on by rubber. Before I heard about homosexuality, I knew I would find other people who liked latex, too. When I went to college, I spent all the money my parents had given me for tuition to mail order two skin diving suits. This was in the middle of Kansas, so when they found out what I had done, there weren't too many excuses I could make. Today I have three or four rubber suits in different sizes and weights of latex. You can't get too hung up about who's a top and who's a bottom in this scene. Frankly, I wind up introducing a lot of people to it, even women.

—James, a gay rubberman

I wore my new, thigh-high waders to the bar last weekend. Some queen in a flannel shirt comes up to me and says, "I thought this was a leather bar. Did you get lost on your way to the masquerade?" I get that kind of attitude all the time. It's socially acceptable for gay men to wear leather who are not committed to it as a serious fetish. You're not some creepy pervert, you're just macho. But if you see somebody wearing rubber, you know that's what gives him a hard-on. I didn't start to relax and have a good time until I wandered into the john and convinced several guys to piss into my boots.

—Frank, another rubberman

I think the turn-on has to do with being infantile, even wetting yourself. As soon as you put it on, you start to sweat, and it encloses you in your own water, like a womb. It becomes a second skin. I feel like I'm melting, heating up and running all over myself, all the sexual fluids being released. When black latex is wet, it looks so pretty. It makes it sleek and shiny. I feel like a seal.

—Cora, a heterosexual "rubberbaby"

The first time I went into a leather shop, I could hardly *see* anything. I was acutely self-conscious, as if all eyes were on me, as if I had suddenly become naked and forgotten how to walk. The smell was overwhelming. My very private, forbidden sexuality was hanging on the walls, lots of it, where anybody could see it or touch it. I couldn't breathe. The handcuffs were obscene; the whips were unbearable; I had to leave before I suffocated.

It actually took two or three visits before I calmed down enough to look around, compare items, and make a purchase. In one corner of the shop, there were a few odds and ends that looked dusty, as if nobody had handled them—weird things, like junk from a garage sale: a couple of yellow or red enema bags and bulbs; a tee-shirt, gloves, and panties with a penis sheath made out of black latex; a gas mask. The overload switch in my head flipped on, as if to say, "Enough, already! Leave something for later!" On subsequent visits, I discovered some catalogs that featured women in all kinds of outfits—evening gowns, maids' uniforms, baby-doll nighties, bras and skirts, catsuits—made of blue, yellow, red, white, and black latex. The colors made it seem frivolous and unreal to me, like a TV commercial for a new brand of laundry detergent. What was sexy about that? Of course anything in black was sort of interesting...so I kept looking at the pictures.

A cat with nine rubber tails that I found at the Los Angeles Pleasure Chest became part of my whip collection. A pair of elbow-length, black latex gloves in my size magically appeared at Leatherworld. I bought them. At Mister S, when I saw a latex hood that looked like it would fit, I bought that, too. And at a garage sale to help *Gay Community News* rebuild after its offices had burned down (I swear this is true), I found a wet suit and bought that.

At the next women's S/M party, I wore all the latex I had, except the hood, which would not go on without pulling out all of my hair. (Incidentally, beware of latex masks or hoods that are sold without nose or mouth holes. Cut breathing holes *before* you put on the mask.) Just putting on all that rubber required a ritual of powdering everything to lubricate it, then slowly inching the fragile material up over my body. Since I didn't have latex tights, I substituted fishnet stockings and tall, patent-leather spike heels. With the zipper about three-quarters of the way up, the wet suit produced great cleavage.

Guests at the party reacted to my latex the way people at McDonald's had reacted to my shaved head. Someone remarked that I looked like a spare tire. But that's okay; the uninitiated will always sneer. I perspired quickly and freely, which made the suit feel slippery but also slightly gritty, barely abrading my skin. I loved feeling it stick to me, then slide, the slight friction always keeping me turned on. And there was a constant feeling of pressure evenly applied from all sides, holding me snug and making me a little breathless. This is the eroticism of a corset (or the corset's modern-day equivalent, too-tight designer jeans), which embraces, constrains, enforces posture and yet can create a strict and commanding presence in the person who wears it. Fucking people while wearing long latex gloves (using water-soluble lube only, since oil-based lubricants will eat holes in latex) was fascinating. The clinging material transmitted sensation much more intensely than leather. When I got home from the party, I washed off all the lube (stepping into the shower in full latex was more fun than the party), dried and powdered each garment, and stored it away from direct sunlight or extreme temperatures. I was a convert.

Why, oh why, is this sexy? I'm not going to answer that question by constructing a theory about infantile trauma caused by soggy Pampers and Mommy's cold hands. Psychoanalytic theories about the origins of sexual preferences never give you hypotheses that can be operationally defined and proved or refuted. Instead what you get are moral statements about the inferiority of "the other" or recycled versions of your own sexual prejudices. A sociological or anthropological approach is more interesting. The more we know about what people do, the more we can understand how that behavior functions in their lives—what the rewards, stresses, and penalties are.

The English are especially good at rationalizing sexual deviation as if it were merely a logical extension of everyday life. I am reminded of an upper-class, British masochist who visited my dungeon and paled visibly when he saw leather whips hanging on my wall.

"What's the matter?" I said.

"Those," he shuddered, pointing. "They're barbaric! Leather is so violent and primitive."

"Well, what would you like me to use?" I asked, being my usual accommodating though sadistic self. He indicated a thin, flexible bamboo cane. "But that hurts much more than a leather cat!" I told him. "Yes—but—I was caned at school!" he sputtered. "It's *civilized.*"

I saw this tendency personified in an issue of the English fetish magazine *Atomage,* which featured a rare photo essay about a "happy couple" dressing up for an outing. Although they were posed so their faces did not show, they seemed like a typical, rather pudgy pair of people getting dressed in a middle-class bedroom. It was just what they wore that was weird. First the man put on his rubber shorts and his rubber undershirt while the woman donned her rubber panties and rubber bra. Then they each put on their rubber stockings, rubber trousers, rubber overshirts, rubber hip waders, rubber gloves, rubber raincoats, and hats. The last photo was a shot of our "well-protected couple" going fishing in the rain and wading up to their waists in an icy mountain stream—"not feeling the weather a bit." Thus, England's foggy and damp climate becomes the excuse for jogging about in eighty pounds or so of Mr. Goodyear's best.

James, quoted earlier, told me, "I think most gay men feel that our masculinity is injured by our homosexuality. Later on we find out that is not true, but in the meantime we develop crushes on masculine archetypes we can emulate and cruise. I think guys who are into leather got imprinted by the cop image, and guys who are into rubber got imprinted by firemen. They're both very macho, very tough, strong, all that he-man stuff. But cop sex is more S/M, more about arresting people and interrogating them. Firemen handle enormous hoses that shoot huge quantities of water under high pressure, and carry each other up and down ladders, then go back to the firehouse to drink beer and sleep in a dormitory together. It's a buddy-buddy thing."

Cora says her attachment to rubber grew out of her interest in infantilism and watersports. "Let's face it, leather is absorbent, and I don't know too many guys who want you pissing all over their leather. But rubber is so easy to clean off. It's the ideal substance to lose control in." When she finds the rare man who will cater to her fantasy, Cora likes to be dressed in diapers and rubber panties, a rubber baby nightie, then put into her "crib," which is her bed covered with a latex sheet. Daddy comes in, gives her a bottle (usually his cock) and punishes her if she doesn't suck on it. She also gets punished if she wets her diapers, which of course she always does.

People who like rigid bondage are also fond of rubber. Generally, these are people who enjoy bondage for the sake of restraint, not pain. By contrast, rope is much more painful than rubber—stretching the body into stressful positions, cutting into the flesh. It takes a long time to mummify somebody in latex bandages or the homey substitute, clear plastic wrap, but when you are done, she or he can't move a muscle. Plastic wrap is nice because you can see through it. Rubber also has links to an ultimate bondage fantasy of complete sensory deprivation, weightlessness, and giving up control over the body's output and input.

One of my favorite images is somebody floating in a glass tank, suited in thin latex, with tubes running in and out of every orifice. Electrodes monitor all vital functions. I sit at a panel covered with dials and blinking lights, and I get to control everything—heartbeat, water intake, when piss is released (and whether or not it is fed back into the body), temperature, motion or stillness, music or silence.

While leather is atavistic, preindustrial, and romantic, rubber is futuristic, technological, science-fictional. It's the werewolf and the outlaw dressed in the skins of predators versus Aquaman and the Creature from the Black Lagoon. Leather is a totem, giving the wearer the power of the animal it once belonged to; rubber represents an impossible wish to merge with the impersonal (and powerful) machine. Rubber does have links to the animal world, but to carnivorous dinosaurs with long, snaking necks, swimming in the primal sea, rather than the saber-toothed tiger or the dire wolf.

With a gas mask or goggles, someone in a latex suit becomes insect-like or alien. Some people want their "second skin" to line their oral, rectal, and vaginal cavities, too—both protecting them and marking them for sexual use. I am reminded of the people in John Varley's short stories who pair with symbiotic creatures that allow them to live in free-fall in the rings of Saturn. The "symbs" enshroud them, enter their mouths and noses, and go through the anus and digestive tract, until the person is threaded like a needle. The aliens provide mobility, nutrients, heat, and sensory stimulation to their human hosts as they float together through space.

Our fascination with both rubber and leather represents homesickness, an awareness of our human vulnerability. We miss the warmth of fur, the safety of a thick hide or heavy scales, but we want to retain the sensitivity, the sensuality of our bare skin.

Of course the two turn-ons can coexist. Most people who are into rubber also own and enjoy some leather. For one thing, leather is the universal signal of interest in S/M. And rubber is very difficult to obtain. It is expensive and often has to be imported from England or Denmark. If you like the physical properties of latex—the shine, the cling—a garment of black kid can be a substitute. Generally, however, it's leatherfolk who put down rubber and avoid any experimentation with it. They just don't see the point. "It looks silly," "It smells weird," "I don't see anything sexy about dressing up in garbage bags," "It doesn't breathe. I get claustrophobic."

The ultimate fetish material has probably not yet been created. It would combine the protective qualities of leather (its effect as armor) with rubber's ability to conform absolutely to the body's shape and heighten sensory awareness; it would make the wearer feel both animalistic and metahuman.

The latex fetish is an excellent example of the way human culture (especially technology) alters human sexuality. The Victorians went crazy over silk and velvet when these were rare textiles. As quickly as new substances are manufactured, somebody eroticizes them. There are small groups of people attracted to PVC (polyvinyl chloride). This also applies to new social identities or roles. When children were considered tiny versions of adults and given work to do consistent with their class and size, pedophilia as we currently understand it did not exist. Prior to wage labor there was no fetish for cruising blue-collar hunks. Now, astronauts and space suits have joined the ranks of fetishes with longer traditions.

Social change also creates nostalgia and a tendency to eroticize what was. This is one ingredient in the leather fetish and the fetish for corsets and other old-fashioned female foundation garments. It makes cowboys and Victorian governesses sexy. Even the yen to wear one hundred percent cotton Levi's 501s is a nostalgic fetish in this era of synthetic fibers. Latex fans and other fetishists are often accused of substituting their fascination with an object or a part of a person for normal, healthy sex. In part this accusation is based on Victorian sexology (especially Richard von Krafft-Ebing's *Psychopathia Sexualis*). Most of Krafft-Ebing's "cases" obtained their loved and prized objects by stealing them, then masturbated over them in private, terrified of being found out. The good professor (who, let us not forget, was convinced that masturbation caused criminal insanity) is also responsible for the myth that women don't have fetishes. This Victoriana gets recycled in some feminist theories of sexuality in which fetishism is seen as oppressive objectification—men using an object or a part of a woman's body to obtain sexual gratification because they fear or hate living, breathing women.

Fetishism is not inherently antisocial or masturbatory (though there's nothing wrong with creative solo sex). Most fetishists would prefer to share their little peculiarities with a partner, and because times have changed, many of us do. Fortunately, an invitation to try on a pair of eight-inch heels is no longer likely to cause a fainting spell and a suit for breach of promise. It is also easier for us to meet one another and to obtain the items we find erotic. Rather than defining a fetish as a substitute for normal sex, it seems more reasonable to me to think about the cues that most people require before they can become aroused. Somebody who starts to lubricate when she smells leather is on the same continuum as a guy who can't get an erection if his partner isn't using birth control; a lesbian who prefers her partners to have very short hair; women who like big cocks; gay men who need the threat of exposure in a quasi-public setting; or antiporn activists who need a half hour of foreplay spent describing the most degrading eight millimeter loop they've ever seen. The fetish is a problem only if it is so unusual that you can't gratify it, if it involves your partner's doing something that is not in her or his best interest, or if you feel so terrible about it that you stop studying and flunk out of graduate school. It is a way to package and accentuate the human body, not an alienating or hostile impulse.

According to another, more academic and leftist theory, fetishism is an example of the way consumer society regulates desire by creating artificial needs, manufacturing products that will gratify these needs, then selling our own sexuality back to us in an adulterated, unsatisfying form. I feel uncomfortable with this theory because it never seems to get applied with as much vigor to reproductive heterosexuality as it does to the paraphiliacs. Besides, you can't say that the sex industry operates in exactly the same way the mainstream, mass-advertising industry does when it markets color TVs and new cars. Christian morality has impeded capitalism from exploiting all the commercial possibilities for sex. Sexual pleasure is a fringe industry—stigmatized or actually illegal. If you don't believe pleasure is contraband, check out the ferocious border wars over nonreproductive heterosexuality—the struggle to keep commercials for condoms and home pregnancy tests off TV, the constant attempts to restrict access to abortion and birth control.

Because profit can be made from illicit sexual pleasure, an erotic black market will exist under all but the most stringent forms of state repression. If the legitimate institutions of society do not foster and support sexuality, organized crime and police corruption will. While this illicit economy allows sexuality to survive in hostile circumstances, it also limits its shape. The Mafia is notorious for its conservative morality—keeping gay bars out of "nice" neighborhoods; shutting down any attempt to make porn that is too kinky. If a black market becomes too visible, it is inevitably shut down (usually by the same corrupt agents of the state who would otherwise allow it to flourish). The same people who protect illegal or stigmatized forms of sexuality will also oppose any attempt to legitimate them.

This has a curious impact on the folks who inhabit the sex world. One's status as an outcast, criminal, or member of an elite gets eroticized. This can be one way to retain self-esteem ("I am special") in the face of a barrage of denigrating messages, but it doesn't begin to make up for the horrible material conditions we are stuck with. As an exploited market, we are susceptible to being sold shoddy merchandise at exorbitant prices, then to being blackmailed for consuming this merchandise.

In a few tiny liberated zones, unusually gutsy perverts manage to create cottage industries that serve other deviants. John Willie's magazine, *Bizarre*, produced in London during the '50s, was a gift to fellow bondage/fetish enthusiasts. Editing it landed Willie in constant hot water with postal authorities. Feminist sex theorist Gayle Rubin told me a very funny story about Willie. When one of the issues of the magazine was confiscated for obscenity, Willie visited the authorities to find out why. An official brandished a copy at him and said, "Look at this woman in the transparent negligee! Her pubic hair is showing." Willie replied calmly, "That's impossible. I shaved her myself that morning."

The gay/straight/bent business owners who cater to deviant communities certainly have their shortcomings, but they are hardly IBM or Exxon. In this country, they operate in a capitalist context that is beyond their control; still, sexual minorities that support these businesses are not merely the products of decadent capitalist corruption.

Of course the interaction between sexuality and culture is not morally neutral. I find the prospect of sexuality's being regulated by multinational corporations as repugnant as our current bondage to the heirs of the Grand Inquisitor (see Lawrence Sanders's *The Tomorrow File* for a chilling vision of a world in which sex is nothing but a commodity). But I have little hope of seeing sexuality freed from social control. It is too volatile for the powers that be to ignore it. Nor do I think sex and culture can be separated. If they were, it would probably impoverish both aspects of our experience.

I do take some consolation in the fact that no matter how rigidly conformity is enforced, opposition always springs into being. Total control cannot be maintained for very long. It is too expensive, too labor-intensive. Under these conditions, sexuality is a map of rebellion and reaction (especially perversions, for all pleasure is to some extent judged to be perverse). It is not simply a diagram of what is forbidden, since that would be nothing but a mirror image of what is permitted. Rather it is a chart of what has been excluded from the discourse, from consciousness, from literature or the visual arts, insofar as we are able to reconstruct and reimagine it. As an intelligent pervert trying to understand the very strange places in which I find myself getting off, I am filling in whole territories of that map, but I can never stop wondering how much we have lost, what we will never know.

*Un*Monogamy:
Loving Tricks and Tricking Lovers
1984

Every time I pick up a gay paper, the same three-inch headline—"Celebrating Gay Romance"—is plastered across the same naked torso, which used to be adorned by headlines like "Swimwear That's Hotter than Summer," "Proud Gay Pecs on Parade," and "Out of the Bushes and into the Gym."

I know women are supposed to melt into a puddle and come apart at the seams (an ideal combination, you must agree) in the presence of moonlight, string quartets, flowers, swans, waterfalls—anything, it seems, other than the naked body of the beloved. Female sexuality (and, by implication, lesbian sexuality) is not supposed to be genitally oriented. I envision some poor woman writhing with a wandering itch that can't be pinned down by a good scratch, crying frantically, "My desire is not located between my legs, it's in my heart. But not my physical heart, it's all over my body. But not really in my body at all, it originates someplace much more spiritual. Like the sky!"

So you would expect me to be pleased by this new gay male trend toward romance. Many lesbians are; in fact, no valedictorian was ever so contemptuous of her knocked-up classmate: ha, ha, at last those frivolous fags have learned they can't get away with being such sluts! But this smugness offends me—and so does the glut of articles about gay romance, because there's nothing romantic about most of them. Well-intentioned writers (and publishers) are prescribing monogamy and trying to make it palatable to people who know better.

I might find this trend even more offensive than do most gay men, because in the lesbian community serial monogamy has been the norm for what feels like centuries. If you ask the typical lesbian how many lovers she has had, she will count how many women she has lived with and give you a number like, "Four." But if you ask her how many women she has had sex with, she will hem and haw while she tries to add it up in her head and give you an answer like, "Well, more than fifty but less than five hundred." Sex researchers who don't understand this dichotomy in lesbian thinking often report ridiculously low rates of lesbian sexual activity.

I have friends who are unable to have sex unless they tell themselves they are madly in love with the women they bed. The hypocrisy of this enrages me. I don't see why I should pledge eternal love when all I want is some exercise in the sheets. It's blackmail. No wonder straight men get so angry at women who think a hard-on is a handle you grab to lead a man to the altar. I'd rather pay cash for sex than be awakened by a distraught phone call from a woman who expected me to marry her just because I spent a few hours figuring out how to make her come. And she has the nerve to accuse *me* of using *her!* Unfortunately, the numerous tantrums and fist fights provoked by women changing dance—or bed—partners make it difficult to think of the local dyke bar as a good place to go for a quiet beer. Because of a plethora of fake romance, the lesbian community has too much melodrama, alcoholism, and impromptu displays of the martial arts—and not enough camaraderie, good sex, or even good dancing.

Monogamy has nothing to do with morality. If sexual exclusivity were an ethical issue, it would be an individual choice. Has anybody ever said to you, "I'm monogamous, and my lover isn't, so we both do what we feel is right?" Of course not, because monogamy is about controlling the *other* person's behavior—social control, not self-control.

I'm also sick and tired of that line about somebody's being too jealous to handle an open relationship. Monogamy does not assuage jealousy. There is always something to be jealous about. If your lover doesn't sleep around, she has friends. If she doesn't have friends, she has a stamp collection. If she doesn't have a hobby, she has a Past. Even if she was a virgin when you married her, you know quite well how low the odds are that you will be the only person ever to receive her favors. Monogamy is for people who *enjoy* making accusations, feeling insecure, spying on their partners, and getting lots of cheap adrenaline rushes when they finally make up with them. If this is passion, give me bleeding ulcers.

Life contains an irreducible amount of existential misery that does not abate even in the presence of your One True Love. The monogamous have yet to learn this. They want to know beyond a shadow of a doubt that they are loved for themselves, in spite of anything they may do or say, and they want never to be alone.

Proving the existence of love is as impossible as proving the existence of God. You know only that you love someone else, not that she loves you. It's a matter of belief or faith, not knowledge, and I would much rather have someone's faith than her faithfulness. Nobody is loved for whom she is. We are loved for how we treat other people, how we make them feel. So don't blame the Other Woman for your divorce—blame the sulking and screaming and china pitching you did when you found out about her.

You are as alone during simultaneous orgasm as you are sitting home while your lover is out on a date. None of us can escape the prison of her own skull, the isolation of possessing an individual consciousness. And if somebody ever got inside the barrier of your skin, you would feel so violated you would violently expel her. Each of us has impossible fantasies of devouring or absorbing the loved one; of splitting, twinning, loving mirror images of ourselves; or of becoming an appendage of the adored Other, since she will not damage or sever a part of herself. This infantile kind of love is really self-love, a narcissistic impulse to have the stimulation and reassurance a loving Other provides, but not the threat of rejection or the unpredictability of another consciousness, another will. This irrational hunger cannot be appeased by possessiveness. Like the national deficit, it has to be lived with.

So when I hear monogamy touted as the solution to what is euphemistically called "the current health crisis," I want to pound my head on the sidewalk. There is a difference between being monogamous and being in love. Staying in love is hard work. Fear (even the fear of HTLV-III) is not enough to make anybody do that much work. It may be enough to make people stay in the same apartment, but so would a low vacancy rate—and that's not romance, either. Ask anybody who shares a rent-controlled studio apartment in Manhattan with an ex-lover.

Because we don't know what else to do about AIDS, the gay press is condemning promiscuity. The "new romance" is supposed to put an end to gay men's callously using one another as objects in selfish bouts of sexual license. Well, if I knew somebody restricted her sex life to me just to avoid disease, I would feel as used as any cocksucker at a glory hole and considerably less enthusiastic about getting the bitch off.

The correct party line is that we now have to be monogamous because if we don't we'll die. But it is the unpredictability, inevitability, and finality of death that makes it difficult for me to stifle a lustful impulse; I never know if I will get a second chance. I don't know how to express love, desire, or admiration without touch. I may have to wear a surgical glove and avoid exchanging bodily fluids, but I will never give it up. The rigors of "safe sex," difficult as they are to remember once you get past Plateau Phase, are preferable to signing a marriage contract printed on paper that will dissolve if they ever find an AIDS vaccine.

By now, you probably think I never fall in love and that I have sex with everything in a flannel shirt. That isn't true. I've been married to (that's lesbian for "I've lived with") three different women, for a total of twelve years of connubial bliss and bullshit. I haven't been able to be monogamous with any of them, which has been a source of great pain and more hair-trigger diplomacy than the SALT talks. God knows I've tried. But the only way I can control myself is to shut off my turn-on to everybody, including my lover. Still, I preserve a very rigid line between my lover (my heart- and house-mate) and everybody else with whom I have sex. That line is romantic love. You could say I am into monogamous limerance.

The sex is better when I'm in love—whether it's giggly in the shower till the hot water runs out, loud and bawdy in a back-room bar, slow as a symphony to reach a crescendo on satin sheets, sneaky under a fancy restaurant table, groping in the front seat at ninety miles an hour until some truck driver blasts his horn and tries to pull us over, or a grumpy quickie to cure insomnia. When I've just barely fallen in love, nothing else matters. The world becomes an assortment of surfaces on which to make love. Not only is my ordinary, everyday, civilian persona head-over-heels for the woman, but every person I might have been or could be is hot for her, too. The pleasure, the excitement, the necessity of colliding and combining with her make the mundane world seem pale and tawdry.

But sooner or later I realize that before I can enjoy another candle-light dinner I'm going to have to wash some dishes. I also have to go to the bank, launder the sheets, and throw out the trash. When I say staying in love is hard work, this is what I'm talking about—the days when I feel more like a janitor than a porn star.

I think all gay people feel like runaways or orphans. My lover is the only home I have. I don't belong anywhere else. Nobody wants us to be together—not our families, not the bishop (be he Catholic or Mormon), not our bank, not the President. Not our ex-lovers, at least until they find new relationships, and sometimes not even our friends, who know we would have more time for them if we weren't reading *TV Guide* and arguing over what to watch tonight. I am stubborn about sticking it out, showing the others they are wrong about us. I take pride in surviving all this hostility. My loyalty is not just to my lover but to the lesbian nature of the relationship. I stay with her and take care of her because that is all I can do to prove that I am still a good woman, a real woman, despite the fact that I will not raise children or keep house for a man.

With a trick, I sometimes think that if I left my leather in a pile on the floor, she'd never notice my leaving the room. I've never tried it— largely because I am reluctant to undress completely with a casual partner. I know she isn't going to be able to get me off the way a lover who solicits and protects my vulnerability can. And I don't particularly want her to try. It's an almost intellectual curiosity, a hunger to take, explore, and please an unknown body and mind. I respect my tricks—I can even be very fond of them—but there's little or no reciprocity.

Why, if sex is so wonderful with a lover, do I bother to tie up friends and strangers and cane their fannies? This might make you laugh, but enjoying other people intensifies my relationship with my lover. I know she won't leave me because she wants somebody else whom she can't have. I like watching somebody else get hot for her; it confirms my own judgment of her high and sinister qualities. I like telling her, "Go ahead, have fun," because it's a token of my possession—you can't give away something you don't have. When we do people together, it turns me on to watch her muscles pump up as she whips or fucks somebody, to know she is watching me when I hold another woman down by the throat and slip my hand all the way inside her. We admire one another's skills and feel doubly desirable because somebody else desires her, me, us. I love this generosity; having so much sexual warmth in my life, I can share it with others. And, to be very blunt, I like reminding her that I have choices—other places to be and people to do. It makes it more difficult for us to take each other for granted.

None of my relationships has lasted more than five years. My monogamous friends shake their heads every time I go through a divorce, and blame it on my hussy ways. But I honestly don't think I could have prolonged any of my relationships by being monogamous. It seems to me the crime is not ceasing to be someone's lover, it is ceasing to be her friend. While romance makes sex especially intense for me, maybe it also guarantees that love will fade. My lovers are my heroes, and I leave when I am disillusioned, when I no longer believe we are on a great adventure and that they have magical powers to heal my wounds. It makes me profoundly uneasy to loathe somebody I literally worshipped when we first met. Friendships don't evaporate this way, not even friendships that include sex. But I don't want to live without the emotional high of adoring one special woman and promising her everything.

So I continue to have an unrequited love affair with a place of my own. I never make coffee without thinking about which cups are mine. When I get depressed, I draw schemes for arranging the furniture in the apartment I imagine sharing with only a cat named Significant Other. I will henna my hair. Then I will throw exotic orgies and invite everyone my lover cannot stand. No one will ever make me cry or compromise my principles (or come, probably) again. In a pristine office, untroubled by requests for a stamp or a batch of brownies, I will churn out volumes numerous as an encyclopedia. I tell myself soberly that life would be better without the emotional roller coaster of romance, her dirty ashtrays and corny Hummel prints, and the less than noble tactics I must use to force her to clean out the trash in her car. I wonder why taking care of one person (myself) seems more difficult than looking after two, and I don't understand why, no matter how hard I work at it, I don't know how to make love stay.

Obviously, I don't have all the answers. Monogamy is not wrong for everybody; nor would I advocate that we stop taking any precautions to avoid AIDS. But AIDS is no excuse for abandoning an attempt to think critically as gay people about traditional morality or to experiment with new ways of living and loving. Attempts to prescribe monogamy are part of a larger attempt to distance ourselves from the unlucky people with AIDS. Damn few of us are really capable of complete fidelity (or lucky enough to be with somebody who inspires us that much). If we condemn all the people who are not mated for life like Canadian geese or beavers, and who get sick, we won't need to feel sorry for them—we can retreat self-righteously, knowing it is their own fault.

I don't want to go back to living in an economy of scarcity, clinging to one woman as if we were the only two lesbians on earth, or to live as if I were the only healthy person in a leper colony. Isolation is as deadly as AIDS.

The City of Desire:
Its Anatomy and Destiny
1991

The city is a map of the hierarchy of desire, from the valorized to the stigmatized. It is divided into zones dictated by the way its citizens value or denigrate their needs. Separating the city into areas of specialization makes it possible to meet some needs more efficiently; it is also an attempt to reduce conflict between opposing sets of desires and the roles people adopt to try to fulfill those desires.

In the city there are zones of commerce, of transit, of residence. But some zones of the city cannot be so matter-of-fact about the purposes they serve. These are the sex zones—called red-light districts, combat zones, and gay ghettos. Although a city's legal code may specify where these areas will be, community leaders will rarely admit that there is anything deliberate about the construction of these areas. Instead they will say they would rather such places didn't exist at all. Yet there is no city in the world which does not have them. In part because of these zones, the city has become a sign of desire: promiscuity, perversity, prostitution, sex across the lines of age, gender, class, and race.

The sex zone does not have an independent existence; no area of the city is dedicated solely to this use. It is usually superimposed upon another area: a deteriorating neighborhood where poor people, especially those who have recently arrived in the city, must live; an area that has very few residents because it is designed to manufacture or transport goods; or one of those offerings to eco-guilt, a city park. The warning, "Don't go into the park after dark," which has achieved folklore status, is more than just a simple notice of potential physical danger. It is also an acknowledgment of the shift in the park's function—which takes place when the sun goes down—from a place where nature lovers eat lunch and children feed squirrels, to a place where one can buy drugs or get one's cock sucked.

The sex zone is just one example of the many types of urban marketplaces that sell goods and services to urban residents. But the sex zone is a black market, and its wares are not limited to sexual pleasures. Most types of contraband appealing to the low end of the market (drugs, stolen goods, counterfeit and gray-market merchandise) are available in the sex zone. In some ways, this black-market status is an advantage to those who operate and profit from it. Many of the commodities offered here would not be sought after in an above-ground pleasure economy because of their adulterated contents or the dangers of enjoying them.

For example, once a piece of pornography is produced, it never completely loses its value as merchandise in the black market. During crackdowns on obscenity, pornography sellers can warehouse their stock until strictures are eased, and then sell it at a high profit even if the clothing worn by the models is no longer fashionable or the magazines have suffered mildew or water damage. Fortunes are made in the sex zone by peddling ersatz or adulterated drugs which could be produced very cheaply in purer and more potent form in the laboratories of pharmaceutical companies.

But most people won't admit that the legitimized pleasures available outside the sex-zone "for free" (a concept which warrants critical examination) may be less prized or enjoyable than the illicit delights consumers hope to obtain when they enter this black market. Perhaps this is because all members of society are supposed to possess automatically the legitimate pleasures, which are in turn supposed to be sufficient to keep any "decent, sane" person happy. It is embarrassing to admit that this supposed birthright has proven elusive and unsatisfying. It is like admitting you are not a human being or, at least, not a good one.

In other words, despite the fact that people are willing to pay inflated prices for sex zone products, even its most compulsive customers pretend that everything for sale there is trivial, worthless, and unnecessary. They pretend, in fact, that this marketplace does not exist at all. So a sex zone must acquire at least a token invisibility to avoid threatening its customers as well as the authorities. This means that if one visits a sex zone at the wrong time of day, it may be unrecognizable. This type of marketplace is usually tolerated only between sunset and dawn.

A hidden market permits its customers to remain hidden. This gives all other neighborhoods in the city double meaning, a hidden semiotic, since their relationship to the sex zone remains uncharted. The most obvious illustration of this unacknowledged relationship is that the ostensibly safe residential enclaves designated for child rearing and monogamous marriage are also full of johns avid for forbidden pleasure. The sex zone is never allowed to flourish within or even in close proximity to the place where most of its customers live. An inappropriately located adult movie theater or bookstore will find its presence, even if completely legal, hotly contested—often by the same people who patronize similar businesses in the heart of the sex zone.

So johns must make an effort to travel to the black market for sex, and the risk of theft or assault they usually face along the way is a threat that most of them accept without protest. The punitive aspects of the sex zone are some of its most irrational—but also most fiercely defended—characteristics.

The map of the city pits responsibility against shiftlessness. Within the sex zone, the privileged are innocent; the poor are culpable. From those who have much, less is expected. Only those who have very little are expected to pay their dues.

The sex zone is an area of resistance and acquiescence to gender polarization and male domination. Often johns and hustlers view the significance of their exchanges in very different ways. For example, a john may assume that a prostitute is fulfilling a passive, traditionally feminine role. The transvestite hooker may feel that he has suborned another man's privileged heterosexual identity and suckered him into paying to be humiliated or at least deceived. He may feel this way even if his true gender is not discerned. The deception simply reinforces the hooker's belief that the john is stupid, a born mark.

The costumes women wear to make themselves identifiable as streetwalkers and to increase the amount of money they can demand from their tricks are often exaggerated versions of mainstream feminine apparel and lingerie. However, this exaggeration does not simply create a form of ultrafemininity but something that is both related and in opposition to it. Hookers and office workers do not wear the same kind of high heels, stockings, skirts, foundation garments, wigs, or makeup, and these items do not mean the same things, either. The two systems of similar signs do not indicate that one can expect equivalent behavior from each class of women. Indeed, their whole purpose is to indicate just the opposite. Any confusion stems in part from the fact that both the performance of menial tasks and the performance of sex for money are gender-linked in our culture.

But an office worker can be paid to do anything except perform sex, and propositioning her is "sexual harassment." By her manner of dress, the hooker marks herself as an outlaw. She can be paid *only* for sex, and has little communication about anything else with her clients. It is interesting to note that the complaint most frequently heard when an appeal is made for stepped-up enforcement of laws against solicitation is that hookers are bold, aggressive, and persistent. The same gender-"inappropriate" behavior that is a necessary part of their trade is also used to argue for the suppression of that trade.

Gay ghettos operate differently from other types of sex zones. They are more likely to be residential districts for gay men as well as places where they can find entertainment. Although johns still enter gay ghettos in quest for pleasurable activities unavailable within their nuclear families, they have better luck scoring if they camouflage themselves as residents of the area.

Gay men comprise the only sexual minority to have established its own enclave in the modern city. The lesbian community is still at an earlier point in its development, although it could be argued that neighborhoods like Park Slope in Brooklyn and Valencia Street in San Francisco are nascent "lesbian ghettos." The fact that male sexuality is recognized to be a valid, strong, organizing principle in men's lives contributes to the ability of gay men to structure their own ghettos. So does their greater amount of money, freedom to travel, and ability to live away from their parents—conditions enjoyed by all men relative to women.

Other sexual minorities—lesbians, transvestites and transsexuals, sadomasochists, etc.—tend to make parallel use of any gay male social space that tolerates their presence. Historically, these sexual minorities have "followed" gay men out of the red-light districts and into the gay ghettos. Before there were gay bars, there were hooker bars and burlesque clubs that tolerated the presence of homosexuals. Some social spaces which can be used by gay men (for example, drag clubs which cater primarily to straight tourists) continue to exist in red-light districts, and other sexual minorities maintain even closer ties to them.

In the black market for sex, sexual minorities are like Third World countries: dumping grounds for poorly produced goods which have little or no relationship to the needs of the people who buy them; pools of cheap labor; and sites for elites who want to go slumming or take exotic vacations.

It is difficult to envision a heterosexual porn consumer paying for a video which shows two unattractive people who are not heterosexual doing something which only vaguely resembles heterosexual intercourse. Nor would they pay for the services of a prostitute who was willing to do everything *except* make them come. Yet this is nearly the only sort of pornography or prostitution available to sadomasochists. And one minority, pedophiles, must settle either for material which depicts youths but has almost no sexual content, or material depicting adult models who might wear youthful attire but rarely appear to be younger than they really are. Pornography which more accurately depicts pedophiles' interests, even if it is homemade only for individual use and not for commercial distribution, subjects them to the threat of horrific legal penalties.

If toys marketed for infants were made as shoddily as most sex toys are, they would be recalled by the Food and Drug Administration. Lingerie sold in sex shops for the stated purpose of wearing during sex—a vigorous and athletic activity—seems constructed to fall apart within the first half hour. Yet it costs many times the price of lingerie sold in department stores. It is ironic that a pair of crotchless pants winds up being so much more expensive than cotton briefs. It is difficult to interpret the existence of sex toys which can injure their users and costuming which deteriorates upon use as anything other than punishment for expressing an intention to have sex.

It is also difficult to envision conformist heterosexuals accepting the low-paying jobs which the staff members of sex clubs, adult bookstores, and gay bars accept with gratitude because such employment allows them to keep their sexual identities full-time (i.e., become lifestyle deviates). Heterosexuals would not tolerate the presence of, say, a well-dressed group of drag queens who invaded a singles bar, took pictures, interrupted couples to interview them about what happened in their childhoods to cause them to become patrons of this bar, pressured them to accept drinks in exchange for this information, and then attempted to pick them up and take them home for a spot of crossdressing. Yet something very like this scenario happens nearly every weekend at many lesbian bars in smaller cities and large towns.

It is understandable that sexual minorities would like to sever their ties to the red-light district and model their aspirations upon the gay ghetto. Since they are unable to control large amounts of their own social space, they attempt to "share" the more protected space gay men have designed for their own use. The assumption with such space is that the customer's money is going to "one of their own." This obviates the need to examine the concept of what one is paying for and whether or not it ought to be a saleable commodity. Currently, a bar or other business that caters to gay men must maintain the appearance of being gay-owned. In fact, most are not. This gives rise to the myth of the "gay Mafiosos" who supposedly own gay bars. It also prompts straight bar owners to employ gay managers and maintain near complete invisibility. One of the punishments for a gay-oriented business which does not show a profit is the sudden visibility of its real owners, who use the humiliation of reasserting their control as well as threatened or actual violence to improve the gay male manager's performance.

There is considerable tension between the gay male majority and its "camp followers." Some gay men simply enjoy the opportunity to reverse their usual position in society, and they become supercilious elites with the right to condemn and limit the parameters of other minorities' pleasures. Some male homosexuals are made uncomfortable by the differences between their own sexuality and the practices or appearances of other groups. To the extent that a gay man has eroticized expressing his sexual identity in an all-male, masculine environment, he will be hostile to the presence of women or crossdressed males. To the extent that a gay man (or a lesbian) has eroticized a sexual identity based on differentiating between two genders and preferring one exclusively over the other, she or he will be hostile to bisexuals, preoperative or nonpassing transsexuals, and to people whose sexuality is based on factors other than gender distinctions—e.g., age differences, the presence of fetish substances like latex or leather, a need for specific sensations like humiliation or pain, erotic play with body fluids, the sexual use of nonhuman animals, etc.

This tension is sometimes eased by the overlapping specialized aspects of gay male sexuality and other deviant sexualities. There are gay male transvestites and sadomasochists, and the establishments which cater to these subpopulations often have less ambivalent attitudes toward heterosexuals or lesbians who share their erotic predilections. These establishments are more likely to be located in the red-light district than in the gay ghetto proper.

There will probably always be cyclically recurring periods of stress when the gay ghetto will not be a safe haven for other sexual minorities. Paradoxically, these conflicts can occur either in response to increased hostility on the part of mainstream society toward the gay ghetto (in the form of police harassment, overt denial of equal civil rights, escalating and unchecked street violence, or forced closure of gay male social spaces), or to token gestures by society indicating an increase in acceptance of the gay male community. Such gestures often encourage some gay-community leaders and members to attempt to "purge" fringe elements or at least disassociate their own groups from those who are more stigmatized, in an attempt to keep and increase their new (and genuinely precarious) status in the city.

To the extent that lesbians and other sexual minorities can organize independent social forces and claim and defend separate social space instead of being restricted to the margins of the gay male ghetto, they will be able to more reliably meet the needs of their own communities and attract and acclimatize new members. But at least three factors mitigate against this.

First, these groups possess very little capital. In a country where the state will not subsidize the formation and self-promotion of sexual minorities, little or nothing can be done to change the amount or kind of territory they occupy in the city without substantial private financial resources. As long as the activity itself is illegal or at least stigmatized, it is impossible to obtain capital by marketing it in the mainstream economy. Much of the black market for sex is controlled by businessmen who are not self-acknowledged members of sexual minorities (for example, the Mafia), so no capital can be funneled from the sex zones into the creation of new types of sex ghettos.

The very structure of at least one sexual minority—lesbians—makes it impossible to package it as a commodity and sell it to johns in a way that benefits lifestyle lesbians, as opposed to female sex workers who are willing to pose for photos or perform in sex shows that depict male heterosexual fantasies about what lesbians do. The fact that some of these models are, in fact, lesbians does not usually alter the kind of images they are used to produce or the poverty of their community. A sexual minority as a whole may also cut itself off from any resources generated in the sex zone by ostracizing members who work there. For example, few lesbians know any sex workers because prejudice against prostitutes keeps dyke hookers in a very small closet. Many leather organizations are hostile to professional dominants and will not allow them to advertise in their publications.

Second, without the support of a well-organized, powerful (or at least visible) subculture, most sexual deviants are unwilling to identify openly with their sexual preference and organize for the interests of those who share it. Isolation begets invisibility, which perpetuates isolation and gives these variations a furtive and unattractive appearance to prospective members. It becomes all the more difficult for newcomers to identify as members of these minorities or even attempt to gain admission into their social spaces.

One strategy for dealing with oppression is to eroticize certain signs which symbolize it and transform them into signs imbued with meaning supplied by the minority. For example, the dangerous neighborhoods and filthy conditions in which leather bars are located have come to symbolize the daring and adventurous nature of the bars' patrons rather than their insignificant social status. Refusing to acknowledge desperation is one way to preserve one's dignity. It may seem to an uninformed outsider or prospective member that this attempt to boost morale means that lifestyle deviants choose or prefer a marginal existence.

In fact, a shift in membership would probably occur if, say, S/M were an above-ground activity; that is, if no penalties followed disclosure of membership in this sexual minority. The members for whom genuine danger and filth are an important prerequisite to arousal would switch to a more persecuted activity or move their current practices to a less protected milieu. However, the number of people who would drop their membership in a sexual minority under such circumstances is probably much smaller than the number of people prepared to join it if they did not have to worry about stigmatization, discrimination, or violence.

Third, the number of people who acknowledge their own membership in these groups is relatively small, even in comparison to the gay male minority. Members of these groups often feel as much hostility toward their counterparts in other sexual minority groups as gay men or even agents of the state feel toward *them*. The needs and goals of other minorities are perceived as being incompatible, even inimical, to their own. This explains the many acrimonious exchanges between lesbians and transsexuals, sadomasochists and pedophiles, etc., and the willingness of some deviant individuals even to cooperate with the state's efforts to suppress other sexual minorities. There are also lines of stress and fragmentation within sexual minorities. The lines of sexual orientation become barriers, even within variations not based on gender. Lesbian, gay male, and heterosexual sadomasochists may identify less with each other than they do with members of their sexual orientations who have no interest in S/M. Boy-lovers may be contemptuous of girl-lovers. Postoperative transsexuals may want to sever all ties with any deviant identity and attempt to form heterosexual partnerships, while others seek to become members of the lesbian or gay male community. Still other transsexuals refuse to "complete" the process of surgical sex reassignment, and thus in some sense remain alienated from any identity or readily labeled group. Horizontal hostility precludes a joining of forces or sharing of what capital is available.

The term "sexual minority" is probably a misnomer since the range of valorized sexual activity is extremely narrow. If these standards were taken seriously and applied without hypocrisy, very few people would escape being labeled deviants of one sort or another. The existence of the sex zone serves to perpetuate a mythology of sexual normalcy which has little or no relationship to the actual frequency of perverse sexual fantasies and practice.

However, this is not a static, immutable situation. For example, the economic status of women is improving, albeit gradually. Even if women did not want to experience the range of sexual pleasure available to men, the fact that they have more money means that there will be a continual effort to design and market erotic opportunities that will persuade women to part with their cash. Because many of these male attempts are inept, and because women do in fact want to make their lives as enjoyable as possible, there will be more rewards for female sex industry entrepreneurs. And if women obtain access to more resources, there will be more material and labor available to create lesbian enclaves.

Some socialist countries provide models for state-mandated repression and persecution of sexual variation, but others provide models for state-subsidized outreach, education, and organization of sexual minorities and the decriminalization (or at least the benign neglect) of practices such as sodomy, prostitution, use of narcotics, and public sex. Even in America, there seems to be some tendency toward a consensus that a state which is going to collect a high percentage of taxes ought to insure a certain minimum standard of living for its citizens. If the American economy were not in recession, more liberal countries might be employed as models for change in the city's social policy toward the sex zone. And we cannot overlook the past and future impact of deviant individuals with unusual amounts of insight or resources who attempt to alter the boundaries of the city, an anatomy which most people accept as if it were the map of their own bodies.

Thanks to Dorothy Allison, for her November 1986 lecture at the National Leather Association convention in Seattle, on the zones in the city of literature, and to Wendy Chapkis for her suggestions.

Sources

Delany, Samuel R. *Dhalgren.* Bantam Books, 1975. *Tales from Neveryon.* Bantam Books, 1979. *Flight from Neveryon.* Bantam Books, 1985.

Rubin, Gayle. "The Leather Menace: Comments on Politics and S/M." *Coming to Power: Writings and Graphics on Lesbian S/M.* Alyson Publications, 1982, 192-227. "Sex Notes for a Radical Theory of the Politics of Sexuality." *Pleasure and Danger: Exploring Female Sexuality.* Routledge & Kegan Paul, 1984, 267-331.

Weeks, Jeffrey. *Coming Out: Homosexual Politics in Britain, from the Nineteenth Century to the Present.* Quartet Books Limited, 1977. *Sex, Politics and Society: The Regulation of Sexuality Since 1800.* Longman Group Limited, 1981. *Sexuality and Its Discontents: Meaning, Myths and Modern Sexualities.* Routledge & Kegan Paul, 1985.

Girls, Go for the Gloves

1992

When Risa Denenberg, a nurse practitioner who volunteers as a health-care worker for lesbians at New York's Community Health Project (CHP), did a small study of lesbian beliefs about HIV transmission, she "assumed I would find the problem is lesbians don't believe we're at risk for AIDS." In fact, 98 percent of the fifty women clients of CHP she surveyed "believed woman-to-woman sex can put you at some or great risk of contracting HIV infection." However, most of her respondents said they protected themselves by reducing their sexual activity—not by using gloves or dams. One-fifth of her respondents said they would not have sex with an HIV-positive woman or weren't sure whether or not they would. Denenberg feels that "there is a real 'us-them' attitude in our community. Lesbians are not having safer sex because they think they can tell who is at risk for AIDS just by looking."

Denenberg says she has participated in "more than thirty safer-sex forums for women; the women's caucus of ACT-UP's contest to rename the dental dam; encouraging women to eroticize safer sex; getting them to role-play discussions about it with each other," and she believes that "these first attempts to educate lesbians about safer sex were a valiant effort, but they were unfunded and doomed to fail. Women think condoms are for men, so they won't put them on their toys. Dental dams weren't made for oral sex. We based our previous efforts on a gay-male model, and now we need to step back and come up with a whole new strategy."

Denenberg's pessimistic view of the lesbian problem of having safer sex was echoed by New York AIDS activist Garance Franke-Ruta. She says bluntly, "Safer sex for lesbians is complicated, and we're unable to deal with it in our personal lives no matter what people tell us about AIDS."

Rita Shimmin, director of HIV services for Lyon-Martin, a San Francisco women's clinic founded to make health care more accessible to lesbians, disagrees. She says, "It's great to have lesbian-specific presentations" and talks about women who stood up at forums she helped produce last year and spoke publicly about having safer sex. However, Shimmin feels that "one-on-one counseling," like the hour-long talks she has with women clients before and after HIV-antibody testing, "is much more effective" than a public forum for changing behavior.

Shimmin defines safer sex as a continuum of decisions that women can make to reduce risk. "We never get perfect," she says, "but you can make progress toward where you want to be." She tells women that the first step is for a woman to find out what her own HIV-antibody status is as well as her partner's. The next step is to consider screening potential partners, based on their histories of risky sex or drug use. Women can become even safer by abstaining from sex that they consider risky. "There are hundreds of sexual and sensual behaviors with no possibility of exchanging fluids," Shimmin chuckles. The next—and safest—step is to "start using barriers—gloves, condoms, dental dams. Your partner's fluids can get on you but not in you." She emphasizes that this process must "begin with realizing you are vulnerable to the virus."

One of the biggest problems health educators face is the myth that lesbians comprise the lowest-risk group for AIDS. Denenberg explains that "the Centers for Disease Control (CDC) has constructed a hierarchy of exposure categories," and a person who falls into more than one category is not represented as such, but placed in the "highest" hierarchy category in which she or he fits. So a gay man who might have been infected with HIV by a blood transfusion is still listed in the category of "homosexual/bisexual contact because it is listed first in the hierarchy." Furthermore, a lesbian PWA who had risky sex with other women and who shared needles would be listed in the IV drug user category because the CDC system "does not list woman-to-woman contact as an exposure category."

Given this biased data-collection process, it is surprising that any information about woman-to-woman transmission of HIV has surfaced. In her article, "Lesbians in the AIDS Crisis," which appears in *Women, AIDS and Activism*, Zoe Leonard lists five cases of woman-to-woman transmission which have appeared in the medical literature since 1984. She also mentions a case in which a man became infected with HIV by having oral sex with a woman. Her conclusion is, "unprotected oral sex between women cannot necessarily be considered safe."

In "Lesbian Exclusion from HIV/AIDS Education: Ten Years of Low-Risk Identity and High-Risk Behavior," a paper written for the Sex Information and Education Council of the United States (SIECUS) in 1991, Rebecca Cole and Sally Cooper say that as of September 30, 1989, the CDC acknowledged 79 cases of lesbians with AIDS and 103 cases of AIDS in bisexual women. There are also 1,242 women with AIDS whose sexual orientations could not be classified because of incomplete responses to survey inquiries. Cole and Cooper claim that "most women's AIDS organizations, large AIDS service providers, and long-time HIV counselors have seen cases in which female-to-female transmission has occurred."

The lack of research on woman-to-woman transmission doesn't bother Jean (not her real name), a thirty-two-year-old, self-employed, black lesbian, "because I have had experiences with women who have other sexually transmitted diseases besides AIDS and don't tell you. I don't want to get any of the little ones, either. That's my crusade. Herpes, chlamydia, gonorrhea, all that stuff—when I read them the list, they decide they'd rather not worry about it, and having safe sex is a big relief."

Celeste (not her real name), a forty-one-year-old African-American writer, said that her current lover was skeptical at first about whether safe sex was necessary. "We still believe lesbians don't get AIDS. Especially for women of color, there's a lot of denial. I told her the risk of woman-to-woman transmission may be low, but it can happen, and I have a responsibility to take care of myself and my partner. Plus, I love using gloves. So we experimented a little bit with gloves and plastic wrap, and she came around."

Negotiations about safer sex can be blunt, raunchy, or completely nonverbal. Marsha (not her real name), a twenty-seven-year-old health-care worker, prefers to be direct. "I don't want to take somebody's sex history and argue about whether or not they're at risk. Who knows if they're telling the truth? It's meaningless. If somebody's interested in me, I just say, 'I'm a safe-sex girl, what about you?' before anything happens." Marsha says she's gotten "mixed responses. One woman accepted it as the status quo. She said, 'But of course.' Another woman told me she'd just taken the HIV-antibody test and was negative, so she would use latex on me if I wanted her to, but I didn't have to use it on her. We didn't go home together."

Matt Rice, a twenty-two-year-old outreach worker for 18th Street Services, a clean-and-sober gay public-health organization in San Francisco, describes herself as "a female-bodied person with transsexual tendencies" and "a big old flirt. I like to talk about sex to make girls nervous. If somebody at a club comes on to me, I'll ask her to tell me very explicitly what she wants me to do to her body. Or I'll tell her exactly what I want to do. I always describe using gloves and lube and putting a condom on my dick. It's just part of cruising."

Belle (not her real name), a nineteen-year-old stripper, doesn't want to waste a lot of time talking about it. "I tuck a glove in the top of my fishnet stockings. So if anybody's hand starts to climb up my leg, they find it and figure out that they have to put it on if they want to climb any higher!"

Safer sex has an unexpected bonus for some dykes who play with rubber. Billie (not her real name), a white lesbian who works as an office manager, said that her sex life has gotten a lot more adventurous since she started "carrying gloves, cutting up condoms, and using finger cots. A lot of girls might like a finger up their butt, but they're afraid it might get dirty. So you just put something on your hand, and when you're through having sex you throw it away. Women are more receptive to using dildos or butt plugs if they know I use condoms on my toys and keep them clean." Marsha mentioned that more of her partners are willing to try rimming if a dam or plastic wrap is available.

Oral sex remains an area where relapse into unsafe sex is very tempting. Shimmin tells a story about a client who indicated that she would be reluctant to use a barrier if she was going down on her HIV-positive partner. Shimmin said, "Do you think there's no risk of getting HIV infection by doing oral sex?" and the client replied, "No, I believe it's risky. But I like it." Shimmin says, "It's important to know how you really feel about safer sex. Women frequently say they know it's dangerous, but they don't want to have oral sex if they can't taste it. I know which feeling is going to win."

Franke-Ruta outlined the reasons why more lesbians are not using dental dams. "Using a dam is not like using a condom. You don't put it on; someone puts it on you. Dams are also about twice as thick as condoms. Putting a barrier against a woman's vulva reinforces misogynist myths about our genitals smelling or tasting bad. Dams taste awful. They are the wrong size. It's very difficult to feel anything through them, much less have an orgasm." Peg Teising, a twenty-two-year-old white dyke activist added, "I think you should use a dam if you don't know somebody's status. But they're so hard to find, I know very few women who use them." Belle commented, "I can't imagine going down on anybody anymore unless she had been my girlfriend for a long time, and we'd both taken the HIV antibody test."

Some lesbians have problems with all latex barriers. Linda (not her real name), a thirty-seven-year-old white lesbian physician, says she does not have safer sex with her lover because "I'm allergic to the powder on latex gloves." Hypoallergenic gloves are available, but they are expensive and hard to find.

Until some clever sex entrepreneur invents a better shield for cunnilingus, some women get around this problem by using plastic wrap. Celeste was especially enthusiastic about this option. "It's always in the house, it's transparent, thinner, I can cut it to just the size I want. I just feel that it gives me more options." Although research on the value of plastic food wrap as a viral barrier is incomplete, food industry studies show that these films prevent the passage of odor-bearing gas molecules, and a recently-completed CDC study showed that they stop the herpes virus, which is smaller than HIV.

Despite their shortcomings, it's important to keep dams, gloves, condoms, and other safer-sex gear handy if you want to avoid relapse. Marsha confessed that she sometimes has had unsafe sex with other women if having safer sex is "inconvenient. I just don't have gloves or dams with me and it's too late to go get some." Jean was adamant about avoiding this type of problem. "If you go out on Saturday night, you know what you're going to do. Have the stuff you need to do it safely in your trick bag."

If safer sex is going to become the norm in the lesbian community, Celeste feels that "lesbians with HIV disease should come forward." Rebecca Cole, the associate director of Astraea, the National Lesbian Action Foundation, has conducted over two hundred safer-sex workshops for women throughout the country and was one of the founding members of the ad hoc group of the Lesbians AIDS Project which successfully lobbied Gay Men's Health Crisis (GMHC) to fund their work. She says there are many reasons why women with HIV infection do not speak out to other lesbians. First of all, there is the intense stigma placed on the activities most likely to infect women—IV drug use and sex with men. "Most lesbians have not been tested. The few who know they are HIV-positive are scared, and they are not accepted. It brings up many issues. Who is a real lesbian? Who do we want in our community? If we were a little kinder to each other and a little more respectful of how complex all of our lives are, then we could listen to each other."

Thor Butkis, a twenty-six-year-old white lab technician and former IV drug user, says the response she's gotten to her positive status varies widely depending on which group of lesbians she's talking to. "I have not had sex with too many vanilla dykes. When I tell them, it's usually okay. They feel sorry for me, but they don't think I'm sexy. The S/M community is already educated and has a better attitude. Safer sex is mandatory at all of their parties, and leatherdykes have safer sex in private, too." The denial about AIDS in the lesbian community makes her very angry. "Unsafe sex is unsafe sex. I know I can give another woman HIV. Even lesbians who work for AIDS organizations think they are just there to help the men but *they're* immune from it."

Many lesbians seem to feel that if they stay away from women who are bisexual, sex workers, or junkies, they don't have to worry about having safer sex. As New York AIDS educator and counselor Sally Cooper says, "It's sad, but for most people—not just lesbians—safe sex right now means convincing yourself that your partner is not infected." Butkis says flatly that this strategy is "stupid. It's just as bad as being homophobic." And she wishes more of the "women I see in recovery, who say they were working the streets and shooting heroin and shooting speed, would get tested and talk more about it. What are they doing with their lovers now?"

Angela (not her real name) is a thirty-seven-year-old German/Italian who is looking for work as a counselor. She became infected with HIV during a gang rape which took place after she overdosed on drugs in a shooting gallery. "Butches have tried to tell me we don't need to use gloves. Today, if they won't have safe sex, I won't do it. I let them know I'm positive, and the only way I have sex is safe sex. How could I live with myself if I infected somebody else? Some of them say no to me, but I have lovers who said yes. I tell them we can make it fun. I think it's exciting to wait and watch a butch put on gloves or cut up a condom if she feels like being oral or put a rubber on a dildo. I don't get yeast infections any more. And using gloves gives you such a smooth ride."

Veronica (not her real name), a thirty-three-year-old white office worker who is also a transsexual, says sadly, "Almost all of the friends that I used to get high with have tested positive." She always tells women who are attracted to her that she's HIV-positive, and "I haven't been turned down yet. I'd like to think it's because they're so hot for my body. Of course, there's some hesitation. I'd be surprised if there weren't. I just wish my lovers would practice safe sex with everybody. My ex had a date with somebody else, and they didn't use gloves. When I pointed out that she really didn't know this girl's status, she was pissed at me. I think everybody ought to get tested. Being a lesbian does not inoculate you against AIDS!"

Would more funding for safer-sex education in the lesbian community help? Edith Peck, a thirty-nine-year-old, white lesbian mother, says emphatically, "More education is needed. Some lesbian porn has safer sex, and that's a good tool." Billie says, "I really appreciated it when Good Vibrations [a sex-toy shop in San Francisco] told me to use condoms when I bought a dildo there. I advocate talking to your friends. We might not listen to experts, but we can encourage each other."

Sadly, Jean Carlomusto, co-director of the 1990 lesbian safer-sex video *Current Flow* that stars porn star Annie Sprinkle and an African-American woman named Shara, says that many lesbian audiences have reacted negatively to her movie because "we used a format that combined porn, advertising, and music videos. Most women just don't want to watch porn. They say there's not enough affection between the two women. I think there should be more movies. One film can't address every lesbian community. For gay male audiences, Gay Men's Health Crisis has pieces that feature Asians, S/M, black men. And all we have is *Current Flow*. It's an unfair burden to place on one piece."

Cole feels that before lesbians can learn safer sex techniques, we have a lot of other sexual issues that need to be aired. "When I do workshops, I try to get women to talk about what stands between us and getting exactly what we want in bed. Fear and shame still have so much power over women. We have to talk about our fantasies, violence, incest, racism, sexism, economics. Dental dams will only make us safe from HIV. We're still sexually unsafe in a million other ways."

Denenberg sees lesbian failure to practice safer sex as part of a bigger question: "Why do lesbians get so little health care? We're dying from breast cancer, we don't get Pap smears. We have to take our own health care seriously before health educators and providers will."

Butkis says firmly, "The information is out there. The education is available if you want it. If people haven't gotten it already, I think it's going to take something blatant. Maybe we need fuck patrols to bust into bedrooms and shout, 'Where are your gloves? Don't put your tongue in there!' I hate to say this, but if a lot more women were dying from it, we would pay attention."

Shimmin reminds lesbians to pay attention to the history of the AIDS epidemic. "Every group that has thought they were invulnerable to the virus and therefore took no precautions has seen a rise in the virus in their communities."

Educational Resources

Current Flow, a four-minute explicit video of two women having safer sex. Send $5 to Gay Men's Health Crisis, Shorts, 129 West 20th St., New York, NY 10011 or call Myrtle Graham at (212) 337-1950. GMHC also has a pamphlet, "Women Loving Women," available for 35 cents. The advice to "use latex gloves when masturbating" is confusing, and readers are told not to use plastic wrap for oral sex. Add 10% for shipping and handling (15% outside the U.S.) to all orders from GMHC. Include a statement that you are over eighteen years of age.

Clips, a thirty-minute collection of three safer-sex lesbian porn vignettes. $34.95 from Fatale Video, 526 Castro St., San Francisco, CA 94114 or call 1-800-845-4617. Add $3 postage and handling and a statement that you are over twenty-one years of age. California residents add 8.25% sales tax.

Latex and Lace, a twenty-two-minute tape of women discussing AIDS and then having a women-only safer-sex party. Rental is $35, purchase price is $59.95, plus $7 shipping and handling. You must include an over-eighteen statement. Multi-Focus, Inc., 1525 Franklin St., San Francisco, CA 94109, (415) 673-5100.

Making It: A Woman's Guide to Sex in the Age of AIDS, English portion by Cindy Patton and Janice Kelly, Spanish translation by Papusa Molina. Illustrations by Allison Bechdel. Ithaca, New York: Firebrand Books, 1987. A humorous, nonjudgmental, and accurate set of directions that explicitly includes women of all sexual orientations.

Women, AIDS and Activism, the ACT UP/NY Women and Aids Book Group, Boston, MA: South End Press, 1990. A radical, useful, and moving anthology that presents the voices of many different kinds of women whose lives have been affected by HIV infection.

"AIDS...and Lesbians" (30 cents), a brochure, and "Rubber Dams" (15 cents), a card, available from Impact AIDS, 3692 18th St., San Francisco, CA 94110, (415) 861-3397, FAX (415) 621-3951. California residents add 8.25% sales tax. The brochure shows you how to use plastic wrap as a safer-sex barrier. The card says, "Plastic wrap has not been proven safe, but it is better than nothing."

Stormy Leather, 1158 Howard St., San Francisco, CA 94103, sells a pack of thirty-six unflavored dental dams for $12 plus $4 UPS charges. They also sell "dammits," a harness that holds a dam in place. Call (415) 626-1873 for prices.

Good Vibrations, 1210 Valencia St., San Francisco, CA 94110, sells packs of six dental dams in either bubble gum or vanilla flavor for $2 plus $3.50 UPS charges. Call (415) 550-7399 for their catalog.

Love and the Perfect Sadist: Can S/M Work in the Context of an Ongoing Relationship?

1992

He was absolutely gorgeous—six feet if he was an inch, long black hair, a well-toned body, and a face that combined the best of several ethnic gene pools. He had just finished paying me a great deal of money for a dominance session, and we had hit it off, so to speak. Sometimes an erstwhile slave can't wait to rip off his dog collar, shove his feet into trouser legs, and scoot for the front door. But this gentleman didn't seem to be feeling any pangs of post-pleasure Christian guilt. So we chatted while he had a glass of wine, put his clothes back on, brushed his hair, and donned his jacket.

I was curious about his motives for answering a "de Sade" ad in our local adult paper, *The Spectator*, and negotiating for a paid scene. It seemed to me that a man who was this good-looking, intelligent, and sensitive could have found a lady who loved him enough to cater to his not very outrageous submissive needs. (He wanted a little bondage—the kind that is mostly ornamental and definitely not escape-proof, some sensual teasing and foot worship, to be made up with lipstick and eye shadow, and the insertion of my very smallest set of anal beads while I talked a bit roughly about raping him. He had come without either one of us touching his cock.)

So I asked him a few tactful questions. No, he was not new in town. He had a Japanese mother, an African-American father, one Hispanic and one African-American grandfather, one Cherokee and one Russian grandmother. No, he did not want to know where he could go to meet other people in "the scene." The idea that there were social groups for adults who liked bondage and discipline or fetish costumes seemed to frighten him. Yes, he had a girlfriend—they were engaged to be married. Had he ever talked about any of this (I gestured at the dungeon) with her? "Absolutely not!" he blurted. "I have to go!" And, like a bunny with a tail wind, he went.

As I packed up my gym bag (yet another heap of lingerie to rinse out, the spike heels too high for a walk to the bus, my makeup kit, tit clamps, a suede whip, Tanith Lee's latest book, and a wire brush), I wondered which part of our encounter was too dreadful for him to share with the woman with whom he apparently planned to share the rest of his life. Was it simply kneeling? Confessing to having wicked thoughts and naughty daydreams? Was it the lipstick? The feeling of warm, oiled, heavy chrome beads being inserted carefully, one at a time? What consequences did he imagine would follow such exposure?

On my way home to the woman who is my lover, I kept thinking about all the men (and the occasional woman) who answered my ad. Most of my clients seemed to assume that S/M was something you literally could not do with somebody you loved or somebody who might also love you. The ideal mistress had to be a stranger. Why?

There are many motives for seeing a professional. Very few people have elaborate dungeons in their own homes or extensive fetish wardrobes. Some people are erotically excited by exchanging money for pleasure. Some of my slaves have had wives who were ill. Others felt they were too old, disabled, or busy to find partners they did not have to pay. But most of them were simply ashamed of themselves and didn't want anybody else to know their dirty secrets.

None of my clients participated in so many scenes as they would have liked. Very few of them ever found mistresses who were compatible or genuinely interested in their needs. Most of them hopped from ad to ad, hoping that every time a new domina opened shop she would somehow work the magic that nobody else had successfully performed.

What could possibly make the guilt, isolation, frustration, and the tiresome chore of living a double life worth it? Respectability, I suppose. ("I'm just like all the other people living in this middle-class suburb. No need to herd your children to the other side of the street if you see me out for an evening walk.") Male privilege, of course. ("I'm the boss, always the boss, completely in charge and on top, during sex and out of bed.") Heterosexual privilege, ditto. ("Poofters are disgusting. You'll never catch anybody putting anything up my butt. Never catch me in red panties and a blond wig. Never see me sucking cock. I'm no sissy, no drag queen, no faggot. I just want my Supreme Goddess to ravish my throat with Her mighty dildo.") Denial, too. ("She's the perv, that girl in the see-through raincoat who paddles slave-boys for fifty dollars. Not me. I was just curious. I didn't really like it, and I won't be back because I can do without it—for at least a week or two.")

This is not solely a heterosexual problem. While many gay leathermen and leatherdykes feel that since we're already out as queers, we might as well go all the way and be out as pervs as well, there are plenty of gay men and lesbians who dream about chain harnesses and latex catsuits but who will never find the courage to make those dreams come true. The ex-Marines, dominant bodybuilders, and spanking daddies who advertise as "models/masseurs" have to get their clients somewhere. And there's enough hostility toward S/M in the mainstream lesbian community to keep potential slave-girls and Amazon mistresses out of the leather shops and porn stores. Many same-sex couples who want to explore bondage and discipline have broken up because of the assumption that it's wrong to play rough with the person on the next pillow.

A good S/M or fetish scene isn't simply a matter of acting out a passage from *Story of O* or duplicating the latest Kim West ad. There is no such thing as a generic B&D fantasy. All the participants have to be comfortable and familiar enough with their own erotic trigger-points to describe them to each other. It may seem easier to say this embarrassing or risky stuff to a stranger. But I believe that it is damaging to one's self-esteem to feel that the innermost self is so far beyond the pale of social acceptability that it can only emerge in a brothel or an alley. Dominance/submission is, after all, a form of sex. And romance makes all kinds of sex so much better. When you know that your loved one sees the truth about you—your secrets and fears—and still love does not fail, it eases some of the loneliness we all carry inside our skulls.

A good S/M scene requires the same qualities—trust, honesty, safety, risk-taking, creativity, personal growth, mutual respect, and affection—that a good relationship possesses. Commercial S/M often takes the form of obsession—trying to create one perfect scenario. Each new mistress or master will be unable to get it just right, so you move on, demanding the same impossible fantasy from the next person you hire. But a committed partner will try harder to give you what you want, and you will be more inclined to forgive any imperfections. You don't have to do the same scene over and over again; you can build on it. It becomes just the first chapter of a long and surprising book. It's the difference between hiring somebody to help you jack off and making love.

So how does one create this sort of relationship? First, understand that most people find themselves in one of two situations: either that of a kinky person paired with somebody who has no apparent interest in the scene, or that of a person who is romantically involved with another self-defined perv.

The first situation is the most common, especially for heterosexual players. It takes patience to get from missionary-position coitus to corset training and high colonics. Try thinking of your partner as a novice rather than as a hostile, disapproving obstacle to your gratification. You didn't simply wake up one day with your head full of bondage positions and verbal abuse. It took you a lot of time to put it all together. We live in a sex-negative and ignorant world. From the time they are very small, women are taught that they will be punished with violence and contempt for asserting sexuality. Men are threatened with the loss of masculine identity if they deviate from the boorish in-and-out ideal. Decent men with some political awareness are often reluctant to try S/M games for fear of becoming piggish. Your partner might need some general sex education and gentle loosening up.

Reading sex manuals, watching erotic videos, taking massage classes, and embarking on field trips to fetish shops are good ways to learn new ways the two of you can express your desire for one another. Always respond positively to your partner's curiosity, answer questions, and treat fears with respect. Remember that we are all much more likely to try new things if they seem fun, easy, and rewarding. If it isn't clear what your partner is going to get out of all this, she or he is understandably going to be reluctant.

This means that you probably have to be the top, at least in the beginning. You can't expect somebody to automatically know what to do with those handcuffs and that riding crop. And don't be lazy—don't do exactly the same things to your partner that you wish some hooded icon of your libido would do to you. Tailor your experimental efforts to your partner's fantasies. Try not to scare the less experienced person. Make sure she or he knows that you'll stop at once if she or he becomes uncomfortable. An initial scene that includes a little bit of kink and a lot of really good vanilla sex will probably make your partner eager to learn some more. A little further down the line, you can mention that you'd like to return the gift of submission and completely serve her or his pleasure.

Sometimes, despite all your efforts, your lover or spouse will be indifferent or negative to your need for imaginative sex. But that need not be the end of the relationship. A neutral partner might be willing to oblige you occasionally or trade favorite activities with you. If the two of you are determined to remain together, your partner may allow you to seek out casual playmates for S/M. But remember that the essence of this sexual specialty is *consent*. If your partner really finds S/M repellent or silly, don't manipulate or coerce her or him. It won't work, and it isn't fair. Separation may be the only sensible solution.

When a man and woman or two men or two women who already own leather jackets and shackles engage in courtship and mating rituals, they still have to decide how to integrate S/M into the rest of their relationship. Very few S/M relationships resemble the fantasy ideal of the distant, cruel owner who carries a whip everywhere, apparently even to the bathroom, and the slave who isn't allowed to wear anything but a collar and does nothing but hang on a cross all day. Both partners might be bottoms (or, more rarely, tops). Even if your role preferences are neatly polarized, it's possible for a bondage bottom to find herself or himself paired with a top who is mostly interested in, say, flagellation. And you wonder why S/M educators talk so much about negotiation and communication skills!

Of course, some S/M couples (or triads or other polygons) do try to maintain their erotic roles one hundred percent of the time, and they usually sign a written contract. It works best when some time is spent discussing the content of the document and when it is individually tailored to a particular relationship, not simply copied out of *Venus in Furs*. A workable contract must include practical matters like earning the rent and keeping the house clean. Very few dominants can afford to keep slaves, and vice versa. As a feminist, I am offended by the notion that the dishes must always be done by the bottom, although I must confess that if I ever found a slave who would really do all of the housework, I might consider wearing my leathers around the clock.

A realistic contract will also include some provision for time-outs, when conflicts can be discussed without S/M roles intruding, and when the bottom can exercise dominant impulses or the top can take a vacation from being a hidebound demigod. I suggest signing the first draft of this document for a limited period of time—perhaps as short as one week. Renegotiate after the two of you have a chance to see if you really enjoy living up to its terms.

Personally, I am not excited by the reality of having a full-time submissive. It's the change in status from autonomous adult to shivering, restrained, helpless flesh that I find exciting. If somebody is already down on the floor, I don't get to have the fun of catching and wrestling her or him down. I don't like what usually happens to bottoms who never get out of role. Although it's difficult to generalize, I've seen quite intelligent men and women become unable to keep their jobs, make the simple decisions involved in shopping for groceries, or maintain good grooming habits. Often they start drinking too much. And they usually become boring and selfish in bed. The unconscious reasoning seems to go like this: "I've given up my independence, so you owe me complete and instant fulfillment of all my S/M fantasies." Constantly harnessing your will to another's inevitably creates resentment that erupts in provocative, rude, even violent behavior.

I would rather do heavy, hot sessions with an eager masochist once a week and walk out of the playroom with both of us feeling very pleased with ourselves than constantly supervise an incompetent dependent and punish her or him for being rebellious three times a day. I've never had a bottom who didn't need to be punished once in the course of our relationship. But if I must punish someone a second time, it's either because we're not compatible or the bottom is incorrigible. In that case, I'll send her or him away. S/M that is always scripted as serious punishment, as opposed to playful discipline or cathartic, erotic humiliation, makes both of us feel badly.

And I don't like what happens to me when I try to become a full-time mistress or daddy. I become rude to waiters, find it impossible to wait my turn in line, don't listen, don't ask questions, can't accept help, and can't admit I'm ever wrong. Top's Disease is so unattractive. I don't feel very believable as a dominant when I'm so rigid and brittle that the smallest inconvenience or demur makes me furious. The same skills that make an S/M scene hot don't really work when you have to pay an overdue telephone bill in person.

Besides, I'm not one hundred percent top, and I don't know any honest masters or mistresses who are. All of the people who wear their keys on the left like to switch from time to time, although very few of us will talk about it. Bottoms who are scandalized by this fact are going to have a hard time keeping any top happy. Do you really want to go under for somebody who has no idea what sort of emotional and psychological state in which she or he is putting you? Do you really want to let somebody hurt you who has forgotten (or never knew) what a squirt of hot wax feels like? If you really love your owner or your sadist, don't you want her or him to be happy—even if that means occasionally rolling over? Or is your devotion such a fragile thing that it can be shattered by any evidence of your top's humanity?

I can't maintain my sobriety if I lie about what I want. Sexual dishonesty will lead me straight back into the destructive habit of abusing drugs and alcohol. Owning my own submissiveness and my sadism, not letting anyone make me feel guilty about either one of them, is a major part of the program I have to work to stay clean. I can't be in a relationship with somebody who doesn't validate this. It's too dangerous for me.

My favorite S/M scenes are based on what both of us want right now, not what we think we should want or what we think we can get. This keeps me from falling back on a rote scene (first you'll kneel and strip, then I'll tie you to the bed, then I'll use the soft rubber whip, then I'll use the soft leather whip, then I'll get out the cane, then I'll turn you over and go for the clothespins, etc.). This means that the onus is not entirely on me. If my partner has read an article on removing hair with hot wax and is intrigued, she'd better say so. It also gives me room to put out my own agenda, instead of simply acting out a script the bottom hands me.

My best relationships run in a similar fashion. One night I might want to be served dinner and then given a back rub and pedicure by a pretty slave girl. On another night, I might want to be a teenage boy who is going to tie up the local cocktease and have his way with her. Or I might be a stern leather daddy showing his boy how to take it like a man. I might want to put on my spike heels, step on somebody's throat, and cane her or him until my arm is tired. On the other hand, I might also want to put on my flannel jammies and watch *Bringing Up Baby*. If I can't have my evenings off with cocoa and animal crackers, I don't want to be your Bitch Goddess.

S/M couples can have the same problems keeping the sex intense that vanilla people face. Running a household and making a living can be so time-consuming that by the end of the day, lacing on a PVC jumpsuit or getting into those leather jodhpurs seems like just one more awful chore. Since I work at home, it's especially important for me to cover the computer, close the office door, and firmly force myself to get out of worker-bee mode. I have to eat, shower, and then lay out my toys and the evening's outfit. The ritual of getting ready for a scene usually becomes a kind of foreplay. By the time my boots and gloves go on, I'm ready to kick ass.

I also need to remember to take vacations with my lover. Getting away from the telephone and the television allows us to remember why we fell in love. Perhaps because I write so much pornography, I tend to forget that I can be inspired by other people's work. If I feel that I'm getting too predictable, I may give myself homework. For example this week my assignment might be to find a place to do a quick scene out-of-doors or figure out how to do bondage in the kitchen instead of the bedroom. Or I might put away the six toys I always reach for and make myself use less familiar equipment.

Having an open relationship also keeps things from going stale. If my partner catches some other top's eye, she is free to return the wink. The thought that some other pair of tender, downy buttocks might get my attention certainly makes her think twice about using her safe word too quickly. If we meet somebody we both like, we might set out to seduce her or him together. When we can find a suitable space to rent, we host play-parties where we can meet new women in the scene and see how other couples are amusing themselves.

We're not immune to jealousy. But I never had a monogamous relationship where I wasn't accused of wanting to sleep with other women anyway. If I'm going to have to go through the trauma and drama, I'd rather get some nookie as well. Of course we insist on safe sex with outside partners, and there are certain people who are off limits to both of us because they don't respect our primary bond with one another. I expect to be asked for permission before my property lies down under someone else's sadistic touch, and I think bottoming for anyone besides my current girlfriend would be asking too much. When my lover comes back to me after having a date with somebody else, I want to hear all the details. I'm enough of a voyeur to find it arousing, and I'm proprietary enough to want to rise to the challenge and take her back again.

Our arrangement may not work for other couples. The point is, you don't have to set up your relationship according to other people's rules. You can learn a lot by playing with other people in the community. A lot of S/M history, traditions, customs, and technique are passed on orally. Most competent mistresses or masters acquired their skills by apprenticing to more experienced tops or bottoms. Playing with other people need not be a painful or threatening experience. It can be an exciting way to make new friends. It's tricky to figure out what limits you need to set—for example, no sex, no romance, no overnight stays—but if both parties follow the rules, nonmonogamy can bring you much closer together and give you a new erotic charge.

Just as I allow a submissive lover time on her own to build a career, go to school, spend time with her family, and maintain her own life, I want to be left alone to do my writing, schedule speaking engagements and workshops, cope with the bills, telephone my mother, and vacuum the rug. I don't expect her to polish my boots when she's got the flu, and I don't want to rise from my sickbed to administer six of the best and a punitive clyster. Taking care of each other when we're ill, depressed, or in trouble is as much a part of loving each other as getting a new leather uniform shirt for Christmas or organizing a very elaborate birthday spanking.

I need that affirmation because I live in a world that tells me S/M is aberrant, sick, violent, and hateful. It is increasingly illegal to depict my sexuality in photographs or movies. S/M literature is always being confiscated, banned, or burned by government officials or prudish, politically correct gay or feminist activists. My ties to blood relations are usually strained to the breaking point. And leather people have a very tenuous, contested position in the larger gay community. I suspect that most vanilla fags and dykes wish we would disappear and that they blame us (along with the drag queens and boy-lovers) for much of the opprobrium they face. If you are publicly identifiable as a perv, you face job discrimination, street violence, and the loss of custody of your children. That's a lot to deal with. It's why every S/M publication, every leather organization or event, and every kinky man or woman I recognize on the street is invaluable to me. I need all the evidence I can get that I'm not alone, not despicable, not crazy.

Someday we will all realize we have more to lose than we have to gain by remaining fearful of one another and hidden away. Before we can even think about changing the negative stereotypes of S/M or creating better, safer, bigger social space for ourselves, we have to find one another. For us, creating satisfying, healthy S/M relationships is as politically radical as AIDS activists' chaining themselves to the axles of a pharmaceutical company's delivery trucks. To amend a once popular lesbian slogan, an army of lovers in latex cannot fail.

Modern Primitives, Latex Shamans, and Ritual S/M

1993

I have a recurring nightmare. I've just tied somebody who's too cute for her own good to my bed. The only light in the room comes from flickering candles. As I approach her, a flogger draped over one shoulder and a bag full of plastic clips in one hand, she stirs, testing her bonds. I wait to hear what she has to say. Will it be fearful? Respectful? Provocative?

Nothing that useful! She whines, "Where's the altar? You never gave me any time to meditate before you tied me up. Can we do some tantric breathing and chanting together before we play? It's the vernal equinox, you know. Those candles should be yellow and blue. Why haven't you cast a circle and called up the appropriate guardians and elements for each of the four directions? Aren't you going to burn any incense? I just love Dragon's Blood, don't you? If you're going to mummify me, you should put crystals over my chakras. And if you're going to hit me, I really want to dedicate my pain to Kali because she's my tutelary deity for this moon cycle. Are those plastic clips? I never let plastic touch my body. Wood absorbs aural vibrations so much better. Wait, let me look at that tattoo on your arm. Oh. It isn't very, well, tribal-looking, is it? I guess you could get some cover-up work done. Are you going to ring a bell to cleanse the air of intruding influences? If you'd just let me up, I could help you smudge the room and cast that circle I told you about earlier."

As I draw my knife to cut her loose, she squeals, "Is that your athame? You know you should kiss it before you put it back in the sheath!" The fantasy ends before I can stuff her into a cab (or a much smaller and darker place). But it leaves me with my wolf hackles up and a bad taste in my mouth.

In fact, my altar is on top of my dresser, where it's been for the last twenty years. I don't burn incense because I've got asthma, and if you see me wearing a knife, it's probably not my athame. The tattoo on my arm will never appear in a coffee-table book about the New Tribalism, but I feel comfortable with its spiritual significance. It depicts Crete's Little Goddess of the Serpents, and I have been her not-so-humble devotee and servant for many years now. The Goddess has tested me, taught me, blessed me, and hidden from me, but never abandoned me. Saying yes to the Mistress of the Universe is an art, a devotion, and a discipline.

Why, then, am I so grumpy about the recent trend in the leather community toward calling your friends your tribe, doing rituals instead of doing scenes, and evoking the ineffable every time a whip comes down? Part of it has to do with the genesis of the term "modern primitives." This apt phrase was coined by Fakir Musafar in 1979 to describe himself and a few kindred spirits in a *Piercing Fans International Quarterly* article. Andrea Juno and V. Vale used it as the title for one of their Re/Search Publications books. A careful reading of *Modern Primitives* makes it plain that Juno and Vale are fascinated with S/M, but they appear to see themselves as P. T. Barnum, touring with a sideshow of freaks.

The book is subtitled *An Investigation of Contemporary Adornment and Ritual*. In the introduction, Juno and Vale outline several motivations that people in modern western societies might have for acquiring permanent body decorations such as tattoos or piercing, or altering the shape of the body with corsetry and other modifications. "Amidst an almost universal feeling of powerlessness to 'change the world,' " they write, "individuals are changing what they *do* have power over: *their own bodies.*"[1] They assert that these practices have value and meaning as art and as attempts to recapture the irrational aspects of human consciousness, and that they exist in opposition to the programming created by the mass media's library of prepackaged images.

The fact that some body modifications, such as genital piercings, are intended to enhance sexual pleasure, is dismissed as a "functional" rationale. Virtually every activity explored in *Modern Primitives* is stigmatized precisely because the people who engage in them are thought to be driven by needs for perverse sexual pleasures. Tattooing, piercing, scarification, and corsetry are usually seen as signs of membership in the S/M community or some other outcast group. One would think that this aspect of body modification's history would merit a little further examination. Without its association with sexual deviance, deliberate body alteration would lose a great deal of its power to attract both attention and disapproval. Vale and Juno have this to say about S/M:

> Today, something as basic as sex itself is inextricably intertwined with a flood of alien images and cues implanted from media programming and advertising. But one thing remains fairly certain: *pain* is a uniquely personal experience; it remains loaded with tangible shock value. The most extreme practitioners of SM probe the psychic territory of pain in

search of an "ultimate," mystical proof that in their relationship (between the "S" and the "M"), the meaning of "trust" has been explored to its final limits, stopping just short of the infliction/experiencing of death itself.[2]

There are so many things wrong with this breezy little stereotype that it's hard to know where to begin to deconstruct it. There are certainly people who would argue that S/M is the result of media programming that is rife with bondage and fetish imagery. And it's questionable that pain has any particular purity or power to shock in a society that gobbles down slasher films by the dozens. The knowledge we might be able to glean about the leather community from a study of "the most extreme practitioners" of S/M (or, at least, Juno and Vale's image of them) is questionable. Their linking of power-exchange sex to thanatos is nothing but a cliché. Our community is interesting (and powerful) precisely because we have chosen to *live*, to fashion relationships, organizations, institutions, traditions, mythology, and norms—in spite of all the voices from outside which tell us we (a) are obsessed with death, and (b) deserve to die.

Juno and Vale are the death junkies, not leather people. Later on in the introduction, they say:

All the "modern primitive" practices being revived—so-called "permanent" tattooing, piercing, and scarification—underscore the realization that death itself, the Grim Reaper, must be stared straight in the face, unflinchingly, as part of the continuing struggle to free ourselves from our complexes, to get to know our hidden instincts, to work out unaccountable aggressions and satisfy devious urges. *Death remains the standard whereby the authenticity and depth of all activities may be judged* [emphasis added.]. And [complex] eroticism has always been the one implacable enemy of death. It is necessary to uncover the mass of repressed desires lying within the unconscious so that a *New Eroticism* embracing the common identity of pain and pleasure, delirium and reason, and founded on a *full knowledge* of evil and perversion, may arise to inspire radically improved social relations.[3]

This Freudian muddle hardly constitutes a clear signpost to utopian Eros. It does bolster the association that already exists in most people's minds between sexual risk-taking and death. It also reifies the notion that it is pathology which impels people to enter the erotic frontier. Rather than examine the ingenious ways that sexual subcultures subvert the mass media and the state in the here-and-now, it points the way toward a vague future when there will apparently be no neurosis, lots of synthesis, no perversity (since that will be absorbed into a new, more healthy sexuality), and even more verbal posturing. Of course we are all suborned and contaminated by the oppressive milieu in which we live. There are practical limitations (economic and legal) as well as limitations of the imagination and spirit in terms of the amount of social change that rebel groups can generate. But the fringes should not be dismissed as if they were nothing more than neurotic lifestyles or phases of arrested development.

Juno and Vale never say exactly what their personal connection is to the "modern primitives" they investigate. It's tempting to label them voyeurs, but a voyeur is at least obviously aroused by what she or he views and is thus linked to it. While interviewing Fakir Musafar, who has personally explored mind- and body-altering rituals from virtually all human cultures and made up a few new ones of his own, Juno asks, "What is your critique of SM?" Musafar replies, "SM, in this culture, is one of the few places people can get started on the road back to their god. In this culture there are very few opportunities for this." This response doesn't make Juno very happy. She comes back at him with the question, "But don't most SM people just get stuck?" Musafar obliges her by criticizing people who do S/M merely to reach orgasm, without ever discovering "a strange new world just this side of orgasm that beats orgasm all to hell."[4]

In her interview with lesbian piercer Raelyn Gallina, Juno makes this revealing comment: "Even though I have problems with aspects of SM society, I think that getting into ritual cuttings and pain could possibly reawaken or liberate a whole world of sensation, depending on the individual—especially if they've suffered a lot of repressive conditioning."[5] In her dialogue with Jim Ward, owner of the Gauntlet, a piercing emporium, she says of people who get branded, "I think some of these people don't have very evolved philosophies."[6] What is her point: that only people with graduate degrees in comparative religion or philosophy are qualified to decide to acquire permanent marks?

Vale is equally snide. In his interview with Industrial-Culture movement theoretician Monte Cazazza, he snipes, "Some people may have just one area of deviancy, like being members of a corset society, but in other cultural areas they can be disappointingly middle class."[7] It would be nice if everyone who had unusual sexual tastes were also politically progressive. This is obviously not the case, any more than it's true that most S/M people are neo-Nazis or, at the very least, have authoritarian personalities. But people who come into the leather community looking for anarchists are just as misguided as the people who dismiss us as a bunch of fascists. A sexual practice which provides mutual pleasure to consenting adults should not require any other justification. It is its own excuse and reason for being.

The issue of how to maintain a daily life, meet survival needs, and function in a hostile world is a difficult one for sadomasochists and other sexual minorities to resolve. We do, after all, need to support ourselves, eat, sleep, and have human connections, like anybody else. Some of us even have children or professional careers, and if we want to keep those things, we usually can't have our faces tattooed. Because people have varying levels of ability to tolerate deviance, and varying levels of ability to hide, some of us are more visible than others as different, strange people.

But, as the law and the mass media know, the most carefully camouflaged kinky person is still a pervert who can be ferreted out, exposed, and used to sell newspapers and increase the number of viewers for the evening news. To insist on a right to privacy, to be free of the scrutiny of reporters, shrinks, neighbors, employers, cops, talk-show hosts, and politicians is thus one of the first political demands made by any sexual minority. Those in the closet deserve at least as much pity as scorn. Furthermore, the fact that we exist in suburbia and the Republican Party as well as in cool clubs and street riots subverts society's bland notions about what constitutes normal sexuality and the assumption that the majority of us endorses those limitations.

Perhaps Vale is "disappointed" by the middle-class members of this hypothetical corset society because he is not particularly interested in the sociology of deviance. You have to be a minority-community member in good standing to recognize the hardship that people endure and the courage it takes to keep on going. These quiet survivors don't look outrageous on a postcard; they don't provide amusing anecdotes for the folks back home.

Vale asks performance artist Genesis P-Orridge, "How do you rationalize the accusation that these [tattoos, piercing, and scarification] are just masochistic or perverted activities? That you've merely just twisted your sensations around so you're now experiencing pain as pleasure?" P-Orridge replies, "I've met genuine masochists and they're usually rather dull, because they don't give you any intellectual explanation at all, nor are they interested in one...I'm interested in *heightened awareness*, and I'm interested in learning more and more about—not just myself, but what is possible through the achievement of—not exactly trance states, but altered states in the true sense."[8] Neither man challenges the idea that there's something terrible—retro, unevolved, mentally dull—about being a masochist or a pervert.

Despite this carefully maintained distance between its producers and its subjects, *Modern Primitives* created a great deal of controversy about Re/Search Publications. The book was even prosecuted for obscenity in England. Faux may not be close enough for rock 'n' roll, but it's apparently close enough for Scotland Yard. Police confiscated a copy from London bookseller Richard Waller's The Book Inn in November 1989. Almost a year later, he received a summons charging him with selling obscene materials. A conviction would have carried a maximum one-year prison sentence. Appropriately enough, Waller was arraigned in the same courtroom where Oscar Wilde was first arraigned for homosexual offenses in 1895 and Radclyffe Hall's pioneering lesbian novel *The Well of Loneliness* was declared obscene in 1928.

The police presented two photos as evidence of obscenity. One showed Fakir Musafar hanging from fleshhooks (inserted through permanent piercings in his chest). The other showed a penis that had been surgically cut in half lengthwise. The defense noted that a nude photograph of a one-thousand-pound nymphomaniac had recently appeared in a popular British tabloid, the *Sport*, and the film *A Man Called Horse* (which was currently running on British television) depicted the same Native American ceremony which Musafar was pictured duplicating.

Magistrate Ian Baker ruled that the book was not obscene, noting, "There is a great deal in it which is likely to shock or offend sensibilities. It may put ideas into people's minds, but I cannot see how it would corrupt and deprave readers."[9]

Modern Primitives has made Re/Search a lot of money. Since it is written in interview format, the company didn't have to pay contributors. With 60,000 copies sold (1,524 in Great Britain), it is one of Re/Search's most popular publications. Vale and Juno say the book allowed them to quit their jobs as typesetters and publish on a full-time basis. Vale calls it "their most influential book."[10] None of that money has come back into the leather community, where it could have been spent to defend the Spanner men, oppose censorship of S/M literature in Canada, or just buy Fakir and his friends some new fleshhooks. Around the time when *Modern Primitives* was being tried for obscenity, professional piercer and tattoo artist Anthony Oversby, whose work appears frequently in the book, was charged with assault in connection with three instances of body piercing. Oversby probably could have used a few bucks. He was eventually acquitted (and as a result of this case, piercing in England is now legal only if the piercer and piercee do not obtain "significant sexual pleasure" from the event).

There's even a legal question about who owns the term "modern primitives" now—its creator Fakir Musafar or the Re/Search impresarios. At the peak of my light-fingered powers, I was never *that* good a shoplifter. Subcultures are always being exploited by the media. Madonna steals from the black drag queens who taught her how to vogue. The movie *Colors* stole from the Crips and the Bloods. Juno and Vale steal from people on the fringe (some of them sadomasochists) who use their bodies to go to an extraphysical, transcendental place. They are no different than the suits on "60 Minutes," who acquire manna by being willing to go to scary places and talk to scary people (who live in these scary places all the time and still get treated like garbage after the microphones and cameras leave).

The ethical issues that arise when journalists interview people whose lives involve conduct that may be illegal (such as addicts and drug dealers, people in cross-generational relationships, sex workers, and sadomasochists) are underexamined. A reporter in this situation has tremendous power over her or his informants. If a journalist takes things out of context, misquotes the informant, reveals identifying information, makes material public that was supposed to be off the record, or otherwise distorts the truth, the informant has very little recourse. Fact checkers don't go to Harlem or the Mineshaft, and outlaws can't usually sue for libel.

The fact that subcultures get raided doesn't mean there's something wrong with the original matrix that engendered the ideas, rituals, language, music, and fashion which are eventually, in turn, bowdlerized and mined for somebody else's prestige and profit. But it does mean that new members are being recruited to the Modern Primitive movement by a book that we did not produce and can't control. (In the Bay Area, once leather people started to think about the dynamics of how *Modern Primitives* was produced, they refused to wear the tee-shirt that was put out to publicize it, or they blacked out the Re/Search logo.) I am deeply disturbed by men and women who wear leather or latex , tattoos, and body piercings, who are ignorant about or even hostile toward the S/M community that created this look. I am also concerned because the Neotribal look has become more important in many quarters of the S/M community than technical competence or emotional safety in play. Generational differences in the fetish subculture are exacerbated by a reluctance to learn from (or teach) somebody who doesn't "look right." We are lined up in different camps with those who think William

Carney's *The Real Thing* was the last word in S/M semiotics looking askance at people with skate-rat buzz cuts and bones in their noses.

But the heart of my disquiet is much harder to talk about than Old Guard versus New Guard signs. Aleister Crowley once cautioned those who seek arcane knowledge: "Those who speak, don't know. Those who know, don't speak." He said this partly because he was an elitist son of a bitch, partly because we really must protect sacred things from being profaned, and partly because there is something literally unspeakable about some profound, transformative experiences. Even if we cannot accurately describe those moments, I think we have to start talking about the uses to which we put them and the ways we try to create them.

It's exciting to live in a time when monotheistic, male-dominated religions are being challenged and people are seeking guidance from the natural world and its Creatrix. Sex is a powerful force, and I think it's healthy for people to counter the prudery of the Jehovah cults by incorporating pleasure into their rituals. But shame is very hard to eliminate. I sometimes see it crop up when spirituality is used to rationalize or excuse S/M. Sex does not need to be justified. Pleasure is a virtue, and as we all know virtue is its own reward. Some of the latex shamans are using occult jargon to sanitize S/M and make it sound like something more refined than a complex and unusual way to get off. This has created a new hierarchy among perverts. If a guy with feathers in his hair is blowing a nose flute while he puts needles in somebody who is standing on a buffalo skin, that trip is assumed to be more important or superior to the naked, greasy folks in a fist-fucking sling who have spanked each other silly and are now oinking their way to a thunderous simultaneous orgasm.

In fact, very few S/M rituals that I've witnessed include genital orgasm for the participants. Is this tantric sex, or is it AIDS phobia? We're trying to touch the face of God, so we can't touch our pee-pees? I don't believe it for a minute. In the last decade, S/M has become less and less about fucking and sucking and coming. People don't want to admit that they hate using condoms or gloves or, in fact, don't have safe sex in private. I sometimes wish we could spend as much time dealing with the sweaty, uncomfortable mechanics of eroticizing safer sex as we do constructing shrines. People are still getting infected with HIV in our community, so it's obvious that what we've done up till now is not working.

The top's function in an S/M scene is to give meaning to what is happening. This becomes even more important when tops and bottoms meet to do sex magic with each other. But many S/M rituals seem to have no clear purpose. Is someone being purified? If so, from what? Is someone being initiated? What is the next stage of life, and why is a partner qualified to bring her or him over the threshold into it? Is the person being healed? Ordained? Blessed? Bound to someone else? A pre-scene negotiation ought to include the answers to these questions, which are at least as important as setting up a safe word.

It's hard enough to keep S/M relationships between mundane tops and bottoms free of unhealthy power dynamics. We dance together in an ever-changing stream of mutual needs and insecurities. When your top also becomes your spiritual mentor, the waters are even more treacherous and muddy. Too many people assume that if you are a chela, apprentice, or novice, you must also be a bottom. Is it possible for someone to enter the tribe of modern primitives without taking on a sponsor who is also fucking her or him? Am I the only person who thinks this encourages an abuse of power?

Very few practitioners of S/M magic have described an ethical component to their practices. It seems vital to ask why we want to generate ecstatic or trance states or become powerful sorcerers, shamans, or witches. Are we seeking our true names? Looking for spirit guides? Asking for solutions to difficult problems? Making amends for offenses against someone else's spirit or freedom? Or are we just trying to feel groovy? Anybody who can afford a hit of MDMA or a bag of heroin can achieve bliss and euphoria. In this hyper-rational, Apollonian society, we need more Dionysian energy to give our lives balance. But you can't exist in a perpetual state of hedonism without becoming an abusive, irresponsible joy junkie. Too much feeling is as bad as too much thinking. We need to always ask ourselves, How do we treat each other? What is right or wrong? Does this make us better, wiser, kinder people? Is our process democratic? Are we accessible to newcomers? Do we do our own shit work or expect others to wait on us?

Power (surprise, surprise) is the crux of the matter here. The only legitimate source of power is responsibility. Other people may try to give somebody power because they think that person is smart or beautiful, or because they want to manipulate that person. But it is always wrong to wield power if you are not prepared to accept the consequences for your actions and do the work it takes to use your strength and authority with precision and fairness. A good leader is many people's servant. If being trained to become a perfect servant sounds too humiliating, you are not strong enough to withstand the temptations of wielding power.

Some people are attracted to magic precisely because it seems like a shortcut to power. No grubby hands, no sore shoulder—just flying with the angels. I compare this to putting sugar in your coffee with a steam shovel. The Goddess helps those who help themselves. If you want a job, get your resumé and your work drag together in addition to burning a dollar bill on your altar. If it's your very last dollar, don't burn it—use it for bus fare to a job interview.

Finally, I have to say that many white practitioners of S/M magic are shameless in their misuse and romanticization of the rituals and mythology of preindustrial societies. A lot of these people used magic simply because they didn't have any other resources. When people in tribal societies perform rituals to make the crops grow, they are expressing their connection to the earth. But they also do magic because they don't have the knowledge or the capital to use fertilizer and other Western agricultural methods. A group ritual to draw off sickness can generate a strong feeling of community and compassion, but a Navajo mother whose kid is dying would probably rather have more doctors on the reservation. From our privileged place as well-fed, white Americans, it's easy to ignore the factors that drive Amazon Indians to work in the sawmills or tempt native women in New Guinea to go live in Christian missionary compounds.

Of course it's better to study the legends of Native Americans, the Maori, Inuit, and African people than it is to ignore them. But we need to be acutely aware of the fact that it is difficult, if not impossible, for us to know exactly what their spiritual practices mean to these people. It is intellectually dishonest to pretend that hunter-and-gatherer cultures were great places to be queer or female. In our bitterness with the homophobia and sexism of twentieth-century America, it's too easy to fantasize that people with less technology were completely free of these ills. Small tribal societies had different rules to govern social sex roles and pleasure-seeking behavior, but those rules were fiercely enforced. Today we probably have more equality between the sexes, more civil rights for sexual minorities, and more knowledge of ecology than you'll find in any group of people that makes a living with fishing nets and blowguns or slash-and-burn agriculture.

While we strive to preserve the interior life of Third World people and learn from their ceremonies, we should never forget that this is their ethnic heritage, not ours. Why aren't more white pagans trying to recreate the magical traditions of the Celts, Spain, Germany, France, Poland, Sweden, and other European nations? There's something bogus about white people who are unable to feel spiritual unless they borrow somebody else's Siva spears and elk's teeth necklace.

Modern primitives live, for the most part, in urban enclaves in the age of the machine. We have to find ways to synthesize the rhythms of nature with our electronic lives. A fuzzy-headed, sentimental longing for a bucolic utopia will not save us from toxic waste or nuclear weapons.

We need a world where we can have both computers and campfires, heart circles and telecommunications, where we can write letters to our government representatives as well as get letters from the orishas. Sex is only one kind of magic. Not all magic is sex, and not all sex is magic. If we wish to follow this path to a golden end, we must pursue other kinds of study and accept other kinds of discipline. The Goddess can be found in the kitchen, the library, a homeless shelter, an office, and on the 22 Fillmore bus, as well as in a solstice circle in a meadow. We also have to recognize that luck and talent enter into this equation. The Queen of Elfland doesn't come for every suitor. It is not fair to scorn those who are not so gifted (or cursed). Instead of praying for extraordinary talents, we should pray for the good sense to fully use all the talents we have been given. You'll need to comfort the sick a lot more often than you'll be allowed to raise the dead.

I hope those who read this essay will not think that I want them to sell their drums or stop looking for ways to celebrate the great cycles of the earth and our own transitions. Looking from the outside, I am not qualified to judge anyone else's spiritual practice or life path. But I think the once tiny family of pagans who do S/M has grown beyond the point where we all know each other and can assume that we share the same values and goals. Perhaps this article will provoke a discussion about how we can pursue spirituality without becoming hopelessly pretentious. It would be sad and silly if we alienated ourselves from other pervy people or replicated bad, old, antisex habits while we're reaching for the full moon and the stars.

Notes

1. Juno, Andrea and V. Vale. *Modern Primitives: An Investigation of Contemporary Adornment and Ritual.* San Francisco: Re/Search Publications, 1989, 4.

2. *ibid.*, 5.

3. *ibid.*

4. *ibid.*, 20.

5. *ibid.*, 105.

6. *ibid.*, 163.

7. *ibid.*, 132.

8. *ibid.*, 169.

9. McKenna, Neil. "London Bookseller Cleared in Sensational Obscenity Trial." *The Advocate,* April 25, 1991, Issue 575, 55.

10. Pepper, Rachel. "Incredibly Strange Books." *The Advocate,* April 20, 1993, Issue 627, 72-73.

Whoring In Utopia

1994

Even people who are supportive of sex workers' rights often assume that prostitution would somehow wither away if women achieved equality with men or industrial capitalism fell on its blemished, bloated face. Whoring, like other deviant and thus "problematic" sexual behavior, is assumed to be an artifact of sexism, American imperialism, racism, insane narcotics laws, Christianity, or whatever institutionalized inequity has the pontificator's knickers in a twist. While large and sweeping social change would probably alter the nature of sex work, the demographics of sex workers, and the wage scale, along with every other kind of human intimacy, I doubt very much that a just society would (or could) eliminate paying for pleasure.

Prostitutes, both male and female, have been with us from the earliest recorded time. The "art of prostitution" and "the cult of the prostitute" are two of the *me* (sacred treasures) given to the Sumerian goddess Inanna by her father Enki, the god of wisdom. When Inanna takes the *me* back to the city of Uruk in the boat of heaven, the people turn out in droves to cheer in gratitude. A hymn to Inanna which describes the people of Sumer parading before her says, "The male prostitutes comb their hair before you. They decorate the napes of their necks with colored scarves. They drape the cloak of the gods about their shoulders." These poems are thousands of years old. In fact, Sumer is the first civilization from which we have written texts. And there's no reason (other than a certain wistful prudishness) to think that commerce and sex won't continue to intersect as long as either has meaning or a place in human culture.

In America today, the sex industry is shaped by several negative forces. First of all, because the work itself is illegal or plays pretty close to that edge, it attracts people who are desperate, who believe they have few or no other choices, and people who embrace the identities of rebel, outsider, and criminal. Very few sex workers are able to be open with their children, lovers or spouses, friends, and families about how they earn their livings. This need to hide puts enormous stress on people who are paid for relieving the stress of their customers.

The existence of prostitution as we know it is based on the compartmentalizations of male sexuality and female identity. There are women whom men marry and with whom they have children, and there are women whom they screw for a set fee. The wife-and-mother class is not supposed to acknowledge the existence of the whore class because that would destroy the "good" woman's illusion that *her* faithful, loving husband does not have an alternate identity as a john. The opportunity for paid infidelity (as long as it is hidden and stigmatized) makes monogamous marriage a believable institution. Of course not every married man has sex with hookers, but enough of them do to keep the black-market sex economy booming.

The illicit sex trade interacts and overlaps with other underground economies such as stolen merchandise and the circulation of illegal aliens. But the most influential of such economies is the narcotics trade. Street prostitution is the only occupation that provides most female (and more than a few male) junkies with enough money to support addiction to the overpriced, adulterated narcotics that our "Just Say No" social policy on drugs has caused to flood the urban environment.

Also, as technology grows more complex and educational opportunities for workers constrict, prostitution has become one of the few forms of employment for unskilled laborers. (Another slot for unskilled laborers, which is generated by laws against solicitation, is on the vice squad. Cops are often the socioeconomic counterparts of the people they harass, blackmail, bust, and control.)

So what would happen to the sex industry if some of these shaping constraints were lifted? What if narcotics were decriminalized and addicts were able to get prescriptions for maintenance doses of good drugs at decent prices? What if prostitution itself were decriminalized *and* destigmatized? If women had the same buying power that men do? If racism no longer forced so many nonwhite citizens into second-class citizenship and poverty? If the virgin/whore dichotomy and the double standard melted away? If everybody had sex education, access to contraception and safe-sex prophylactics, and we no longer believed sex was toxic? Wouldn't the free citizens of this wonderful society be able to get all the sex they wanted from other free agents?

Of course not! One of the dominant myths of our culture is that everybody longs to participate in romantic heterosexual love; that it is romance which gives life meaning and purpose; and that sex is better when you do it with somebody you love. We are also taught to assume that romance and money are mutually exclusive, even though the heroes of romance novels and neogothics are almost always as wealthy as they are handsome. It would be foolish to deny the existence of romantic passion and lust, but it would be equally foolish to ignore the people who prefer to fuck as far away as possible from the trappings of Valentine's Day. These people don't enjoy the roller coaster ride of romantic love. And there will always be people who simply don't get turned on in the context of an ongoing, committed relationship. Some of these people make trustworthy and affectionate, permanent or long-term partners as long as they're not expected to radiate a lot of sexual heat. But in a more sex-positive society, these folks might be able to have both marriage and paid sex without the guilt and stigma of being diagnosed as psychologically "immature" or "incomplete."

It's also possible that prostitution would become romanticized and idealized. The relatively new reality of women as wage earners has generated enormous tension in heterosexual relationships. This hostility has been exacerbated by divorce laws which continue to force men to pay child support and alimony while depriving them of their homes and custody of their children. In a world of prenuptial agreements and lawsuits for breach of promise and sexual harassment, the "good" woman who was once valorized by men as a suitable candidate for marriage and motherhood is increasingly perceived as a leech and a liability. More men may come to believe that "nice girls" are revolted by sex and will take all their money, while "fallen women" like cock, like sex, and want only a hundred dollars or so. The current media obsession with supermodels needs only a little push to turn into an image blitz popularizing glamorous courtesans and hookers with hearts of gold and ever available cunts-without-commitment.

Even in a just society, there probably would be plenty of people who were simply too busy to engage in the ritual of courtship, dating, and seduction. A person with a job that requires a great deal of travel, for example, may not have a stable enough living situation to connect with and keep a steady lover or spouse. Some of these harried businesspeople will be women. While male sex workers—whether they identify as gay or straight—today service an overwhelmingly male market, I can't imagine what would stop women who could afford it from beckoning the prettiest boys that money can buy to their executive limos, helicopters, and hotel suites. This new job market would have a tremendous impact on the parameters of male heterosexuality, identity, and fashion. Straight men are currently defined mostly by the things that they do *not* do (wear dresses or bright colors, get fucked, suck dick). But in a buyer's market, proactive behavior is at a premium. Female customers would prefer to be serviced by men who actively demonstrate their ability to please women and their arousal at the thought of doing so. The word "slut" would lose its gender.

There will always be people who don't have the charm or social skill to woo a partner. In a society where mutual attraction and sexual reciprocity are the normal bases for bonding, what would happen to the unattractive people, those without the ability or interest to give as good as they get? Disabled people, folks with chronic or terminal illnesses, the elderly, and the sexually dysfunctional would continue to benefit (as they do now) from the ministrations of skilled sex workers who do not discriminate against these populations.

The requirements of fetishists can be very specific. People who have strong preferences for specific objects, acts, substances, or physical types would probably continue to find it easier to meet their sexual needs by hiring professionals with the appropriate wardrobes or toolboxes of paraphernalia. Furthermore, a great many prostitutes' customers have fetishes for paying for sex. It's the sight of that cash sliding into a bustier or a stocking top that makes their dicks get hard, not the cleavage or the shapely thigh. Many fetishist scripts are simply elaborate forms of sublimated and displaced masturbation that do not offer anything other than vicarious pleasure to the fetishist's partner. For example, a shoe fetishist's girlfriend may not be particularly upset about her or his need to be kicked with white patent-leather pumps with thirteen straps and eight-inch heels, but performing this act is probably not going to make her come. Especially in utopia, there would be no reason for someone to play the martyr and try to be sexually satisfied by an act of charity. Cash would even the bargain and keep the fetishist from becoming an erotic welfare case.

The first experience one has with physical pleasure has a dramatic impact on the rest of one's life as a sexually active being. In a better world, virgins and novices would probably resort to prostitutes who specialized in rituals of initiation and education. A talented sex worker could introduce brand new players to all of their sexual options, show them appropriate ways to protect themselves from conception or disease, and teach them the skills they need to please more experienced partners. This is a sensible antidote to the traumatic rite of passage that "losing your cherry" often is today.

An encounter with a hooker is already a standard part of the traditional bachelor party. The groom must pay tribute to the wild woman and subsidize her freedom before he is allowed to lay claim to a bride he can domesticate. If whoring were not stigmatized, it could be used to celebrate all kinds of holidays. A visit with an especially desirable and skilled sex worker would probably make a great gift for grandma when she came out of mourning for her deceased husband. A pregnant wife could thank her husband for being supportive and patient by giving him a weekend with the girl or boy of his dreams. Paid vacations could include sexual services. Bar mitzvahs and other puberty rites would be obvious occasions for incorporating orgasms for hire.

Since human beings are a curious species, and many of us need adventure, risk, and excitement, I would hope that the sex industry would continue to be available to fulfill those needs in positive ways. The thrill of arranging several sexual encounters with people you don't know very well certainly seems more healthy to me than big-game hunting or full-contact sports, which are high-risk activities sanctioned by our society. The story of the hero who meets a beautiful stranger and wins her favors is archetypal. If we are fortunate, we encounter the anima/animus in our beloved. But until that magical moment, those of us who require refreshment, insight, and sexual nourishment could pay for receiving that blessing. We may have an innate human need to take that mystical journey of transformation into a stranger's arms.

Perhaps sex work would even find its spirituality restored. Those who wished to worship icons of womanhood, manhood, or intersexuality could perform these sacred obligations with sex workers who were guardians of the mysteries of the human heart and loins. The Great Rite, the ancient sacred marriage between earth and sky, teaches us to respect the ecology of the natural world. Perhaps the Sierra Club could sponsor an annual *hieros gamos* as part of its major fundraising drive. Of course, the performers in such a majestic pageant would have to be compensated for their efforts.

It's obvious that the range of people who sought out sex for money would change dramatically in a kinder, gentler world. But what about the people who would do sex work? I wonder if the boundaries between whore and client might not become more permeable. The prostitute's identity is currently rather rigid, partly because once you have been "soiled" by that work you are never supposed to be able to escape the stigma, but also because such rigidity creates clarity for the heterosexual male. He is what the prostitute is not (male, moneyed, in charge, legitimate, normal). In a world where women were as likely to be clients as men; sex workers were well paid and in charge of their own lives; and prostitute were as valid a social identity as Senate majority whip, there would be less need for the high walls between "good" and "bad" people, "men" and "women." Everybody might expect to spend a portion of her or his life as a sex worker before getting married, if she or he didn't want to be thought of as sexually gauche. Perhaps there would be collective brothels where people could perform community service to work off parking tickets or student loans. A stint in the community pleasure house might be analogous to going on retreat.

The people who took up sex work as a profession would be more likely to pursue the erotic arts as vocations, just as priests and artists do today for their professions. They would be teachers, healers, adventurous souls—tolerant and compassionate. Prostitutes *are* all of those things today, but they perform their acts of kindness and virtue in a milieu of ingratitude. The profession would attract people who like working for themselves, who are easily bored, who want a lot of social contact and stimulation. It would also attract dramatic, exhibitionist performers and storytellers. As computer technology is used for sexual purposes, sex workers will need to be computer literate. The ideal sex worker might be somebody skilled at creating virtual realities, programming environments, characters, plots, and sensations for the client. This programming ability might become more compellingly sexy than a pair of big tits or a ten-inch dick.

Sex work would also attract stone butches of all genders and sexual orientations—people who want to run the fuck but are not interested in experiencing their own sexual vulnerability and pleasure. Often these people are the most adept at manipulating other people's experiences. They are more objective about their partners' fantasies and do not become distracted by their own desires, since their needs to remain remote and in control are already being fulfilled.

There are other social changes which would continue to alter the dynamics of the sex industry. In a society where everybody was doing work they enjoyed for fair wages, the meaning of money (and work itself) would change. It would cease to be a gender marker, for one thing (I am male, so I earn a paycheck; you are female, so men give you money). This change is already underway. In a postindustrial society where power was cheap or free and survival was no longer an issue, money might even cease to be a marker for social class. I believe human beings would still have the need to group themselves into smaller tribes or social units based on affinity and common interests, but the parameters of these groups would change. People would have new, now unforeseen, ecological slots as "those who pay/give" or "those who get paid/receive" for possessing certain characteristics or performing different activities.

Unfortunately, it's doubtful that any of these visions will be realized. As AIDS paranoia grows and nation-states continue to consolidate and extend their power, it's much more likely that sex workers will face harsher penalties and stepped-up law enforcement campaigns. In a few radical locales, prostitution might be legalized and subjected to strict government regulation as a social experiment to control AIDS and other sexually transmitted diseases. People seem to be suckers for anything that promises to make them safer, whether it's motorcycle-helmet laws or the Brady bill. But there is no guarantee that making the federal government the greatest pimp of all would do a goddamned thing to make sex work a better career or to protect the health and safety of the customer. In such a system, prostitutes would be like mill workers in late nineteenth-century England.

But a state that believes it has the right to send young men off to die in a war or conduct above-ground testing of atomic weapons in populated areas eventually will try to take over the hands, mouths, dicks, cunts, and buttholes that are sex workers' means of production. So the halcyon, golden days of prostitution may be happening right now. This may be as good, liberal, and free as it gets. So you might want to visit your ATM, take out a couple hundred bucks, and hurry to the red-light district now, before it becomes as antiquated as a Wild West ghost town.

PHYLLIS CHRISTOPHER

About the Author

Pat Califia is well-known as a sharp critic of repressive American attitudes toward sexuality and pornography, a long-time activist for gay rights and the right to free sexual expression, and a lecturer on sexual politics. She has authored twelve books and published numerous articles and essays in national publications, including *The Journal of Homosexuality, The Advocate, Co-Evolution Quarterly, High Times, Brat Attack, Taste of Latex, Skin Two, Invert: The Journal of Gay and Lesbian Sensibility, On Our Backs, Drummer,* and *The Spectator.* She lives in San Francisco where she is completing her M.A. in counseling psychology at the University of San Francisco.

Index

Grateful acknowledgment is made to the following publications in which these essays originally appeared in slightly different form:

"The Age of Consent: The Great Kiddy-Porn Panic of '77": *The Advocate*, October 16, 1980, pp. 19-23, 45. "The Aftermath of the Great Kiddy-Porn Panic of '77": *The Advocate*, October 30, 1980, pp. 17-21. Reprinted as "Man/Boy Love and the Lesbian/Gay Movement" in *The Age Taboo*, Daniel Tsang, ed., Alyson Publications/Gay Men's Press, 1981, pp. 133-146.

"Public Sex": *The Advocate*, September 30, 1982, pp. 18-21, 24.

"The Obscene, Disgusting, and Vile Meese Commission Report": *The Advocate*, October 14, 1986, pp. 42-46, 108-109.

"Victims Without a Voice": *High Times*, December 1985, pp. 32-36, 66, 68-69.

"Among Us, Against Us—The New Puritans": *The Advocate*, April 17, 1980, pp. 14-18. Translated into the Danish and reprinted in *Umoralske Opstød*, Dorte-Maria Bjarnov, ed., Forlaget Juvelen, 1986. Revised and reprinted in *Caught Looking: Feminism, Pornography And Censorship*, published by the Feminist Anti-Censorship Task Force, New York, 1986.

"See No Evil: An Update on the Feminist Antipornography Movement": *The Advocate*, September 3, 1985, pp. 35-39.

"Feminism, Pedophilia, and Children's Rights": *Paidika: Issue 8—Special Women's Issue*, Vol. 2, No. 4, Winter 1992, pp. 53-60.

"A Secret Side of Lesbian Sexuality": *The Advocate*, December 27, 1979, pp. 19-23. Unauthorized reprint in *ZG80*, No. 2, special issue on "Sadomasochism: Its Expression and Style," Great Britain. Reprinted with permission in *S and M: Studies in Sadomasochism*, Thomas Weinberg and G. W. Levi Kamel, eds., Prometheus Books, 1981, pp. 129-136. Also reprinted in *Skin Two*, Issue No. 6, 1986, as "The Power Exchange," pp. 21-22, 33.

"Feminism and Sadomasochism": *Heresies*, Sex Issue, No. 12, 1981, pp. 30-34. Reprinted in *CoEvolution Quarterly*, Spring 1982, pp. 33-40. Reprinted in *News That Stayed News: 10 Years Of Coevolution Quarterly*, Stewart Brand and Art Kleiner (eds.), North Point Press, Jan. 1986.

"Genderbending: Playing with Roles and Reversals": *The Advocate*, September 15, 1983, pp. 24-27. Translated by Betty Paerl into Dutch and reprinted in *Slechte Meiden #1*, 1983.

"Gay Men, Lesbians, and Sex: Doing It Together": *The Advocate*, July 7, 1983, pp. 24-27.

"Beyond Leather: Expanding the Realm of the Senses to Latex": *The Advocate*, May 29, 1984, pp. 26-28, 52.

"Unmonogamy: Loving Tricks and Tricking Lovers": *The Advocate*, November 13, 1984, pp. 26-27.

"The City of Desire: Its Anatomy and Destiny": *Invert: The Journal Of Gay And Lesbian Sensibility*, Vol. 2, No. 4, Winter, 1991, pp. 13-16.

"Girls, Go for the Gloves": *The Advocate*, August 13, 1992, Issue 609.

"Love and the Perfect Sadist": *Skin Two*, 1992, pp. 42-47. Reprinted as "Love & SM" in *The Spectator*, Vol. 29, No. 23, Issue 752, 2/26-3/4/93.

"Pagan Passions! On Modern Primitives, Latex Shamans, and Ritual S/M": *The Spectator*, Vol. 30, No. 16. Issue 771, 7/9-15/93, pp. 3, 12. Reprinted in *Skin Two*, January 1994, pp. 90-92. Also reprinted in *The Masquerade Erotic Newsletter*, January/February 1994, Vol. 3, No. 1, pp. 2-5.

"Whoring In Utopia": *Gauntlet*, Vol. I, 1994.

Books from Cleis Press

SEXUAL POLITICS

Good Sex:
Real Stories from Real People
by Julia Hutton.
ISBN: 0-939416-56-5 24.95 cloth;
ISBN: 0-939416-57-3 12.95 paper.

The Good Vibrations Guide to Sex:
How to Have Safe, Fun Sex in the '90s
by Cathy Winks and Anne Semans.
ISBN: 0-939416-83-2 29.95;
ISBN: 0-939416-84-0 14.95 paper.

Madonnarama:
Essays on Sex and Popular Culture
edited by Lisa Frank and Paul Smith.
ISBN: 0-939416-72-7 24.95 cloth;
ISBN: 0-939416-71-9 9.95 paper.

Public Sex:
The Culture of Radical Sex
by Pat Califia.
ISBN: 0-939416-88-3 29.95 cloth;
ISBN: 0-939416-89-1 12.95 paper.

Sex Work: Writings by Women
in the Sex Industry
edited by Frédérique Delacoste and
Priscilla Alexander.
ISBN: 0-939416-10-7 24.95 cloth;
ISBN: 0-939416-11-5 16.95 paper.

Susie Bright's Sexual Reality:
A Virtual Sex World Reader
by Susie Bright.
ISBN: 0-939416-58-1 24.95 cloth;
ISBN: 0-939416-59-X 9.95 paper.

Susie Sexpert's Lesbian Sex World
by Susie Bright.
ISBN: 0-939416-34-4 24.95 cloth;
ISBN: 0-939416-35-2 9.95 paper.

LESBIAN STUDIES

Boomer: Railroad Memoirs
by Linda Niemann.
ISBN: 0-939416-55-7 12.95 paper.

The Case of the
Good-For-Nothing Girlfriend
by Mabel Maney.
ISBN: 0-939416-90-5 24.95 cloth;
ISBN: 0-939416-91-3 10.95 paper.

The Case of the
Not-So-Nice Nurse
by Mabel Maney.
ISBN: 0-939416-75-1 24.95 cloth;
ISBN: 0-939416-76-X 9.95 paper.

Dagger: On Butch Women
edited by Roxxie, Lily Burana and
Linnea Due.
ISBN: 0-939416-81-6 29.95 cloth;
ISBN: 0-939416-82-4 14.95 paper.

Daughters of Darkness:
Lesbian Vampire Stories
edited by Pam Keesey.
ISBN: 0-939416-77-8 24.95 cloth;
ISBN: 0-939416-78-6 9.95 paper.

Different Daughters:
A Book by Mothers of Lesbians
edited by Louise Rafkin.
ISBN: 0-939416-12-3 21.95 cloth;
ISBN: 0-939416-13-1 9.95 paper.

Different Mothers:
Sons & Daughters of Lesbians
Talk About Their Lives
edited by Louise Rafkin.
ISBN: 0-939416-40-9 24.95 cloth;
ISBN: 0-939416-41-7 9.95 paper.

Girlfriend Number One:
Lesbian Life in the '90s
edited by Robin Stevens.
ISBN: 0-939416-79-4 29.95 cloth;
ISBN: 0-939416-8 12.95 paper.

Hothead Paisan:
Homicidal Lesbian Terrorist
by Diane DiMassa.
ISBN: 0-939416-73-5 14.95 paper.

A Lesbian Love Advisor
by Celeste West.
ISBN: 0-939416-27-1 24.95 cloth;
ISBN: 0-939416-26-3 9.95 paper.

Long Way Home: The Odyssey of a Lesbian Mother and Her Children
by Jeanne Jullion.
ISBN: 0-939416-05-0 8.95 paper.

More Serious Pleasure: Lesbian Erotic Stories and Poetry
edited by the Sheba Collective.
ISBN: 0-939416-48-4 24.95 cloth;
ISBN: 0-939416-47-6 9.95 paper.

The Night Audrey's Vibrator Spoke: A Stonewall Riots Collection
by Andrea Natalie.
ISBN: 0-939416-64-6 8.95 paper.

Queer and Pleasant Danger: Writing Out My Life
by Louise Rafkin.
ISBN: 0-939416-60-3 24.95 cloth;
ISBN: 0-939416-61-1 9.95 paper.

Rubyfruit Mountain: A Stonewall Riots Collection
by Andrea Natalie.
ISBN: 0-939416-74-3 9.95 paper.

Serious Pleasure: Lesbian Erotic Stories and Poetry
edited by the Sheba Collective.
ISBN: 0-939416-46-8 24.95 cloth;
ISBN: 0-939416-45-X 9.95 paper.

REFERENCE

Putting Out: The Essential Publishing Resource Guide For Gay and Lesbian Writers
by Edisol W. Dotson.
ISBN: 0-939416-86-7 29.95 cloth;
ISBN: 0-939416-87-5 12.95 paper.

POLITICS OF HEALTH

The Absence of the Dead Is Their Way of Appearing
by Mary Winfrey Trautmann.
ISBN: 0-939416-04-2 8.95 paper.

AIDS: The Women
edited by Ines Rieder and Patricia Ruppelt.
ISBN: 0-939416-20-4 24.95 cloth;
ISBN: 0-939416-21-2 9.95 paper

Don't: A Woman's Word
by Elly Danica.
ISBN: 0-939416-23-9 21.95 cloth;
ISBN: 0-939416-22-0 8.95 paper

1 in 3: Women with Cancer Confront an Epidemic
edited by Judith Brady.
ISBN: 0-939416-50-6 24.95 cloth;
ISBN: 0-939416-49-2 10.95 paper.

Voices in the Night: Women Speaking About Incest
edited by Toni A.H. McNaron and Yarrow Morgan.
ISBN: 0-939416-02-6 9.95 paper.

With the Power of Each Breath: A Disabled Women's Anthology
edited by Susan Browne, Debra Connors and Nanci Stern.
ISBN: 0-939416-09-3 24.95 cloth;
ISBN: 0-939416-06-9 10.95 paper.

Woman-Centered Pregnancy and Birth
by the Federation of Feminist Women's Health Centers.
ISBN: 0-939416-03-4 11.95 paper.

FICTION

Another Love
by Erzsébet Galgóczi.
ISBN: 0-939416-52-2 24.95 cloth;
ISBN: 0-939416-51-4 8.95 paper.

Cosmopolis: Urban Stories by Women
edited by Ines Rieder.
ISBN: 0-939416-36-0 24.95 cloth;
ISBN: 0-939416-37-9 9.95 paper.

Dirty Weekend: A Novel of Revenge
by Helen Zahavi.
ISBN: 0-939416-85-9 10.95 paper.

A Forbidden Passion
by Cristina Peri Rossi.
ISBN: 0-939416-64-0 24.95 cloth;
ISBN: 0-939416-68-9 9.95 paper.

In the Garden of Dead Cars
by Sybil Claiborne.
ISBN: 0-939416-65-4 24.95 cloth;
ISBN: 0-939416-66-2 9.95 paper.

Night Train To Mother
by Ronit Lentin.
ISBN: 0-939416-29-8 24.95 cloth;
ISBN: 0-939416-28-X 9.95 paper.

The One You Call Sister:
New Women's Fiction
edited by Paula Martinac.
ISBN: 0-939416-30-1 24.95 cloth;
ISBN: 0-939416031-X 9.95 paper.

Only Lawyers Dancing
by Jan McKemmish.
ISBN: 0-939416-70-0 24.95 cloth;
ISBN: 0-939416-69-7 9.95 paper.

Unholy Alliances:
New Women's Fiction
edited by Louise Rafkin.
ISBN: 0-939416-14-X 21.95 cloth;
ISBN: 0-939416-15-8 9.95 paper.

The Wall
by Marlen Haushofer.
ISBN: 0-939416-53-0 24.95 cloth;
ISBN: 0-939416-54-9 paper.

We Came All The Way from Cuba So
You Could Dress Like This?: Stories
by Achy Obejas.
ISBN: 0-939416-92-1 24.95 cloth;
ISBN: 0-939416-93-X 10.95 paper.

LATIN AMERICA

Beyond the Border: A New Age in
Latin American Women's Fiction
edited by Nora Erro-Peralta and
Caridad Silva-Núñez.
ISBN: 0-939416-42-5 24.95 cloth;
ISBN: 0-939416-43-3 12.95 paper.

The Little School: Tales of Disap-
pearance and Survival in Argentina
by Alicia Partnoy.
ISBN: 0-939416-08-5 21.95 cloth;
ISBN: 0-939416-07-7 9.95 paper.

Revenge of the Apple
by Alicia Partnoy.
ISBN: 0-939416-62-X 24.95 cloth;
ISBN: 0-939416-63-8 8.95 paper.

You Can't Drown the Fire: Latin
American Women Writing in Exile
edited by Alicia Partnoy.
ISBN: 0-939416-16-6 24.95 cloth;
ISBN: 0-939416-17-4 9.95 paper.

AUTOBIOGRAPHY,
BIOGRAPHY, LETTERS

Peggy Deery:
An Irish Family at War
by Nell McCafferty.
ISBN: 0-939416-38-7 24.95 cloth;
ISBN: 0-939416-39-5 9.95 paper.

The Shape of Red:
Insider/Outsider Reflections
by Ruth Hubbard and Margaret Randall.
ISBN: 0-939416-19-0 24.95 cloth;
ISBN: 0-939416-18-2 9.95 paper.

Women & Honor:
Some Notes on Lying
by Adrienne Rich.
ISBN: 0-939416-44-1 3.95 paper.

ANIMAL RIGHTS

And a Deer's Ear, Eagle's Song and
Bear's Grace: Relationships
Between Animals and Women
edited by Theresa Corrigan and
Stephanie T. Hoppe.
ISBN: 0-939416-38-7 24.95 cloth;
ISBN: 0-939416-39-5 9.95 paper.

With a Fly's Eye, Whale's Wit and
Woman's Heart: Relationships
Between Animals and Women
edited by Theresa Corrigan and
Stephanie T. Hoppe.
ISBN: 0-939416-24-7 24.95 cloth;
ISBN: 0-939416-25-5 9.95 paper.
